PLAYBOY'S
BOOK OF
SPORTS CAR REPAIR

PLAYBOY'S
BOOK OF
SPORTS CAR REPAIR

by
Arthur Darack

WIDEVIEW
BOOKS

ACKNOWLEDGMENTS

We wish to thank the following companies for permission to reproduce illustrations: General Motors Corp.; Ford Motor Co.; Chrysler Corp.; McKay Datsun; Nugent VW, VW of America; Toyota Motor Sales Co., Ltd; Nissan Motor Co., Ltd.; Fiat Motors of North America, Inc.; Audi Volkswagenwerk.

First Edition

Library of Congress Cataloging in Publication Data

Darack, Arthur.
    Playboy's book of sports car repair.

    Includes index.
    1. Sports cars—Maintenance and repair.
I. Playboy.   II.Title.
TL236.D37   629.28 722   80-50173
ISBN 0-87223-597-1
ISBN 0-87223-602-1 (pbk.)

Anne Kostick was the editor for this book. Brenda Darack was the designer. Hammond Litho Inc., Northbrook, Illinois, set the Times Roman type.

Contents

INTRODUCTION

Sports car maintenance involves some subtleties not present in family sedans. Engines, often the same, are attached to suspension systems, and body structures altogether different in purpose and somewhat different in design. In recent years, sports cars are following the fuel shortage syndrome that has taken its toll of bigger cars, with the result that similar modifications have been visited upon sports car engines. Lovers of sports cars have seen their engines decline in authority, while their car bodies and suspension systems have remained more or less the same. This has not posed a fatal dilemma for the sports car, since engine power is rarely tested in so light a body as the sports car typically possesses. The effect on the traditional sports car enthusiast is less clear, since one of the charms of the sports car has been its extra reserves of power in relation to weight and size. Reserve power confers authority, as any owner of an oil well knows. When it diminishes, one may be hard pressed to assess the consequences, fully. Yet sports car owners are not less realistic than others in relating to environment, and one purpose of this book is to relate them ever more intimately into their car's environment. That includes the power hungry aspects of it, the comforts of it, the pleasures and bliss its perfect functioning confers.

Keeping up a sports car is not exactly like keeping up a mistress, in the French use of that term; it is much more predictable. The French mistress system (which may be disappearing, according to the authority you consult) depends on insouciance, unpredictability, and enslavement by an overwhelming attraction. The sports car maintenance system is out to banish all these habits of behavior, but to wind up with something similar—an overwhelming attraction, or so it is claimed, yet one perfectly legal, and dedicated to the idea of saving energy, performance, environment, and the face of things. It will not be necessary to point out dissimilarities between this aim and the mistress system.

The sports car lover does not normally possess inhibitions about fixing his/her car, as is usually the case with the suburban car lover. That creature has been so propagandized about the dirt and difficulty of it, that merely taking a tire inflation reading is considered a major breakthrough in self-achievement and realization.

The sports car problem centers around the sub-

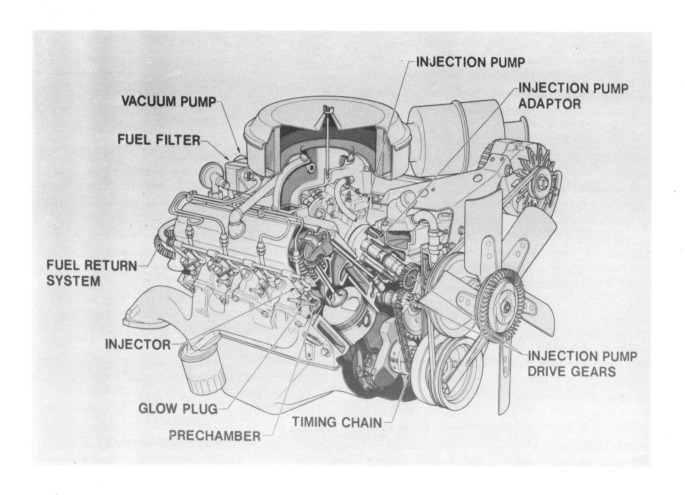

1

tleties of adjustment and the reluctance to take them on, for fear of gumming them up, and what is worse having no one to blame but oneself. That entails the corollary view of the unique character of adjustment involved in the sports car—that each car has a Platonic arena of adjustment unlike any other, and if you discover a mechanic who is privy to the secret you have approached deity.

However, sports car mechanics are not exempt from human failure, and the cars themselves are assembled by the same people and robots, armed with cloned specifications, who put together your family Platypus Eight, with its room for groceries and gear.

That sobering view is what animates the purpose of this book; the sports car is no more exempt from home auto repair than the easiest Subaru. Two systems may raise hackles here; the fuel injection systems that have proliferated, and the turbocharging systems. It will be alleged that these are not for amateurs.

These systems are becoming increasingly familiar on the family sedan, the car that spawned the home repair industry, so we will skirt the issue decorously, noting it but also tackling it in appropriate chapters.

Otherwise, the only problems are catastrophic ones; too many sports car mechanics are unwilling to face up to the weight of the car, and too willing to take chances with it. We shall insist that throughout every job requiring work beneath the car, the essentials of safe suspension be observed. These are; never less than two jacks, positioned in such ways that the failure or release of one cannot lead to the failure of the other. You can also use ramps, which are good for some jobs, not for others, but do have good security to recommend them, if you buy quality ramps. We will discuss tools later on.

Why, it may be asked, is fixing sports cars any different from fixing any other car, or anything else, for that matter? The answer is that sports cars have been positioned in the general psyche to belong to a romantic area not invaded by practicality. To equate working on a sports car with (say) rodding out a malfunctioning sink is to introduce the cesspool into the garden. Old habits of thought change slowly, but they change. Since Arab oil has fastened its stranglehold on world economies we have all had a change of mind about oil and its uses, oil and its users. We no longer think it funny that Arab oil merchants can buy the world's economies to suit their whims. We also no longer think it funny that wasting oil is whimsically endearing. And yet an untuned engine wastes gas on the order of 10 to 20 percent. If all the world's engines were tuned today, the world would be out of the Arab oil jungle tomorrow. At any rate, we would have a start toward a realistic conservation ethic. For reasons of this sort,

we no longer consider it demeaning to work on our cars.

In addition to the philosophical, political, and aesthetic dimensions, there is the purely financial aspect. Sports car repair is one of the costliest services you can buy, approaching medicine in per-minute (or hour) rate. Labor rates of $50 per hour are common, and will go higher. Anything a car needs will be interpreted to require an hour of labor, partly because most repairs take almost that long, and partly because it isn't worth anyone's time to bother with lesser problems, if you are a professional in that problem. Like doctors, mechanics are not satisfied to treat only the symptoms you describe; they also must treat those they discover.

In addition to saving $50 per hour at least, each time you change a light bulb, or replace spark plugs, you also can save on the parts. At the garage you pay healthy retail prices, which means at least a 40 percent markup over wholesale costs. So, spark plugs will cost you $1.25 to $2.25 each, but if you buy them on sale from Sears, Wards, Penneys, or K-Mart, you can get them for roughly half that price. The same cost breakdown holds for other parts. To replace a pair of MacPherson struts can cost $200 in a garage; but the J.C. Whitney catalog sells them for $34 a pair. An electric fuel pump costs $25 to $35 in the catalogs; if you have a fuel pump replaced you will receive a bill for about $100. The cost goes up if the pump is in the gas tank and the new one is installed there. But if you do it yourself and put the new one in the engine compartment, the cost will be the price of the pump — about $25.

The U.S. Government says the costs of auto maintenance and repair are roughly a third of the total costs, and the only one you can alter to your advantage. Because the cost of parts at wholesale is low, you can save all the labor costs, which come out to almost 90 percent of total maintenance and repair costs. For reasons of this sort, home auto repair, even of sports cars, is now very much on the agenda.

You may say "but where can I do the work, since I live on the 28th floor of a condominium?" Obviously you can't do it on the 28th floor. Many people fix cars on the street; others take them to parks (in good weather), and rented garage space is possible. The best solution is your own garage, where you can store any tools and equipment you acquire. You may think the private garage is an impossible luxury in a world which doubles its population every 50 years, or so. But the money you save on car repairs could be one way of affording more living and working space. Admittedly this is a thin solution, but you may not live in an area where you can rent stalls in garages. We can solve all the other problems of your car, but this one resists easy solution, if you don't have a garage.

Chapter One

Preliminaries

TOOLS AND EQUIPMENT

You will be surprised at how many tools you can buy if you wander through a tempting display in a Sears or Wards tool department. You will also be surprised at how few tools you actually use on any given repair job. The socket wrench is the basic tool, and you can buy a set for as little as $10 or as much as $500. Obviously these are aimed at different users and levels of need. The professional mechanic uses the $500 set, the small set is for the occasional fixer. You need something in between, but much closer to the $10 set.

Check out the Penneys, Wards, Sears, and other catalogs, then compare what they offer with what you can buy in your local hardware store. But don't buy anything until you discover how much resolve you possess for entering the auto repair world. You may have no stomach for it, past the oil change and grease routines. For that you need very few tools. Oil change and grease are, however, rites of passage into auto repair, and a test of faith. If you can stomach it, these tasks can clue you into your ability to try others. They are among the easiest and messiest, whereas most things you can do to a car involve delicacy and tact, analysis, and patient corrective measures. Engine tuneup involves surgery, whereas changing an exhaust system—muffler, tailpipe, exhaust pipe, resonator, and tailpiece—is unskilled labor. Most work is closer to surgery. A carburetor is delicate, but so are brakes in their own way, and the repair of an alternator is like the repair of any sophisticated electronic gear; it takes strat-

3

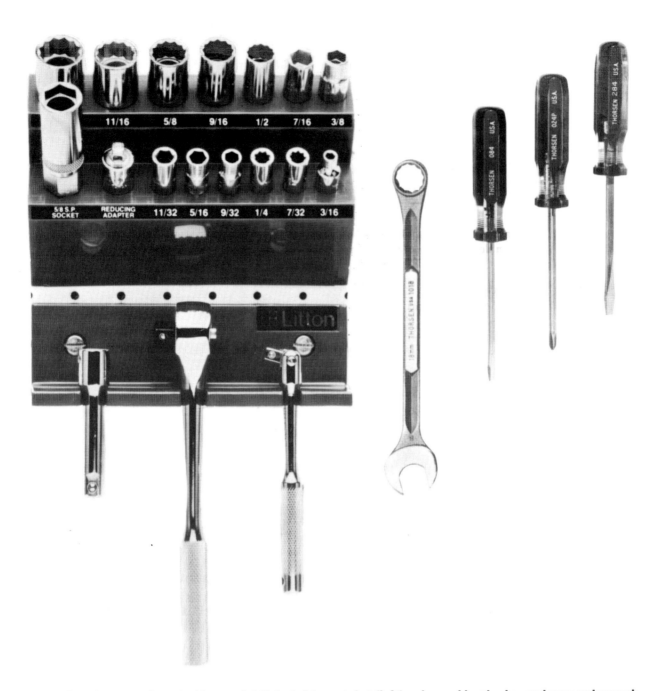

A small socket wrench set by Litton, with ¼-inch drive ratchet (left) and a combination box and open end wrench on the right, with assorted screwdrivers. Tools like these, along with other small hand tools, are common in car work.

egy, tactics, expertise, and special tools. So car repair is not a single issue; that is why garages specialize and so do mechanics. You, however, must learn to do it all.

Once past the socket set, you need a few small hand tools, including a set of screwdrivers, both the phillip's type and the standard blade. You'll need several kinds of pliers, including wire snippers, vise pliers, and the ordinary kitchen variety. But you'll also need the electrician's needle-nose type, which gets into small places.

Several open-end and box (closed) wrench sets, from very small sizes to larger, are necessary, and if your car is an import this, and all other fixed tools, must be metric. (But soon everything from Detroit as well is going to be metric.) You'll also need an adjustable ("crescent") wrench or two, but start with one—a fairly large one with good capacity, say about a 12-inch size.

Probably you already own all these tools, but the chances are that you don't own several jacks. One of these should be a heavy duty scissors jack, another

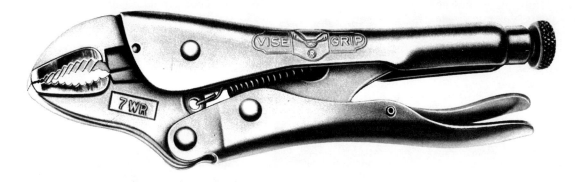

A vise pliers like this one can substitute for a bench vise in some situations where the heavier tool may be specified. But this one can do many other jobs the bench vise can't.

should be a small hydraulic jack, and a couple of sturdy bumper jacks are good to have around, including the one that came with the car. (Most car jacks for sports cars lift from the side. Okay, but you need all the others.) Don't buy any flimsy jack; buy only top quality, such as you find at the stores we list above—Wards, Penneys, Sears, J.C. Whitney, and plenty of others.

What about test equipment?

To begin, you don't need any. If your car has a mechanical distributor (with points that open and close) you'll need a timing light, if you do any job in which timing is disturbed. But you don't need an expensive one—the inexpensive, neon timing light, which costs about $4 or $5, will do. It won't work in bright sunlight, but it will work in any shaded area. You don't need a timing light with electronic ignition.

Engine analyzers, compression testers, vacuum testers, and all the other fancy gauges you see in garages, are window dressing, as far as you are concerned. You can set engine revolutions per minute by ear, as your grandfather did on his Model "T", and get it about right. If it's wrong it will tell you soon enough, by symptoms we'll discuss. You can tell about engine compression, also, and as for voltage, ohms, amps, and continuity of electricity, we'll consider their uses, as we go along. An engine analyzer that can measure all these electrical matters can be useful, indeed, indispensable. Don't buy one, however, until you're certain you'll need its services. Also, many electrical tests can be made without expensive equipment, as we will see when we get there.

As you go along, you'll add such items as a variety of hammers, tools for separating suspension and steering members, exotic wrenches that fit only one kind of nut or bolt, and a selection of bolts, nuts, washers, cotterpins, and electrical fasteners.

One tool you will also need from time to time is a quarter-inch drill, but the chances are you already have one. A bench vise sometimes comes in handy but you will be surprised at how much gripping you can do with a vise pliers.

A metal saw will be useful once in a while. All the equipment in the world won't eliminate buying parts, small tools, and fasteners for every job you do. It's the nature of the beast, but don't buy anything that you think might come in handy some day. The chances are it won't. The point of this and any buying advice is that there are almost always better things to do with your money than what you contemplate doing with it under the stress and enticements of the moment.

WHAT'S A SPORTS CAR?

If you have done any work at all on any car—or even a lawn mower with gas engine—you are perfectly prepared to get started on a sports car, or any other. You will notice that we have avoided defining what we mean by a sports car, as long as possible, not because we don't know what it is, but because the terms are used to mean different things. Everybody admits that the Datsun "Z" cars, or the Chevrolet Corvette, are sports cars. Almost everyone admits the British Leyland MG, MGB, etc., qualify. So too the Fiat and Porsche entries. But what about cars like Scirocco, or the Chrysler-Plymouth Omni-Horizon sports cars? We plan to define them all in, and if you object on aesthetic or other grounds you will have to allow our utilitarian definition. Once we limit the discussion to mechanical principles, the luxury of definition is dissolved. It's a tactile way of defining a problem of the intellect out of existence by the body. In a sense it's the old mind-body philosophical principle resolved pragmatically; either they do meet or they don't, and progress is impossible unless they do.

The luxury of spending the whole of human history attempting to define a tiny aspect of it—argument over a philosophical theory—simply won't do in auto repair, though sometimes when you take the car in it appears that that is what is going on. Your car won't start, or makes a sinister noise, as of incompatible parts clashing. The luxury of mulling over a definition of the problem won't work here; only work will work, and if you are still worried that the sports car is different enough from the jalopy to instill inhibition in you about tackling it, remember that according to the Department of Transportation, 53 percent of all professional jobs are either botched or needless.

Also, because most work revolves around familiar systems such as exhaust, ignition, starting, cooling, brakes, and suspension details similar to what goes on in large cars—for while the suspension systems differ considerably in size and weight, the basic details do not—you shouldn't be intimidated. Once you've seen one water pump, you've seen them all, despite differences of size and design. A large Mercury Marquis water pump, though almost as big as half the Fiat Spyder engine, does exactly what the pump on the Fiat does—push water around the engine. Exactly similar considerations apply to other features.

Engines, as we've noted, are either identical to larger car engines, or very similar. Carburetion, when it is fuel injection, may differ, but as we noted, fuel injection appears to be gaining converts, so it helps to get some familiarity with it.

Since Ford gave up the sports car ghost when it converted Thunderbird to a "personal luxury" car, all aficionados agree that only Corvette qualifies completely. (There is overlapping in these definitions.) That car has occupied an almost iconic niche in American car articles of faith, as the genuine article. That it has been innovative in appearance and performance, cannot be denied. It has also been ahead of the pack in some engineering trends, as we will see. But it remains a Chevrolet, in design and execution—that is to say, a highly tested, carefully engineered vehicle. Chevrolet earned its dominant position in the mass market with popular virtues of thrift and reliability, comparatively speaking, and in the U.S. context. The Corvette surrendered thrift to the usual sports car performance values, but its reliability quotient has been similar to other Chevrolets.

For many years the Corvette engine was the tried and true Chevrolet V-8, 327 cubic inch, usually with a 4-barrel Carter carburetor. Early in its career, however, the Corvette received a fuel injection system on some models. Also—and this was many years ago—General Motors experimented with multiple carburetors, not only on the Corvette, but also on a car that was highly regarded as a sporty make, the Corvair. That car didn't make it into the 70s, and while its advanced engineering caused many a tantalizing look back, no element of it was revived (the idea of an aluminum engine surfaced in the Vega, but nothing else of the Corvair engine found its way into that equally ill-fated car).

The Corvette was used as a high performance experimental car. In 1957 it had received the first U.S. fuel injection system, a mechanical system quite unlike the electronic systems now in use elsewhere in the industry (but not in the Corvette). Corvette lovers contend that the Corvette masterpieces were precisely those early years, and that everything after 1957 was a decline. Be that as it may, the Corvette remains a symbol of what a giant corporation can do for a tiny group of enthusiasts with dedication and a dream—the idea of super mobility in a machine designed and executed around the highest precision demands. It may not always attain these standards, and in recent years the old Corvette fans think it has become a somewhat effete symbol, but it remains the only one of its kind from a U.S. manufacturer.

(Porsche is by V.W., which has a plant in the U.S., but is not predominantly a U.S. manufacturer.)

If Corvette has had a long, innovative career, Ford's Thunderbird was short and meteoric, as a sports car, but long and genteel as an established "personal luxury" car. The sports car aura dissolved into the lap of luxury. Early Thunderbirds are collector's items rather than cars, and all the recent ones are simply part of the market. They have a staid suburban profile.

The Lincoln/Mercury division of Ford shows even less interest in sports cars, though it has no lack of sporty models, such as Capri (which it used to get from Germany but now makes in the U.S. as a twin of the sporty Ford Mustang). The Capri is interesting because it uses a 4-cylinder engine with turbocharging to enhance performance enormously, thus appealing to the sports car lover, while not exceeding normal gas burning by a 4-cylinder engine.

The 4-cylinder engine also figures in Chrysler's sporty versions of their Omni and Horizon, the Omni 024 and Horizon TC3. Chrysler has not sought sporty imagery in the past. But their adaptation of the Rabbit engine as a base power plant, and their own 4-cylinder version of it, will lend these engines to sports car use if Chrysler so desires.

In fact, the new General Motors V-6 engine, an option in the Citation and its fellows up the G.M. line, is the power plant sports car fans look upon covetously, as the performance engine of the new decade. This engine, coupled to a turbocharger and fuel injection meets the requirement of "dynamite," a term not readily translatable but containing the components of ecstasy, furiously quick acceleration, endless reserves of power and "performance" (another untranslatable term).

American Motors Corporation has been in the sports or sporty car field in the past with Javelin and others, remaining in the sporty field with its AMX, which is the sporty version of the Spirit. Spirit is the successor to Gremlin. AMX competes with Pontiac Firebird, Chevrolet Camaro, and sporty cars of that stripe.

Most of the sports car action has come from abroad, with Italian cars such as Alfa Romeo and Ferrari starting the parade, and more recently the Japanese cars leading it. No single car dominates this field.

Mazda's RX-7 and the Datsun Z cars comprise the Japanese contingent, along with Toyota which recently entered the lists, showing Celica Supra.

Porsche, with its 911, 924, and 928 lines, can show a wider range of sports cars than any other manufacturer, both in price and design.

British Leyland Motors, with MG and MGB, has held a dominant share of the lower and middle priced sports car market. Britain's Jaguar is the high-priced Leyland car, costing well above $25,000 at this time, and who is to say what it will be later. There may be no "later" for Jaguar's XJ-S, the sportster or luxury GT car as the aficionados title it. It is a high-powered gas guzzler, like the Corvette with the big V-8 engine, and cars of this ilk will have difficulty in the gas-rationed future, no matter how much affection they inspire. Because their numbers are small in the general market they can endure as monuments and occasional transportation, but they will no longer play innovative roles as they did in the past. Whether they have a future in the bottom line calculations of their manufacturers is a question only time will answer. We may believe and hope they will, but fervor counts for little in these calculations.

Consider some of the counts against the XJ-S. It has a 244 horsepower V-12 engine. It runs at 80 miles per hour as effortlessly as your typical engine goes 30. It gets about 10 miles per gallon, when all we hear is that cars of the future must get 40, and one of the ways they do that is through careful driving at reduced speeds.

No matter; plenty of people will say a concert grand piano is also reckless of materials compared with a spinet and no chief of state has decreed that the Brahms B-flat Piano Concerto is henceforth to be played on the spinet. It may happen, given the parlous political state of the times.

The Japanese cars have been highly favored in recent decades, thanks to innovative engineering, quality control, and the special Japanese genius for getting things right. Mazda, Datsun and Toyota congregate at the top of this field. Datsun and Toyota

have half the cylinders of the Jaguar, whereas Mazda uses the rotary engine, a very special number indeed. In matters of horsepower, the Toyota rates its 156.4 cubic inch engine (2563 cc) at 110, whereas the Datsun checks in at 168.0 cubic inches (2753 cc) at 135 horses.

REGULAR MINOR MAINTENANCE

Changing oil and grease and other minor maintenance procedures are not often expensive tasks when done by professionals, but they are often done badly or overlooked when you count on their being done. That can lead to expensive trouble. An oil filter, replaced incorrectly, can leak, leading to low oil levels or worse. Battery cables, allowed to corrode, can prevent starting or charging, or cause a loss of charging. Minor maintenance, such as greasing door window linkage, which nobody will do excepting for steep rates because so much labor is involved, may not be classed as minor because of the labor cost. However, the home maintenance on such work costs you a few pennies' worth of grease and at least an hour of your time. It will enable you to work the windows easily, especially the one that sticks most—the driver window. That one gets most work, hence needs most grease—and causes most trouble. For reasons best known to auto designers, there is no easy way to grease an automobile window cranking mechanism. Electric windows are no exception; they require grease on occasion, which if it is overlooked can lead to the burnout of the motor, and a huge, difficult, expensive job. Greasing of the windshield wiper system is another such job.

Replacement of PCV valves, exhaust gas recirculation valves, fuel filters, air filters, and other common devices, can be done at home at a minimum of cost and bother, whereas professionals find them

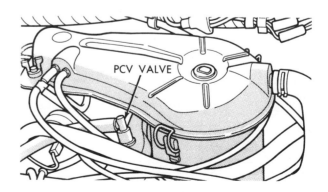

A PCV valve like this one is usually near the carburetor, with a hose coming out of it. The valve itself is usually in the rocker panel.

easy to overlook. All of them, overlooked, spell trouble.

So it follows that minor maintenance is minor only in respect to cost and materials involved. It can save your car and your wallet, over the long haul.

One other minor maintenance aspect should be stressed; the checking of components for wear. From tires to carburetors, such regular inspections can prevent every conceivable problem. Nobody does this nowadays. Also, you can't trust such inspections to willing but unknowing gas station attendants. Sophisticated knowledge often is required. Not many gas station attendants qualify. (No insult is intended here; the young people who work at gas stations endure more public disaffection than their meager rewards should allow, and their exposure to society's late night evils—when such hours prevailed—should have earned them combat pay, and the celebrations that accompanied the safe return of national saviors in past wars.)

BELTS

The first aspect of checking routine components begins with belts. That is because belts turn alternators, which supply electricity; steering pumps, which when present provide directionality; air conditioners; and water pumps, which keep the engine cool and alive.

Not all cars have air conditioners or power booster pumps for steering. Indeed, in the lean years we enter, fewer and fewer power boosters will be the rule, since they burn gas, with the exception of the power brake booster, which works off engine vacuum power.

Belts should be checked about every four or five months. But when you check belts, check the systems they touch—the water, electrical, and the others.

How do you check belts? By visual inspection of the inner surfaces. That's where the wear occurs, first. So open the hood and look first at the belts, to see whether there are any loose strands, then look for frayed edges. If these checks reveal nothing, grab the belt you're examining and twist it sufficiently to see the underside—the side that rides in the pulleys. Twist it to see whether it has any cracks. If there are small cracks of rubber only, they don't count. You're looking for deep cracks in the fiber. Because you can't examine the belts inside the pulleys, turn the ignition key on and off quickly to expose the belts in the pulleys. It may take more than one turn of the ignition key. As a general rule, if the belts are more than three years old, replace them.

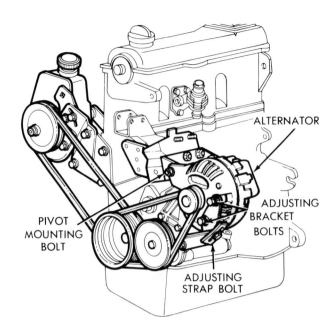

Belts must be tightened so that they can't be pushed more than about a half-inch in on the longest belt reach.

Is it hard to replace belts? Mostly no, but some belts can be a terrible pain. Since all makes and models differ slightly as regards the fasteners and adjusters on belt pulleys, a moment's study will tell you where to begin.

On Corvette the alternator, water pump, and power steering follow standard General Motors practice. The alternator adjuster is a half-moon clamp with one adjusting nut at the half-moon clamp and a through bolt at the opposite end of the alternator. Both must be loosened with a socket wrench, at which point you can push the alternator forward, freeing the belt. When replacing any alternator belt it is important to use care if you use a metal prying rod against the soft metal of the alternator. To obtain proper adjustment of the new belt, pull back on the alternator with one hand as you tighten the adjusting nut with the other. If you pull hard enough you can obtain correct belt tension. If you don't, the alternator will tell you quickly enough. It simply won't charge properly, and if the belt is loose it will make noises which it didn't make before. Foreign cars differ little from G.M. in belt fasteners and adjusters.

Belts are driven by the engine crankshaft pulley, which is at the front behind the radiator usually, but it can also be elsewhere, depending on the type and configuration of the engine. On VW engines, which also include Audi and Scirocco, belts are usually over on the passenger side, and not readily accessible. That's where the transversely mounted engine harmonic balance wheel is found. With most of these engines the fasteners can be loosened without

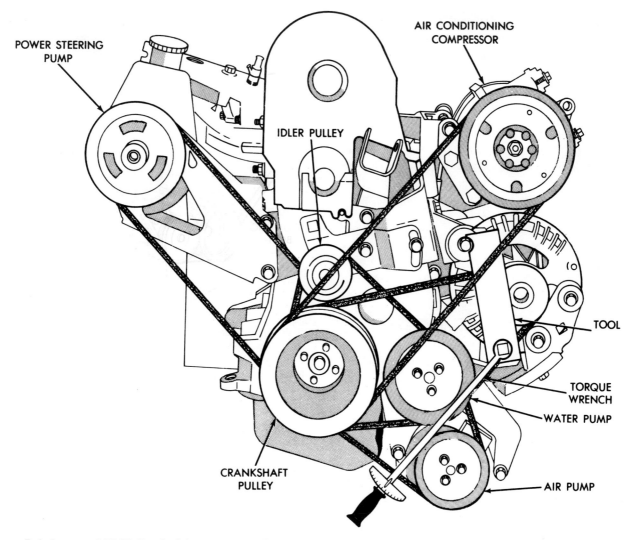

POWER STEERING PUMP

AIR CONDITIONING COMPRESSOR

IDLER PULLEY

TOOL

TORQUE WRENCH

WATER PUMP

AIR PUMP

CRANKSHAFT PULLEY

Belt layout of 1980 Omni with power steering, air conditioning, and an air pump. Four belts must be adjusted; the most crucial and most difficult is the alternator belt.

unusual trouble or exertion, simply by loosening the opposing retaining bolts or nuts. But alternator belts on some cars sold in California require that in order to get the alternator belt off you have to remove the air injection pump belt first. Even that isn't a big chore; you simply loosen the bolts and push the pump in as far as it will go. There is invariably some order of removal and installation of fan belts that must be followed, and it differs from year to year, but if you look at the belt fasteners the order will quickly reveal itself.

The new belt or belts should be tightened so that when you push in the belt it should not move more than about a half inch. More than that means it is too loose; less means too tight. Too tight will ruin components; too loose could prevent proper charging if it's an alternator belt, or adequate cooling if it's the water pump belt, or correct refrigeration if it's the air conditioner, or hard, jerky steering if it's the power steering pump.

Though Chrysler's Omni/Horizon is based on a VW Rabbit engine, their component placement is their own. Alternator belt replacement is similar to VW but different enough to warrant special mention. A splash shield held by four long, slender bolts—two at the front near and below the radiator, and two above and below the fender—must be removed first. To do so requires that four bolts be loosened on the air conditioner and it be pushed in—down. The four bolts are obvious enough if you look closely—three are on top, and one is down below, alongside the radiator.

A through bolt and single bolt and clamp underneath hold the alternator and belt in tension. That single bolt—14mm—is on a sliding clamp. Loosen the through bolt and the bolt and clamp and pull the alternator away from the front of the car. Put the new belt on its pulleys. You will discover quickly that you work in an awkward place where it is difficult to get enough pressure on the alternator to force it back. It is vital that the belt be tight—so tight that it cannot be pushed in on its upper turning surface more than ½-inch. To get it that tight requires that you look directly up under the alternator (crawl under the car which needn't be jacked) and find a surface that you can push against with a sturdy screwdriver or a bar of some sort. There is one such surface. That is about the only way to do the job; holding the alternator while you tighten the clamp bolt. Warning: don't drive the car unless you get the belt right. The belt will quickly go to ruin, discharging the battery and stranding you. Also, buy only an original equipment belt or better.

One aspect of belt maintenance involves the pulleys. A misalignment between pulleys on a component and the turning wheel—say the alternator pulley and the harmonic balance wheel—can develop, for one reason or another. In the case of an alternator, a belt-pulley misalignment can cause squeaking noises. It will ruin the belt and since the bent pulley usually is itself a symptom of internal wear, it will also cause alternator failure. But if the bent pulley is the result of a worn or damaged pulley or the pulley bracket, that should be replaced. Visual inspection should tell you where the trouble lies. Bent pulley symptoms can arise in any belted component. With the water pump it usually is caused by the wearing out of the bearing and its packing and that shows up as a leak along with the out-of-center pulley operation. Push on the water pump pulley and probably it will have excessive play. Power steering, air pumps, and air conditioning pulleys can also develop misalignment, which visual inspection usually will reveal. Squeaking is one symptom, common to all such cases, but it is not positive proof of the cause. Squeaks can be caused by many other defects, both major and minor.

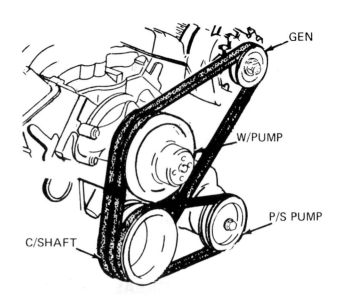

A Corvette belt layout.

Never save money on fan belts—buy only the best, and buy the correct belt. The new belt width must match, front and back the one it replaces.

When replacing belts or simply examining them, look around the components touched by the belts. They are all key parts.

We've already mentioned the alternator and its squeak. A high, whistling sound given off by an alternator can indicate that it is overcharging. This will also show up as a battery that uses excessive water. But it means that either the regulator is faulty and needs replacement or adjustment, or one of the alternator diodes is burned out. If the noise goes away after the engine runs for a short time, don't worry about it. But if it does not, and if the battery water symptom shows up, the alternator will need attention—or the regulator.

If your car has power steering, check fluid levels whenever you examine the belt. Turn the cap off the top and look at the dipstick. Add automatic transmission oil if it's low.

When you look at the water pump, examine the entire cooling system for leaks. First, look underneath the water pump for telltale signs of coolant leak—green droplets from the anti-freeze or moisture. Push on the center post pulley. It should be firm without side motion. Examine all water bearing hoses, beginning at their clamps. Hoses should be without cracks and corrosion at the clamps. Feel the hose; the texture should have some "give" to it. It should not be rocklike. If it is very hard that means it's brittle, and that means trouble. So replace such a hose. And usually when you replace one water hose, replace them all. We'll get to that later, in the cooling section.

Power steering, alternator and water pump are the belted components that can cause radical break-

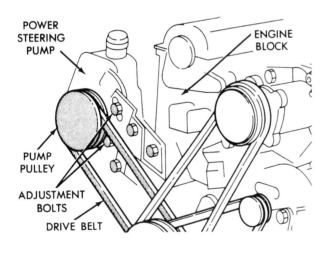

Power steering belt adjustment bolts.

down. You can drive a car without the power steering pump, but not for long or very safely. Without the alternator, the battery will run down quickly and the engine will quit. Without the water pump the engine will be destroyed very quickly. That is why these three belted components must be checked regularly and their belts replaced at the first sign of wear.

Other belted components—meaning the air conditioner or the air injection pump—don't disable the car when their belts break. But some cars become difficult to drive when the air injection pump stops working, and the most radical thing that happens when the air conditioner quits is that you gain from two to six miles per gallon of gasoline.

SUPPLEMENTARY GREASING AND OILING

Regular greasing and oiling includes fairly complex tasks such as changing automatic transmission oil—which isn't a common sports car routine but it happens—and the changing or checking of manual transmission oil, which can be complex in some cars. But it also includes the lubrication of some things that never get done unless you do them yourself.

This group includes doors, deck lids, hoods, hand brake linkage, and one mechanism that is not sup-

posed to need lubrication, but does—the windshield wiper linkage. Lubrication of doors requires grease and oil, the grease for the heavy wear at the hinges, the oil for locks. Use Lubriplate or any light grease on the door hinges; use regular engine oil for the locks. Push the grease generously into the hinges. If there is any sign of rust, use naval jelly or other rust neutralizer, then put some primer on the area and finish with spray paint, which you buy according to paint number listed on the paint information plate inside the engine compartment.

Doors, deck lids and hoods can be greased easily enough. Never oil or grease any part of the carburetor linkage, and even if you can see that the carburetor butterfly valve is sticking, because of carbon formation, don't use oil or grease on it. That will simply add to the formation, even though it will cause an initial freeing of the valve. Any part of the carburetor that doesn't move freely is a sign that the carburetor needs overhauling.

Also, don't ever put grease or oil on any of the pulleys we've been discussing above—the belted components. Any pulley that isn't operating properly has to be replaced.

Parking brakes need lubrication at the foot lever inside the car's driver area, and at the rear of the car, underneath, where the brake cables attach to the divider-adjuster clamp, and at any other friction area you can see. Be careful about putting much grease on

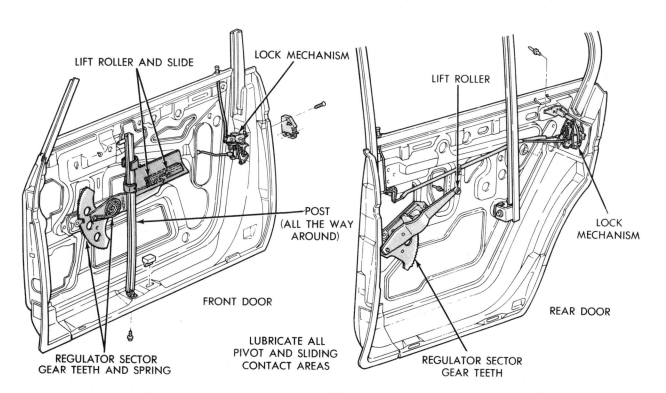

Car doors contain many moving parts and sliding surfaces, all of which need lubrication. They rarely get it because you have to take the door hardware and pad off.

11

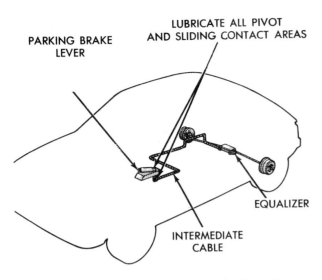

Lubrication points on a parking brake cable.

the cable inside the brake drum itself. A thin film of grease is okay, but too much will inevitably ruin the lining (or pad). Admittedly you won't have occasion to worry about parking brake lubrication very often. It becomes a job only when operation stiffens objectionably.

Lubrication of window mechanism and windshield wiper linkage becomes necessary after two or three years, and sometimes long before that. I have seen new cars with windows that wouldn't roll, thanks to no lubrication at the factory.

To lubricate door mechanism requires removing the window and door cranks, and any other hardware, so as to remove the door pad or covering. Arm rests are bolted on from below. If you lie on the ground, with the door open, and look up at the arm rest you will see two or more fasteners. They may be a bolt head, a phillip's head screw, or a standard screw head. Remove them and the arm rest usually will follow. Sometimes you will find an unusual ornamental border that might be a press fit. Prying off is the usual tactic, but such materials usually are fragile so use great care. Sometimes arm rests are part of the door opening handle, and that has to be unbolted. These inside handles may be held by a variety of fasteners, including snap rings. Snap rings are more common with window crank handles. If that is the case, push in on the door pad until you can see the snap ring. Turn the crank handle until the ends of the snap ring are accessible to a screwdriver or whatever tool is best. You may have to improvise a tool, unless you own a snap ring pliers. Screwdrivers usually work, however. You have to force the snap ring up and out of its groove, then peel it off. The crank handle will then pull off.

You will also have to remove any door lock stem at the top of the door frame. Unscrew it, counter-

clockwise. It will take a lot of turning off. Once all this hardware is removed, you will discover that the door pad is fastened by little tension spring fasteners. Pry each one out with a screwdriver carefully, so as not to bend the door pad out of shape, inserting the screwdriver between the door pad and the door frame. Then you will discover a heavy paper gasket between the pad and the door mechanism. Tug gently at the paper and its cemented surfaces will pull away. If the door has a speaker mounted in it, or if it is a power door with an electric motor and the typical switches, you have to work around these devices. If you deal with electric door switches, their removal requires pushing in on the door pad to expose the holders, which may be anything from snap rings or other tension devices to concealed screws, plastic tabs or what not—the range is puzzling and varied.

Door-mounted speakers may have to be unbolted before the pad will come out. Two or three metal screws usually hold them. Make a note of any washers or gaskets so that you can get them back in the right order. Also, note the right place for the right screw. Some doors will have quite a variety of fasteners, and it makes sense to get them back exactly as they were, even though some interchangeability may be possible.

Once all these steps have been taken, you are ready to do the lubrication job. Lubricate every gear tooth you can find, and also lubricate the window runners and the little plastic wheels that turn on them. These wheels have a habit of sticking and getting ground off on one side, so that they cannot turn or be turned in the runner. Unfortunately, no provision is made for replacing only the plastic wheels. If you are willing to do the job you will discover that it is hard to get replacement parts. The man at the parts counter will say you have to buy a much larger component, and the installation of it will be a major job. The best thing to do is to get the wheel turning, the track greased, and button it back up. Usually, the window will work about as well as if the wheel actually turned perfectly. One other cure is possible, if there is room in which to operate; file the wheel off if there is something to file. Admittedly that solution is less than ideal, since the time and labor involved become formidable with no guarantee of success.

Sometimes you can buy these plastic wheels. In that case, the job isn't quite as painful. But getting the old one off isn't all that easy. It requires forcing the wheel off.

You will discover that you have to crank the window up and down in order to get the grease into every needed area—and you are greasing all moving surfaces, and oiling those you can't reach with grease. Simply put the window crank handle back on, temporarily, for the raising and lowering of the window during greasing.

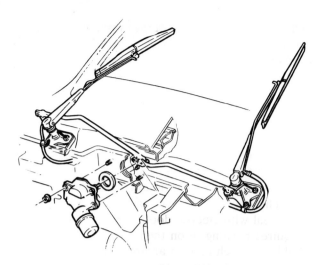

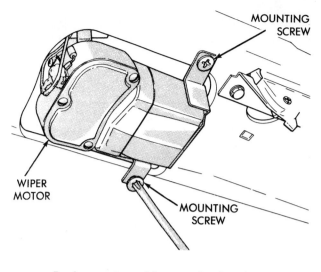

Windshield wiper details where lubrication is useful.

A wiper motor with mounting bracket.

If you deal with an electric window, the problems are slightly more complex, but essentially the same. You want to grease every geared surface that you can reach. But you can't reach them all, since the motor has a pinion gear in it that is encased. Removing an electric motor solely to grease it isn't recommended, unless the window no longer works quickly enough, or properly in other respects. In that case, it is a job that calls for an assistant. It will be discussed later.

Check out the inside of the door for rust. Check it out also to make sure that the drain holes are open. Remove debris and rust, and put some anti-rust paint inside at the bottom, and anywhere else you see rust.

None of this greasing is called for in the manufacturer's maintenance charts, but it becomes essential after a while. Greasing the door's hinges, however, are scheduled maintenance, yet nobody will deny that the inner mechanism failure is at least as annoying.

Greasing of the windshield wiper mechanism is not called for but is actually frowned on; it is supposed to be lubricated for "lifetime." However, it is not specified whose lifetime.

Lubrication of linkage, bushings, and gears, can involve a lot of peeling away of the compartment in front of the windshield. So it should only be undertaken when the wiper loses its flexibility or develops unusual eccentric behavior.

When such behavior appears, look first at the motor to make sure that it is not at fault. The motor normally is located in the engine compartment, bolted to the firewall. It can be unbolted easily enough—three or four bolts retain it. But it will not then fall into your hand, because it is linked to some kind of drive mechanism that in turn moves the two wiper arms. A ball joint sometimes is used at the link

between the motor and the drive arms. Without grease any ball joint wears out; this one is no exception. But other kinds of linking joints are used here, and some of them are bolted so that you can remove the motor without burrowing into the linkage arms.

In any case, disconnect the motor from the linkage and turn it on. If it runs powerfully and without obvious difficulty, the only problem is in the linkage—lack of lubrication. In some makes, the linkage is up under the dash, and difficult to reach. In most makes, the linkage is between the firewall and the windshield. The cowl in front of the windshield must usually be removed, and that may entail removing an ornamental bezel of some sort. Metal screws, cunningly concealed, must be removed. Some of these bezels may have rain gaskets between them and the windshield frame. Don't misplace or spoil the gasket.

Once you dig out the windshield links, fill the coupling joints with grease. Lubriplate or something similar is good here. Use an improvised applicator—say a small screwdriver—rather than a grease gun, unless the gun will do a better job. When you use a grease gun on an area without fittings you are in effect spraying or pumping a small glob of grease. It makes up in coverage what it lacks in precision.

You can test the results by pushing the arms back and forth, looking for binding spots. If the bushings to which the windshield wiper arms are attached seem to bind, the only cure is replacement.

The motor itself has a set of gears that may profit from grease. Some motors are sealed, however, and do not accept any such procedures. Their only cure is replacement.

The windshield washer unit is usually a separate operation that does not normally require lubrication, only replacement of all or part of it. But most windshield wiper components rarely require replacement, and a little preventive lubrication will prolong their life appreciably.

All these minor preventive routines can be done with a minimum of fuss and tools, though peeling away the cowling in front of the windshield may be a bit of trouble. They do require getting your hands dirty in grease. Now we proceed to regular oil change and grease.

SPECIFIED LUBRICATION

Engine oil change nowadays is specified at from 3,000 to 7,500 miles. But there is always the qualification that if you drive in unusually dusty areas, or pull a trailer, or impose other heavy duties on the engine, it will appreciate a more frequent change of oil. Let us be clear about this; engine oil is the key to long engine life. If it is clean, always under pressure, and in the correct amount, you can expect far more engine durability than if one or all of these conditions is not met frequently or even occasionally. Dirty engine oil wears out an engine more quickly than anything else you can do to it. Too little engine oil isn't good for it either. Don't drive an engine with a disabled oil pump—it would warn you via the oil pressure gauge. But oil pumps are extremely simple, durable devices, and their absolute failure rate is so low as to be a meaningless statistic, hence nothing to worry about. When the oil light on the dashboard comes on, check oil level at once. If that's okay, don't assume a malfunctioning oil pump; far more commonly it will be a malfunctioning signal sender on the engine. The sender, on the engine block, should be removed, cleaned off and replaced. The electrical connection often gets corroded.

Oil change is a simple, messy job. So is specified greasing. They are the most important things you can do to your car if you want to keep it in its best possible condition. They prevent rapid wear. They cannot prevent deterioration of the various components in the electrical system, none of which receive lubrication. But they can prevent early wear of the engine, transmission, and the rest of the drive train, including the suspension system and the wheels.

Is there any point in doing your own lubrication, since it doesn't cost all that much at the corner gas station?

Quality control of the job is the key point. If engine oil is cold when it is drained, much of the damaging sludge remains behind, and so much of the value of the oil change is lost. When you leave your car to be greased and oiled, you have no assurance that this

will not occur. When you bring the car to the station and wait for it, the oil is warm, and if the oil change occurs without prolonged delay the new oil will do the job.

That's the first aspect of quality control.

The second is greasing. For the most part, professional grease jobs will not encompass the extracurricular greasing we've talked about—the doors, deck lids, etc. Certainly nothing will be done about window mechanisms, or windshield wiper linkage. Professional grease jobs usually are limited to filling up what grease jets are provided. Fewer and fewer grease jets are provided on new cars; they are a vanishing tribe. In the old days you greased and oiled everything from distributors to rear ends. Grease jets on the suspension system were as common as fleas on an alley cat, or smiles on a Miss America contestant. That is changed; grease jets have given way to "lifetime" lubrication which, as we've noted, does not solve the problem. "Lifetime" isn't spelled out; is it lifetime as with a California Redwood, or as in the case of "rulers for life" in small South American and African "republics?"

But all turning or moving surfaces need some kind of lubrication at points of friction, otherwise they wear out, quickly or slowly as the case may be. Yet rapid wear in some situations is intolerable, for example, in the cases of the window cranking mechanism or the windshield linkage, or even in hood locking and lifting devices. That is why do-it-yourself grease is a justifying task.

Strut suspension systems have eliminated most front end greasing, but not all of it. A few grease jets in the steering linkage continue on, and some idler

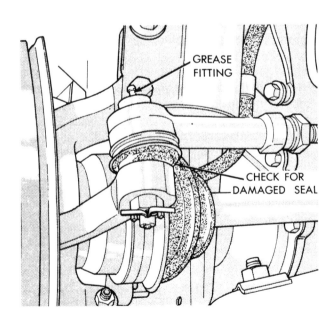

Front end grease fitting.

14

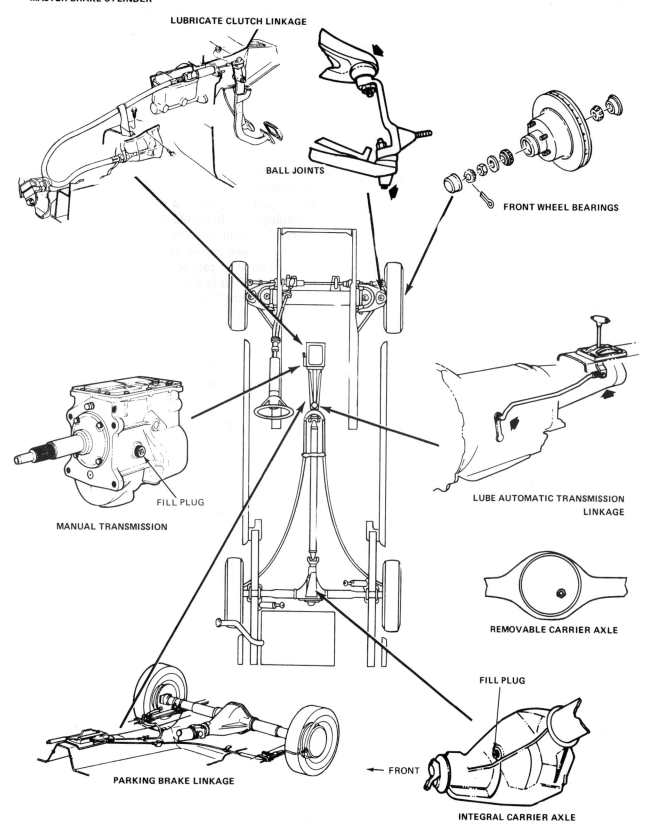

MASTER BRAKE CYLINDER

LUBRICATE CLUTCH LINKAGE

BALL JOINTS

FRONT WHEEL BEARINGS

FILL PLUG

MANUAL TRANSMISSION

LUBE AUTOMATIC TRANSMISSION LINKAGE

REMOVABLE CARRIER AXLE

FILL PLUG

PARKING BRAKE LINKAGE

◄— FRONT

INTEGRAL CARRIER AXLE

Specified lubrication points on a typical front engine/rear drive layout.

arms, which may not have jets for reasons best known to their designers, require regular grease— you simply raise their rubber or plastic skirts and douse them with grease, using the grease gun in this case, even though there is no fitting. One wonders, in the case of idler arms and other skirted components that require grease for which no simple provision has been made, whether they were designed by male or female designers with hangups over the skirt feature. (No one has been able to come up with a replacement for these miniskirts.)

Strut suspension systems do have their grease requirements, as you can see by the rubber bloomers around the two wheel velocity joints, and around the rack and pinion steering gears—rack and pinion is the usual but not invariable steering device to go with the strut suspension. These rubber or plastic grease containers sometimes wear or tear, or (despite propaganda to the contrary) simply run out of grease. Their replacement, at the wheels or the steering, requires major teardown in most cases. However, there are those who say it isn't more involved than exposing the inner wheel bearings on the typical U.S. car with its disc caliper that has to come off for greasing. And some of these strut suspension grease containers can be refilled without major surgery. But the usual problem is replacement caused by tear or wear, and that's a big job.

Change of oil in any small car can be dangerous simply because many people think that the car "can't hurt" if it falls off the jack. But a 2,000 pound car is as deadly as any Lincoln Continental, if it falls on you. And oil change in a sports car always (or almost) requires that the car be jacked up, unlike many big cars, which can be drained without lifting them.

So, the invariable rule applies—at least two jacks, or a jack and jackstand. Also, you want the oil to drain completely, so the car should be jacked in a way that tilts it towards the drain plug, if that is possible, and it usually is.

Remember that the oil should be fully warmed; that means the car should have been driven about 20 minutes.

In buying oil you need to consider the climate in which you drive, as well as the type of oil specified for your car. In cold climates you would do well to use 5W-30 or 10W-40. In warm areas a single grade such as SAE 20 or 30 will do. SAE means "Society of Automotive Engineers," just as API means American Petroleum Institute and NLGI means National Lubricating Grease Institute, the latter two designations often found on grease cans. The SAE grade number identifies viscosity of an oil, which means its ability to flow or resistance to flow, and the lower numbers are specified in colder climates, but obviously the oils which combine properties of high and low numbers have advantages not possessed by one or the other, and that is why they are more expensive.

The most expensive oil is any synthetic, for example Mobil I. Such an oil is okay if your engine has no leaks and is in new or tip-top condition. Though the synthetics usually don't need changing or should be changed at about 25,000 miles, they cost so much more that a leaky engine is too wasteful of dollars and oil. A good synthetic will pay for itself in lowered engine friction, hence better gas mileage and a more durable engine. If you have a leaky engine it is well to replace the leaking gaskets, if that's all there is to it, and use synthetic oil.

As for grease, buy a good quality bearing grease so identified by one of the organizations noted above. Bearing grease should be heavy and sticky. A light, white grease for such things as deck lids and doors, is also necessary. For special grease applications such as the constant velocity joints of strut suspension systems, a molybdenum grease is recommended. This grease is a lithium grease containing a molybdenum disulfide additive that reduces friction. Battery terminals can be greased with a petroleum jelly or simply a silicone spray.

No matter what anyone says, you shouldn't drive engine oil more than 7,500 miles, unless it is a synthetic such as Mobil I, which can be driven 25,000 miles between changes.

Grease also has its limits. Wheel bearings will rarely endure more than 15,000 miles without drying up dangerously. Bearings in need of grease can seize and the wheel and axle can grind off at any speed.

VW and Audi recommend these lubricants: Cars before 1975 use oils lettered SD, SE or both for the engine. After 1974 the letters should be API/SE. Most familiar brands qualify. As to viscosity, VW recommends a multi-viscosity oil such as 10W-40. Manual transmission oil should be SAE 80W or 80W/90. Automatic transmission oil should be DEXRON preceded by the letter B and with a five-digit number.

Mazda recommends multi-viscosity oil that is non-detergent. Mazda suggests that if you drive in below-zero temperatures for any length of time you had better use a 5W-40 or 5W-20. Rotary engines require more frequent oil changes. Mazda recommends change at 4,000 miles. Mazda transmission oil should be changed every 12,000; also rear axle oil should be replaced at that mileage. Mazda suggests that ball joints be lubricated every 32,000 miles or two years; wheel bearings at the same mileage.

Corvette requires oil change between 6,000 and 7,500 miles, or every four months (always whichever comes first). Use multi-viscosity oils, unless you plan continued high-speed driving. Then use a 30 or

40 viscosity oil. Automatic transmission oil should be changed every 24,000 miles. Corvette also recommends checking rear axle lubricant every four months or 6,000 miles. Positraction gears require a special lubricant. Others use SAE 90.

Front wheel bearings on Corvette should be greased at least every 24,000 miles.

Porsche did not recommend multi-viscosity oils in the past, but in recent years such oils have been used increasingly. Given the mobility most drivers expect to pursue, it is impossible to follow the elaborate specifications handed down by Porsche in the past, limiting you to certain temperature zones with matching viscosities. If, for example, you lived in Chicago where you would use SAE 10 or 5 in the winter, and decided to drive south to get away from the terrible weather, you would first have to change your Porsche's oil to SAE 30. But, of course, if you changed it before you left, you would be guilty of a terrible no-no; driving with SAE 30 in Chicago in winter, which could be a criminal offense depending on the clout of Porsche dealers there.

If your car is a Triumph you must change its oil every six months or 6,000 miles, grease the chassis at the same intervals, and the steering rack and pinion assembly at those times.

One may generalize and say that it is better to err on the side of caution when it comes to lubrication of cars, and it is clear from the above data that most sports car manufacturers specify similar intervals and similar kinds of lubrication. The Mazda rotary is different, but that's a different animal, excepting for its transmission and suspension-steering details.

Lubrication procedures differ little from make to make.

You should either consult a lubrication diagram for your make and model, or simply draw up a list.

The Corvette for example, has these lubrication points: Front suspension; steering linkage; steering gear; air cleaner; front wheel bearings; transmission; rear axle; oil filter; battery; parking brake; and brake master cylinder. To these, we add all the other non-scheduled lubrication points already discussed above.

Corvette is, of course, a front engine/rear drive format, without the strut suspension that changes lubrication patterns.

The Saab, a car which doesn't fall precisely into sports car lore and definition yet is a sporty car by most standards, lists these lubrication points: carburetor damper oil; manual transmission oil; automatic transmission fluid and final drive fluid; brake and clutch master cylinder hydraulic fluid; power steering reservoir; and suspension systems.

The Saab is unusual in that it is front drive yet does not employ the strut suspension but rather the traditional upper and lower control arms, with coil spring, in this case above the upper control arm. It does, however, have rack and pinion steering. Control arm suspension, characteristic of most U.S. cars until recent Omni/Horizon, and G.M. "X" cars, requires lubrication at all linkage joints. Idler arms, ball joints, pitman arms and tie rods, all have or should have grease jets, or those miniskirted grease cups we've talked about. In some of these cases, lubrication is made at the factory for long mileages—Chrysler's 36,000, for example—at which time you must then install grease jets for the next lubrication. Such installation is no big deal. In addition to the suspension members, steering linkage in typical control arm suspension systems may have several grease jets.

Most front drive cars have strut suspension, unlike the Saab. This eliminates control arm and steering linkage lubrication because of the use of the permanently lubricated "boot" or whatever it's called at each wheel and over the rack and pinion steering box. But, as noted, these boots tear often enough to require effective replacement strategy, which we'll discuss.

Some strut suspensions don't eliminate all lubrication points. You simply have to look around for grease jets, or grease skirts, and lubricate them. However, don't put grease on bushings that anchor sway bars and other stabilizing rods. These bushings have rubber-steel joints and couplings, and grease would ruin the hard rubber. When these bushings wear out, the only cure is replacement.

Indeed, cars with upper and lower control arm suspension systems usually require bushing replacement along about the third or fourth year. At that time, you can expect the upper control arm bushings to be worn sufficiently to interfere with wheel alignment. If allowed to go on, the entire rubber part of the bushing wears off and the front end becomes a "clunker." Bushings in the lower part of the suspension—for example, at the pitman arm—show up less as clunking noise than as poor steering and wobble. Upper suspension bushing wear can also show up as wobble.

It isn't necessary to go prospecting for grease jets; you can see them wherever there is any sign of grease or grease buildup. But first, change oil.

It will be necessary to jack up the front end of most cars to get at the oil pan under the engine, but obviously if the engine is elsewhere you go there. The oil pan should always be checked for gasket leaks when you change oil. Be wary of accusing the oil pan gasket without a thorough check of other possible culprits. Oil leaks can start at the top of the engine and trickle down from the rocker panel or other gasket-lined components—around the fuel pump in some cars, from the oil sender and various other devices that plug into the engine. Also, the transmis-

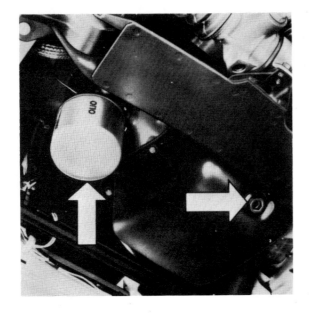

VW lubrication points—engine oil drain and filter.

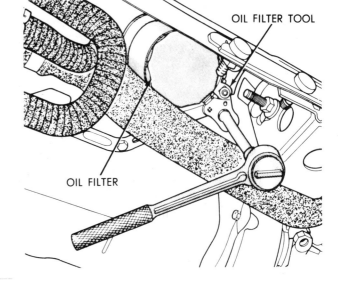

Oil filter tool for getting into and out of tight places.

sion and clutch are notorious candidates for oil leaks.

The only way you can track down an oil leak is to clean off the engine, then run it and look at suspicious areas.

Meanwhile, loosen the oil plug on the oil pan just below the engine, with a socket wrench. Put a pan underneath, then remove the oil filler cap above and remove the oil plug. You have to do it once or twice to learn how to avoid getting a sleeve full of oil, as you turn out the oil plug. The reason you remove the oil filler cap is to obtain more freedom of flow from the oil; otherwise engine vacuum will make the flow sluggish.

Let the oil drain, then tighten the plug. Don't over-tighten it.

Should you change the oil filter? Every other time. The filter, which is a round can somewhere along the side or bottom of the engine, may require a band wrench to get it off. You can improvise one by winding a piece of rope up around the can, and twisting that, and sometimes you can even twist it off by hand if you hold belts in Indian wrestling.

The oil filter will be full of oil; put the pan below it, then remove it gingerly, open end up. When installing the new filter, be absolutely certain that you first lubricate the gasket with fresh engine oil, checking first to ascertain that the new filter is identical with the old—not necessarily the same manufacturer, however. Tighten the filter as specified in the directions. If the gasket is separate from the filter, put it in place, after rubbing oil over both sides of it, and tighten the filter with great care, to make sure that the gasket is seated correctly. Many engines have been ruined when this precaution was not followed

—the oil gushed out, the driver couldn't believe it was happening, the glowing warning light notwithstanding.

When you're under the car to remove the oil, look around at various components that you don't otherwise see. First look at the inner surfaces of the tires, for bulges. Then look at exhaust system components—crossover pipes, muffler, tailpipe, and whatever is in the system. You are looking for holes and other signs of wear. At the engine, check the coupling of the exhaust pipes to the engine. This can be anything from pairs of ball joints, to a single pipe coupling of some sort. The joint usually has a gasket and some type of flexible coupling. Look for exhaust gas leaks—signs are either obvious looseness or discoloration from hot exhaust gases. Usually you can hear such defects—various noises from hissing to booming. Look at the bottom of the water pump for signs of leaks. Look for signs of anti-freeze leaks at all the hoses.

You should check suspension components. Shock absorbers, whether the isolated types in conventional systems, or the strut type that is integrated into the big component, should be dry and without sign of leak. Oil leaks are a sign of terminal wear.

Refill the engine with the specified amount of engine oil and remove the jack, jack stand or whatever else you used (remember the rule; when doing under-the-car work, use a jack, jack stand or two jacks. Or, if one jack has to be under the suspension system, for raising it and lowering it, independently of the car's frame, or under the engine for some special reason, you must still use an added support for the frame.)

Porsche oil change entails different directions. Loosen the drain plug, then loosen the ten nuts holding the oil strainer cover in many 912 models. When oil drains out, clean and replace the drain plug. Then remove the ten nuts holding the oil strainer cover (in many 912 models). You must replace the gasket. This requires cleaning off the gasket surfaces carefully. Liquid gasket removers are available. Once you clean off the surfaces, including the cover and magnetic filter, check the cover for warping. Straighten it out or replace it if you can't get it straightened. Put the new gasket over the engine studs, and replace the strainer, with its opening fitting tightly around the oil tube in the engine, which also has a gasket that must be replaced. Tighten securely but not very tightly, otherwise the surface will be warped and the cover will leak.

In various 911 models the components are slightly different. The oil strainer, cover and two gaskets are circular, but you do the same thing to them. The oil sump or tank is on the right side of the engine compartment.

In the 914/6 there is a line between the engine and the oil tank that must be drained. Once the oil sump (or tank, as Porsche calls it) has been drained, move the pan over and under the line between the engine and oil sump. Two open-end wrenches will be needed to disconnect the lines and drain the tank. Disconnect the lines and push the tube downward into the pan so it will drain. Tighten the lines with the open end wrenches, then do the same cleaning and gasket renewal job on the oil strainer and cover, as directed above on the other models.

Draining and replacing oil in the transaxle of any Porsche model is also a fairly frequent requirement, and easy to do. Remove the filler plug under the transmission, then fill the gear box up to the point where it starts to squish out. Normally this will require a special suction gun different from the long tubular grease gun but resembling it somewhat.

The replacement of oil filters on any Porsche model is required at every other oil change, at every 10,000 miles on others, and at varying mileage on still others. So consult your manual for your make and model specifications.

Porsche oil filters fall into two types—the removable, throwaway cartridge which is located in a housing on top of the 912 engine, and the spin-off, throwaway types common to all U.S. cars.

With the cartridge you deal in a messy operation, and one that requires extra care with the gasket. You remove the cover retaining bolt and cover. Turn the cartridge and lift it out of the housing, using rags or paper towels to minimize oil drippings. To remove the rest of the oil from the housing, use either a suction gun, or soak it up with a rag, then clean out

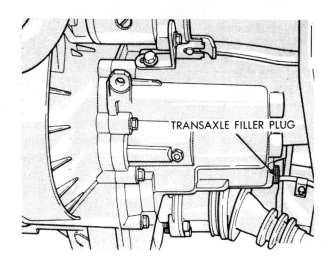

Transaxle filler plug on Omni/Horizon.

the housing. Put oil on the new gasket and install it on the cover. Carefully position the cover on the housing and tighten the bolt. After you add oil, check carefully for leaks. Disposing of the oily rag is your problem; ditto the oil.

The spin-off, throwaway filters in the 911, 914/6, 914, and other models, are found in the engine compartment or at the bottom of the engine. The spin-off filter normally requires a wrench to remove it, and unlike U.S. car manufacturers (who recommend hand-tightening) Porsche suggests using the wrench to tighten the filter—carefully. Draw up the filter with the wrench securely, but not very tightly. Always check for leaks around the filter, by running the engine for a minute or two. Check it also, after the first hard driving episode.

Mazda's rotary engines require oil change more often than piston engines—about twice as often, or between 3,000 and 4,000 miles. Engine oil change is similar to most other cars—the oil plug at the bottom comes out in the usual manner. The oil filter should be changed every other time.

On many Mazda rotary engine sports cars the oil filter is at the top of the engine, easily replaced. Don't use a band-wrench to tighten it; use your hands.

On the Fiat X-1/9 (and other Fiats) it is recommended that the filter be changed at each oil change. In fact, that's probably good advice for any car. Oil filters are inexpensive and new ones don't saddle you with the dirty oil in the old one.

Oil change in the various Triumph sports models is recommended in the six months or 6,000 mile formula. Both the cartridge type replaceable filter and the spin-on, throwaway types are used. As always with any replaceable filter, the trick is to get the gasket correctly in place and the center bolt free of leaks.

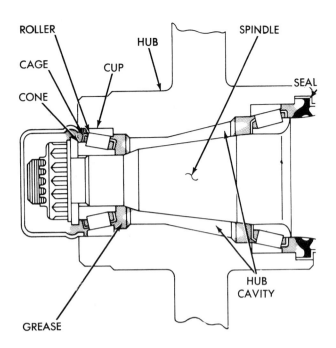

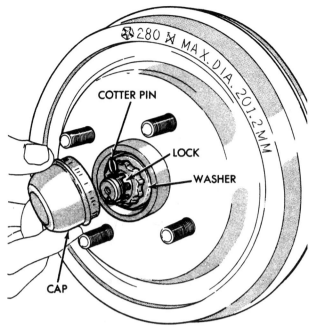

Cross-section of wheel bearings showing grease spots.

Grease cap removed to show wheel fastener details for greasing.

Grease requirements, as we've noted, vary throughout the sports car repertory of makes and models, because of differing suspension systems. Front drive cars generally don't require regular front wheel bearing lubrication, nor do they have many grease points. But Corvette and other front engine/rear drive cars require regular wheel bearing and suspension grease. If brakes in front are disc, as they usually are nowadays, we'll deal with bearing grease in the brake chapter. Removing the caliper to get at the inner bearings is a specialized task, to be taken up under "brakes."

In drum brakes the job is easier.

To grease front wheel bearings, jack up the car securely. That means at least two jacks holding the frame up, and a jack stand under the suspension system. That's the safe formula. Many people recommend using only jack stands, but there are horror stories of jack stands collapsing, and the formula above is foolproof or fail safe. Jack stands are useful as subsidiary supports in any job such as this one where you may bang the car around a little bit. But a scissors jack and hydraulic jack in tandem with the jack stand make up the safest possible lift. You can buy hydraulic jacks for very little money and the scissors jack that comes with the car is perfectly okay as a third of the support. Buy only top quality jack stands. You can look at them for ruggedness characteristics as well as checking out their load capacity.

Wheel bearings on all drum brake assemblies need regular greasing, no matter what you hear. Bearings, by their nature, cannot be greased "for life," unless they have constant sources of supply which are not interrupted. That is the theory of the boot grease containers on strut suspension and on rack and pinion steering systems. Drum brakes have no such sources of supply.

To get at virtually any drum brake you have to remove the so-called "dust cover," which is a thin metal bowl covering the large nut, cotterpin and washer which hold the bearing and wheel in place. It isn't necessary or even advisable to remove the tire, first. The dust cover comes off by prying it, beginning with a thick screwdriver and working around the rim, then tapping it with a rubber hammer. That will knock it off. Remove the cotterpin which sometimes goes through the nut or in other cases (for example, VW Rabbit, Scirroco, Dasher, etc.) it goes through or with a separate nut lock. Some nut locks don't have cotterpins. Incidentally, you have to pry off any outer wheel covering to get at the dust cover—anything from a usual aluminum or other wheel cover to the small plastic covers that are found on some cars.

Once the lock nut or cotterpin are out, turn off the large nut, using your fingers or an open end adjustable wrench. In order to pull the wheel off without wrenching or putting damaging force on the bearings and their races, because of the weight of the tire and wheel, put a tire iron or any prying tool—a piece of sturdy wood—underneath the tire and guide it off so that no pressure is pushed onto the bearings. If the

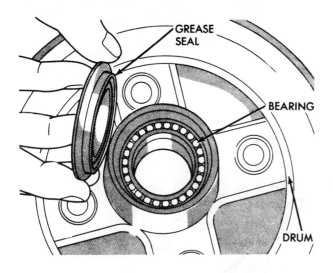

A grease seal to hold grease into wheel bearings.

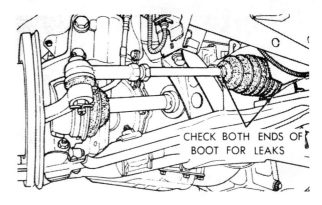

Constant velocity joints on front suspension must be checked for leaks and repaired when they occur.

wheel won't come off, it means the parking brake is on. If it is, release it only after blocking a wheel, if you haven't already done that. Block the wheel opposite the one you're working on.

With the wheel off, fish out the front bearing if it hasn't already fallen into your hand in the process of getting the wheel off. Now lay the wheel down and pound out the grease seal, if such there is. The grease seal will, in some cases, hold the bearing in, loosely. To pound it out, use the wooden end of a small hammer against the seal and down through the wheel axle chamber, and hit it once or twice sufficiently to drive out the seal. But put a rag under the working area so that when bearing and seal come out they land softly.

Examine the bearings and the races (what they turn on) carefully for wear and other imperfections —cracks and other blemishes. If you see nothing, and the bearings haven't been noisy, they should be cleaned along with all the surfaces around them. Soak the bearings in a de-greasing solution of anything designed for it—from kerosene or gasoline to trade brands such as Gunk. Use a soft brush to loosen hardened grease. Once everything is shiny, push grease into the bearings. You can buy a small tool to do this or use the palm of your hand. Put a lot of grease into the palm of your hand, and then push the bearing into the grease, again and again until grease is coming out of every pore of the bearing. Bearing grease, as noted above, should be very heavy and sticky. A once-over-lightly greasing will not do the trick.

After the bearings are full of grease, install them as they were, and add grease inside the housing, but don't overdo it. See that there is plenty of grease on and around the two races, and behind the large washer in front behind the dust cover. But don't put grease in the dust cover.

When you put the wheel back on, again use the pry bar to guide the wheel so that the bearings don't get scuffed or scratched.

Wheel bearings run out of grease between 10,000 and 30,000 miles. Don't overlook them; dry bearings are dangerous.

Rear bearings on front drive cars are very similar to front wheel bearings on cars with drum brakes. If your car is front drive, you have the same expectation of a bearing grease job on the rear wheels as you would have on a car with drum brakes in front, and with the control arm suspension systems of the front engine, rear drive power train.

If bearings and races show wear, either from grinding noises, or from visual inspection, you must replace both the bearing and the race at fault. It isn't necessary to replace both bearings if only one is faulty.

To replace a wheel bearing, you must drive out the old races and drive in the new. If you clean away the grease from the inner surfaces of the races you will see access paths to them where you can use a drift and hammer to drive them out. These access paths are at opposite sides of the race so that you can pound on the race equally at either side. Otherwise you won't get it out.

You shouldn't pound on the new race, however. Use a block of wood over it and pound on that. If you can't get it to bottom out using only wood, find an old pipe that will fit over the race, or use a large socket and a piece of wood to protect the socket. Try to avoid using the drift (punch), because it can scuff the edge of the race.

To grease inner bearings on disc brakes requires removing the caliper. That will be discussed under ''brakes.''

Grease all places that have jets provided, and places where there is no provision for a grease gun, but a requirement for grease. We've covered most such places.

Chapter Two

Engine Tuneup

A brief description of what happens in an engine electrical system may aid in understanding why regular tuneups are needed.

Points and condenser (or the electronic equivalents of the points) are in effect a kind of dam or switch. They build up an electrical charge, which comes to them from the coil. The coil takes in 12 volts from the battery and changes it into much higher voltage—from 20,000 to 30,000 or more, depending on the type of system. That voltage goes to the distributor's points and condenser. Their action is what enables the coil to build up the high voltages. They dam, store and discharge the increased voltage to the spark plugs for firing.

The coil has two circuits, a primary and secondary. When you turn on the ignition the voltage goes from the battery to the primary circuit of the coil, then on to the points and condenser. As you can see, one of the point leads is a ground, which completes the circuit. The circuit is completed when the distributor turns to open the points; at that instant, the voltage leaps across the opening gap, propelled by the magnetic force in the primary circuit of the coil which forces an increase of the voltage in the secondary circuit, and that voltage, in turn, is what actually is fed to the spark plug being fired. The condenser's function is to store excess voltage from the points when they open, preventing the points from fusing, melting, or breaking down. If that happens, the gap is closed or altered and the plugs cannot fire.

The primary circuit must be broken, otherwise the secondary circuit will not possess sufficient voltage to fire the plugs.

Wear on points, condenser, and plugs is enormous, from the time you turn on the ignition. It is surprising that they last as long as they do, since each engine revolution fires half the plugs, and the points, condenser and coil must produce the required voltage charge at every opening of the points, and every high cam lobe push on the points.

In electronic ignition something similar happens, though there are no contacting surfaces to wear away. Also, electrical components wear out for other reasons.

Corrosion, breakdown of insulation, vibration which causes wear on all components, and the incessant dust and dirt, all conspire against the electrical system.

TUNEUP SCOPE

Engine tuneup is an activity aimed at restoring like-new performance, to the extent possible. Aside from the fact that new cars often arrive with defects that require some of the ministrations of engine tuneup before they behave in a manner befitting their age, the fact is that once a car is driven past eight or 10,000 miles, virtually every part of it has suffered irretrievable wear. This has nothing to do with quality control—theirs or ours (European, Japanese)—or workmanship. It has to do with the state of the art and with materials that wear out, especially friction-bearing materials and surfaces.

It is as true of Japanese cars as of American or German. It is a reflection of entropy, or the natural unavailability of resources due to internal processes.

Tuneup in any car may be a major job involving basics such as compression and engine rebuilding, or it may be a minor but essential job involving spark plugs, points if any, and carburetor adjustment. Carburetor adjustment can also lead to carburetor rebuilding, in which case the tuneup becomes more than minor but less than major. In music there are minor modes considered "darker," and carburetor rebuilding would place the tuneup in that category— darker, minor.

Parts involved in minor tuneup are; spark plugs, points, distributor cap, rotor, condenser, air filter, spark plug cables, battery and battery cables, belts, PCV valve and air filter.

Valve lash is included in engine tuneup, though it's a separate job and can be done anytime within the mileage specifications of the individual car. In some cars it's complex and requires special tools. But tuneup generally isn't difficult, though it may be painstaking and require much time in the matter of carburetor rebuilding.

Engine tuneup is needed when simple accumulation of mileage dictates it. But tuneup is also needed when various symptoms appear. Basically, these include hard starting, poor acceleration, stalling, poor idling, and generally bad performance at almost any speed—if the car will start at all.

Spark plugs

Spark plugs, their behavior, characteristics and appearance, continue to be the key to engine tuneup. Electronic ignition has prolonged the life of spark plugs. With mechanical distributors rather than electronic, the life of a spark plug isn't much more than 10,000 miles, if that. Electronic ignition increases spark plug life, up to 20,000 miles or more.

Eight of ten cars on the road today need new spark plugs. Because they don't get them, their engines burn vastly more gasoline than if new plugs were installed. In cars with mechanical distributors (points and condensers), fuel consumption goes up with wear on these components. Tuneup corrects such needless gas consumption.

Spark plugs, when new, also cut down on emissions—up to one half, in fact. You can save almost three out of every 20 gallons of gas with an engine tuneup consisting of new spark plugs primarily, new points if applicable and emission control maintenance.

Spark plugs with mileage over 20,000 should almost always be replaced, even if they pass the appearance test. That test is a simple visual inspection, after removing the plug (which may or may not be simple), to check on the color of the electrode residue and the condition of the electrodes. If what is on the electrodes is a light tan or chalky color, and the buildup isn't great, and if the electrodes aren't worn off noticeably, it is probable that the plug has been firing properly and will continue to do so, if you clean and gap it correctly.

If the plug has a wet, black deposit on it when the engine is cold, and has heavy mileage as well, the chances are great that the plug is simply worn out. You can't always see a defective plug. Indeed, it is common that a plug will look good to the naked eye but be defective, and it can happen with relatively new plugs, though it is much more likely to occur with plugs that have heavy mileage. So, if your engine develops a lope or miss, and you are puzzled by a visual inspection of the spark plugs that shows

NORMAL

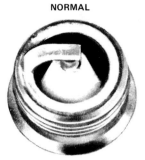

IDENTIFIED BY LIGHT TAN OR GRAY DEPOSITS ON THE FIRING TIP. CAN BE CLEANED.

WORN

IDENTIFIED BY SEVERELY ERODED OR WORN ELECTRODES. CAUSED BY NORMAL WEAR. SHOULD BE REPLACED

GAP BRIDGED

IDENTIFIED BY DEPOSIT BUILD-UP CLOSING GAP BETWEEN ELECTRODES. CAUSED BY OIL OR CARBON FOULING. IF DEPOSITS ARE NOT EXCESSIVE, THE PLUG CAN BE CLEANED.

OVERHEATING

IDENTIFIED BY A WHITE OR LIGHT GRAY INSULATOR WITH SMALL BLACK OR GRAY BROWN SPOTS AND WITH BLUISH-BURNT APPEARANCE OF ELECTRODES, CAUSED BY ENGINE OVERHEATING. WRONG TYPE OF FUEL, LOOSE SPARK PLUGS, TOO HOT A PLUG, LOW FUEL PUMP PRESSURE OR INCORRECT IGNITION TIMING. REPLACE THE PLUG.

PRE-IGNITION

IDENTIFIED BY MELTED ELECTRODES AND POSSIBLY BLISTERED INSULATOR. METALLIC DEPOSITS ON INSULATOR INDICATE ENGINE DAMAGE. CAUSED BY WRONG TYPE OF FUEL, INCORRECT IGNITION TIMING OR ADVANCE, TOO HOT A PLUG, BURNT VALVES OR ENGINE OVERHEATING.

FUSED SPOT DEPOSIT

IDENTIFIED BY MELTED OR SPOTTY DEPOSITS RESEMBLING BUBBLES OR BLISTERS. CAUSED BY SUDDEN ACCELERATION. CAN BE CLEANED.

Spark plug wear and tear.

nothing wrong, try replacing the plugs. That's easier than rebuilding the engine, which is a common prescription under the circumstances.

Some conditions of radical wear in spark plugs include electrodes burned off or joined together—the gap filled in—by corrosion. These are rare and caused by pre-ignition in the case of the burned off electrode, or the wrong plug or a worn out plug in the case of the electrodes fused by corrosion buildup. Burned electrodes are also caused by incorrect ignition timing—too much advance—or too lean a carburetor setting and (rarely) spark plugs not torqued properly.

Pre-ignition, which is the igniting of the combustion chamber mix before it is scheduled to occur, or "run-on," in which unburned gases continue to ig-

nite from burning carbon accumulations after the key is turned off, are signs of various defective conditions. They can be caused by the wrong spark plug, low octane fuel, lean gas/air mix, incorrect engine timing (too advanced), poor engine cooling, or simply an engine with worn rings, valves, etc.

Heavy oil deposits that foul the electrodes are the usual sign of worn valves and rings. A new set of plugs won't cure the problem but if you don't want to do an engine overhaul you can buy plugs that will fire through oil.

Visual tests

Distributor caps, spark plug cables and conden-

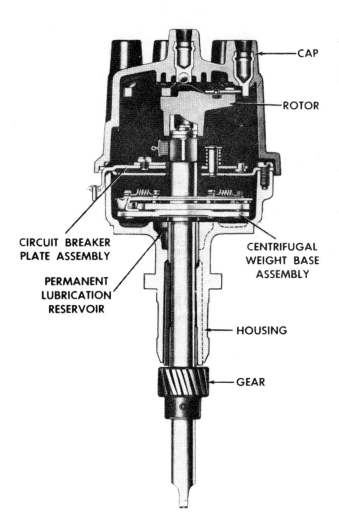

Details of a typical distributor.

CAP

ROTOR

CIRCUIT BREAKER PLATE ASSEMBLY

PERMANENT LUBRICATION RESERVOIR

CENTRIFUGAL WEIGHT BASE ASSEMBLY

HOUSING

GEAR

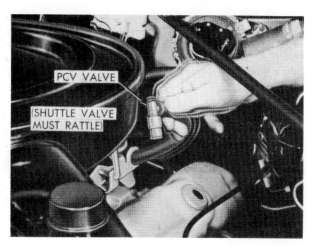

A PCV valve.

PCV VALVE

(SHUTTLE VALVE MUST RATTLE)

sers all may seem perfect to the naked eye, but any one of them can be defective and cause a repertory of weird engine symptoms that defy analysis. A hairline crack in a distributor cap, hard to see even in clear daylight, a defective condenser which no visual inspection can reveal, or cracked insulation and other wear or corrosion on spark plug cables, can make it difficult or impossible to start an engine, to accelerate or obtain any efficient performance from it. Symptoms like mulish, bucking behavior, backfiring, or constant and sudden engine failure, can be caused by these ignition components. With electronic ignition, which doesn't have points, the distributor cap can also crack and produce these symptoms. But if the electronic module of these newer distributors conks out the engine will show no sign of starting or running whatsoever.

You can actually see bad spark plug cables if you open the hood and run the engine in a dark place. The cables will give off arcing flashes of electricity at worn spots, if the spots are close enough to a ground on or near the engine. But there can also be cross-

firing between cables that are incorrectly routed. If cables have deteriorated from wear there will be other symptoms such as an engine miss, backfiring, or weak acceleration.

You can see the wear on belts, if you twist them around sufficiently to expose the underside that gets all the wear in the pulley grooves, and flick the ignition switch on and off once or twice to push them out of the pulleys so they can be seen entirely.

You can also see a dirty carburetor, when you remove the top of its air filter housing. If there's a lot of dirty black accumulation inside the throat it needs cleaning at least.

A PCV valve can be checked roughly by removing it and trying to make it rattle by shaking it. If it rattles loosely it is probably okay; if it doesn't produce such a noise it is almost certainly defective. PCV valves must be replaced conscientiously, otherwise you risk engine damage. They don't function much beyond 15,000 miles, so they should be replaced earlier.

The high tension coil cable from the center pole of the distributor to the coil should also be inspected for cracks and corrosion. Look too at the smaller wires to the coil, one of which usually goes to the battery, the other to a side post on the distributor.

Battery cables themselves wear out at the lug joints after a few years. Battery posts should be cleaned regularly along with the lugs and the battery surface.

To clean battery posts and lugs on the side mounted types, simply unbolt the lug and use a wire brush on all surfaces. Top mounted lugs must be unbolted and gently pried off. Push a large-bladed screwdriver in the slot, after you unbolt the lug, and gently pry the two sides apart. Under no circumstance do you use force on the battery post—it will break, ruining the battery. Small pullers are available inexpensively. The screwdriver will break open the corrosion that usually builds up, and enable you to get the cable off easily. The pullers hold the post in place while pulling up on the lug.

Wire-brush or sandpaper all the lug-post surfaces.

Also, wash off the battery top or, in the side mounts, the lug surface, with baking soda and water. Filmy corrosion builds up to the point where there is sufficient electrical contact between posts to keep the battery discharging all the time and eventually running it down. Use distilled water to fill the cells.

Tuneup procedures vary as to specifications; spark plug and point gaps differ, as do timing specifications. The actual processes also differ from make to make, despite their basic similarities.

VW Scirocco spark plug replacement begins by marking the cables with a tab of some sort so you get them back on the right plugs. Firing order is 1-3-4-2, with No. 1 plug on the side of the engine nearest the fan belts and the oil filler cap. (That's the right side viewed from the driver's seat.) You needn't mark them if you can remember them.

To remove spark plug cables, take a screwdriver and pry gently at the bottom of the boot, against any part of the engine that allows you the slight amount of leverage needed—very little. If you simply grab the cable and pull the boot off, you may pull the cable out of the boot, thus ruining it, and you'll still have the problem of getting the boot off. So pry it off.

To remove the spark plug, use the ratchet, a long extension, and the spark plug socket. If the plug has been tightened excessively, as too often happens, give the ratchet a sharp tug or punch with your open hand. With slight persuasion the plugs will come out.

Examine all of them for the symptoms we've noted. But don't get alarmed if you see black carbon deposits on one or two of them, whereas the others might have the normal tan chalky color. Black carbon may mean merely that the plug isn't firing because it is defective, not because the cylinder is defective, or because of too rich a mixture from the carburetor.

Examine the spark plug cables carefully. Any cracked boot requires replacement of that cable. The same prescription applies to the cable, though if its boot is okay you can, if you wish, tape up a cracked cable. But the cost of new cables is so little, their function so basic, that it is poor economy to attempt to salvage worn cables.

If the spark plugs have low mileage, clean them off with a spark plug file or a finger nail file or sandpaper, gap them with a feeler gauge, scrape out the inside carbon around the center post, without disturbing the post, blow out the debris, and replace the plug. Because the cylinder head is aluminum, start the plug in by hand to make sure you don't strip the

threads. Aluminum is delicate in these matters. If you can't start one or more of them by hand, put the plug inside the spark plug socket, attach the extension rod, and turn it slowly and carefully until you can be certain it has started in correctly. To make sure that there is no obstruction on a re-used plug, clean its threads off with a wire brush before installing it. The new one won't need such treatment. Put a few drops of oil on the threads.

Gap the new plugs according to specifications, install them, tighten them securely but beware of force. They should be easy to loosen with the ratchet wrench, if you have any doubts about it.

New plugs are gapped to the most commonly used specification, so it often happens that you don't have to change the gap. But all gapping tools have a U-shaped bending tool on them for any adjustment needed. Don't push on the center post. You obviously gap only the outer, exposed electrode.

The most important thing to remember about spark plug installation is to keep the socket centered so that it doesn't break the porcelain. That ruins the plug. It's not a terribly expensive mistake, but it's a nuisance to have to go back to the store for only one plug. It's also embarrassing.

When you replace cables, get them on tight by pushing down on the boot until it resists pulling off—a test you don't wish to apply strenuously.

Distributor

Distributors on the Scirocco, Dasher (and Rabbit), have their condensers mounted outside, as do most 4-cylinder cars (not enough space inside, unlike bigger engines).

You will replace the condenser, and the points and, if necessary, the rotor and distributor cap.

To gain access it is necessary to remove the two retaining clips on the outside of the distributor cap. Pry them open with a screwdriver. Lift off the distributor cap without disturbing the cables. If one comes loose, put it back or tab it. In a bright light—preferably sunlight— examine the inside of the distributor cap for hairline cracks. Feel around it with a finger. Sometimes you can feel such a crack without seeing it. Examine the outside carefully, also. Any crack will cause "arcing" (short circuiting) sooner or later. Remove each cable, one at a time, from the top of the cap. Clean out the cap "towers," one at a time, cleaning the cable as well. Look for insulation cracks on the cables.

If the cap requires replacement, move the cables, one at a time, from the old cap to the new one, starting by lining up the cap with the clip fastener as a guide.

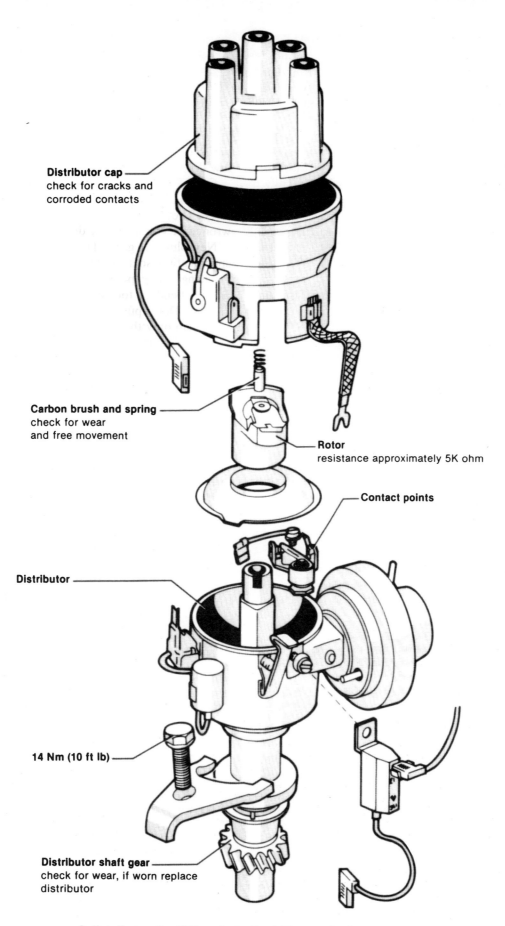

Distributor cap
check for cracks and
corroded contacts

Carbon brush and spring
check for wear
and free movement

Rotor
resistance approximately 5K ohm

Contact points

Distributor

14 Nm (10 ft lb)

Distributor shaft gear
check for wear, if worn replace
distributor

A distributor for VW engines, Ford Pinto and others.

Unscrew the condenser.

You must make a decision now, whether or not to remove the distributor from the engine. If you don't remove it, you work in cramped quarters. If you do remove it, you must mark the relationship of the rotor to the rim mark of the distributor bowl, and some point on the engine, otherwise you disturb timing to the extent that the car won't start.

If you choose to remove the distributor, turn the engine by using the wrench that will grasp the center of the crankshaft pulley, turning it clockwise until the rotor of the distributor points to the slash mark across the rim of the distributor housing. This marks the No. 1 cylinder firing position. That is the way you return the distributor—the rotor tip pointing to the mark on the bowl. Don't move the engine while the distributor is removed. That will upset timing.

If you decide to remove the distributor, proceed as follows. Once the distributor cap is off and the rotor tip pointing to the mark on the bowl, remove the rotor and the dust shield. Examine the rotor, the carbon brush and spring, for wear and signs of arcing, as well as cracks. Below the distributor bowl is a hold-down clamp and nut. Release the nut and remove the clamp. Detach all wires and tubes coming in and out of the distributor, and remove the distributor from the engine.

It isn't necessary to remove the distributor in order to perform the necessary disassembly tuneup routines, but they are the same whether the distributor is inside or outside the engine.

The points connect to a clip at the side of the distributor. It snaps on and off—pull it off. One screw anchors the point set to the plate below. Before removing that screw with any screwdriver that fits, place a rag around the plate below the points, to close up any hole into which you might drop the screw.

Release the point set by removing the small screw.

Note that if you remove the distributor from the engine, you also remove the vacuum advance mechanism with it. Pull off the rubber tubing, but leave the vacuum advance alone.

To install the new point set, first rub some grease around the distributor cam lobes—a very thin film of grease that usually comes in a capsule with the new point set. Next, notice that the point set can be installed only in one way, with a pin on the bottom going into a slot on the breaker plate below. Tighten the point set retaining screw lightly and install the wire and connector you removed.

If you removed the distributor and you now have the point set installed, you must next install the distributor.

Replace the distributor into its housing, taking care to install the washer in the shaft opening to the engine block, if you removed it. First, turn the distri-

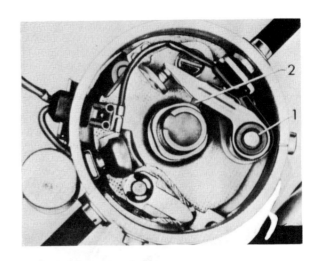

A distributor showing contact points (1) and rubbing cam (2).

butor shaft to the No. 1 cylinder marking on the housing, then turn it away from the mark about 18 degrees clockwise. Now insert it into the gears; the rotor should turn back to the No. 1 cylinder mark as the bottom slot of the distributor shaft goes into the oil pump drive gear. If it does not, remove the distributor and look at the oil pump drive. It should be parallel to the engine crankshaft. If it isn't, insert a screwdriver into the slot and turn it. Then insert the distributor. Seat the distributor, check the mounting flange so that everything fits perfectly, and make sure that the rotor tip faces the No. 1 cylinder mark. Install the hold-down clamp and bolt, and the distributor cap. Tighten the clamp sufficiently to keep the distributor bowl from turning.

If you are not certain that the engine is at the desired position—the distributor rotor pointing to the No. 1 cylinder—remove the oil filler cap and look at the cam lobes just below the oil cap. Both cam lobes of the No. 1 cylinder are exposed and should both point up. If they do not, turn the crankshaft as before with the socket wrench one complete revolution, which should produce the desired stance. This procedure also will work to start the engine if for some reason you have disturbed engine timing with the distributor out of the engine.

The points must now be adjusted. Turn the crankshaft with a wrench until the fiber rubbing block on the contact point set rests on one of the peaks on the distributor cam. This is the widest open gap between the two electrodes. Use a feeler gauge and if the gap is not the prescribed .016 (.40 mm), insert a screwdriver into the adjusting slot on the contact plate and turn it until the feeler gauge just goes between the points. Now tighten the hold-down screw on the point plate, but don't tighten it too much—securely, not aggressively.

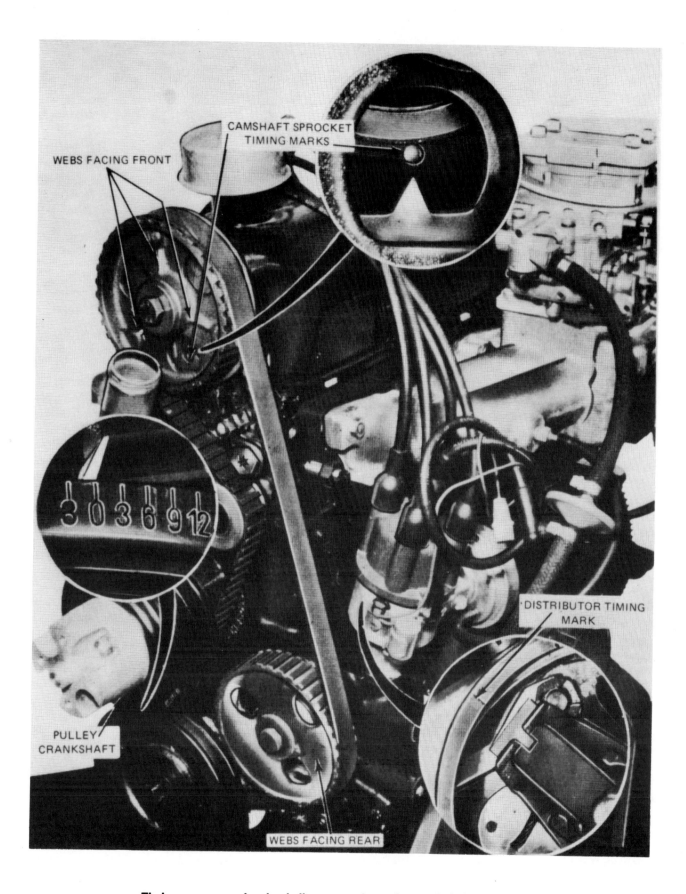

WEBS FACING FRONT

CAMSHAFT SPROCKET
TIMING MARKS

3 0 3 6 9 12

DISTRIBUTOR TIMING
MARK

PULLEY
CRANKSHAFT

WEBS FACING REAR

Timing sequence showing indicator marks on harmonic balance wheel.

29

Now it is necessary to time the engine.

Engine timing requires a timing light. The engine should be at operating temperature. It isn't necessary to remove the vacuum advance hose from the distributor. It is necessary to time the engine when the idle speed is very low, running smoothly. If the idle is too fast it will not be possible to time the engine accurately. The idle adjusting screw on the side of the carburetor will usually produce the desired results—a turn or two counterclockwise. It's the screw nearest the throttle linkage coupling that obviously pushes on it. If turning the idle screw only produces a rough idle at very slow speeds that's one customary sign of a carburetor in need of overhaul. If it's too rough you won't get precise timing results, though you can get it close enough until such time as you can get around to doing the carburetor.

Attach a neon timing light—the cheapest type, perfectly accurate but it can only be used away from sunlight and that's no handicap when you consider the price (about $5)—following instructions. If the timing light is neon you attach it to the No. 1 spark plug cable (which you have removed) and the spark plug. It will have two leads, one of them fitting the spark plug cable end, the other one fitting the plug itself. Other, more expensive lights, either plug into an electric wall outlet— that's the AC type—or are attached to the battery and the No. 1 spark plug. That's the DC type, unsurprisingly.

The No. 1 spark plug on inline engines, whether sixes or fours, is the plug nearest the radiator, or in transversely mounted engines such as Rabbit, it would be the one nearest the alternator and the crankshaft balance wheel. In engines such as Subaru, which is an opposed 4-cylinder, it will be marked.

Scirocco and Rabbit with manual transmissions are timed in one way; with automatic transmission there are slight differences. Also, early models (1974) have minor variations of componentry from models since that year. The placement of the Computer Analysis TDC sensor is the chief difference. In those early models the sensor was on the bell housing with an attached cable. Later on the sensor was put on the driver side away from the bell housing; it has no further interest for the home mechanic.

On early cars, disconnect the wire that runs from the sensor on the bell housing. Then unscrew the plug. It it's tight, take a block of wood to it and tap it open with a small hammer, counterclockwise. VW sells a special tool for just that one task. Don't buy it.

On all models, including the most recent, you do have to remove the plug since it conceals the timing marks on the flywheel.

Once the plug is removed you can see a pointer mark in the hole which is supposed to coincide with the correct timing mark; it is 3 degrees ATDC

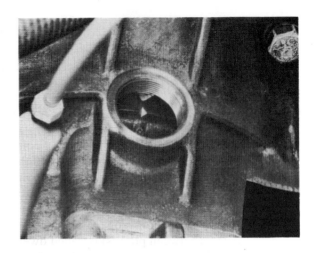

Timing mark on VW engines.

("after top dead center"). That mark, on the flywheel, may have to be found and brightened with chalk before the timing light will pick it out. But, first try to find it with the timing light.

With the timing light installed, and the motor running slowly and smoothly (and at normal operating temperature), aim the flashing light down into the hole, making sure you don't get near anything that's moving. If the light flashes on the TDC mark in exact coincidence with the pointer, engine timing is correct. But if it misses, or you are unable to find it at all, loosen the hold down bolt below the distributor and with the light in place and the engine running, slowly move the distributor bowl until you do see the TDC mark. Then tighten the hold down clamp. If the bowl is stuck, use slight force.

If you are unable to find the TDC mark with the flashing light, you'll have to find it by turning the crankshaft as before until you do, then marking it with chalk. This could take a lot of turning—always clockwise. If you've never done it before you may find it similar to looking for a needle in a haystack—if you've ever done THAT before. It may take more patience than you have.

But the TDC mark is there and as you turn the crankshaft you may have to use a flashlight to find the mark. That means a tiny turn, then moving to the timing hole with the flashlight.

The basic difference between stick shift VW's and automatics in this procedure is a trivial one—the configuration of the TDC marks— the stick shift TDC mark is circular, the automatic is a line. Otherwise you do the same things. Note: if you never succeed in finding the timing mark it means you don't have the No. 1 plug.

There is one test it is well to make, once you get timing in order. That is the throttle valve gap in cars with fuel injection. Simply disconnect the green hose from the distributor, with the engine idling, and watch the timing mark; it should move forward. If it does not shift, the valve is not doing its duty.

Engine timing on VW cars includes Rabbit, Scirocco, Dasher and Audi Fox; they're all timed more or less alike.

Adjusting for dwell is usually prescribed. Dwell consists of that fraction of a second when the coil builds up for its next discharge at contact point opening. In other words, when the center pole of the distributor turns, rubbing against the moving point arm, it builds up voltage in the coil between the raised cam lobes, then discharges the voltage when the raised lobes push the points open. The time between lobe points (between pushes) is called dwell. If you adjusted the points correctly with the feeler gauge the chances are that you've also gotten the dwell adjustment correct. But if you didn't it will show up in poor performance and gas mileage. Generally, point adjustment, if done conscientiously, will also take care of dwell. Conscientious adjustment means nothing more than getting the point adjustment at the precise highest point of the lobe. But if the distributor is worn, and there's too much "play" in it, an exact dwell adjustment is impossible. When you suspect that to be the case—and it will happen only after very high mileage—the cure is to rebuild or buy a rebuilt distributor. One easy test is to turn the center pole by hand, noting how much "play" it has. It shouldn't have much—just enough to rub the points open and closed.

To actually test for dwell requires a dwell meter. You can buy inexpensive dwell meters; usually an engine tester has a dwell meter attached to it. To use a dwell meter you must pull off the vacuum control rubber hose from the distributor and plug it—with a pencil end or anything. A selector switch will indicate the number of cylinders you will use—your car's number. Connect one meter lead to the coil terminal of the distributor (the center post), and the other meter lead to a ground, which is any engine bolt, screw, nut, etc. Run the engine at normal idle speed and check the reading. Dwell readings on an 8-cylinder engine should be between 26-32; 6-cylinder readings will be between 36-45 degrees, and 4-cylinder will be about 40. But follow specifications for your car. As engine speed is increased, variation in dwell readings should be slight or nonexistent. Anything over 3 degrees, as you push on the accelerator linkage, probably means a worn distributor—the gear, bushings, shaft, or breaker plate. It can also mean something wrong in the electrical circuits—high resistance. That could be almost anything—coil, condenser, points, wiring, fusebox.

There is one exception to the statement about dwell variation over 3 degrees; in some old Ford distributors (Auto-Lite) there can be a dwell varia-

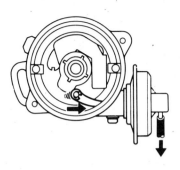

Toyota vacuum advance check.

tion up to 12 degrees without fault.

Thus timing and dwell can be set on virtually every car with a mechanical distributor. Electronic distributors do not require it. Both dwell and timing are set electronically and don't have to be reset, unless they are set incorrectly at the factory, or their timing is disturbed. Timing can be checked using a timing light, as above, and change of setting is performed also in the same way—the nut or bolt holding the distributor clamp is loosened, the distributor bowl turned slightly until the timing marks line up.

You can check both vacuum and centrifugal advance, if after you complete engine timing and tuneup you find that the car isn't performing as it should—more or less as it did when new. To check the vacuum advance, turn the plate under the points as far as you can by hand, counterclockwise. It should spring back quickly. The vacuum advance is checked for leaks by disconnecting the hoses, then turning the same plate back in the same way. While holding it back, cover the hose connections with the fingers of your other hand. Release the plate; if vacuum is right the plate will not return to its original position until you release the hose connections.

Centrifugal advance can be checked by turning the rotor clockwise as far as you can. When released, the rotor should return to its original position, smoothly and quickly. If not, the mechanism needs cleaning, or the distributor needs replacing (or rebuilding).

Replacement distributors (with yours in return) can be purchased for $35 to $50. You can rebuild them yourself for the price of the worn parts, which would be about half. But the job requires a few special tools, which you may not have, some skill and fair amount of labor. It is not recommended as a matter of course, unless you want to acquire expertise in the art.

Since any rebuilt or new distributor will come with new points and condenser installed, it might be sensible to check vacuum and centrifugal advance before going ahead to install new points and condenser in the old one.

Examine the rotor and cap carefully in bright sunlight for cracks, wear, and signs of "arcing" (electrical short circuiting) or carbon tracing—tiny black carbon lines. These flaws condemn either part. When they go bad, rotors in these cars can prevent engine firing altogether, so don't save on rotors.

It is a fact that once you get practice, you can time these engines by ear, moving the distributor slightly back and forth, listening for the best engine idle. You can't move the distributor very far without the idle deteriorating, so you aim at a mid-point.

We have presented in step-by-step elaboration everything you need to know about cars manufactured by Volkswagen insofar as simple engine tuneup goes. Every manufacturer has individual nuances of parts placement, of removal, replacement, adjustment, and testing. But the principles do not vary, since all engines (excepting rotaries, in some cases, and diesels) conform to standard behavior patterns of internal combustion engines with pistons and valves, even those with fuel injection.

Porsche Tuning

Engine tuneup in Porsche follows the general considerations already discussed above as to spark plugs, cables and distributor components. Individual differences occur. Some Porsche rotors, for example, are held by a screw, instead of the usual press fit. Porsche does recommend removing the distributor when you replace points, but it isn't absolutely essential.

In Porsche 914 models timing is set at 5 degrees BTDC ("before top dead center") but requires a special timing light ("static" light). When you get timing correct the light goes out. To set timing requires that you get the right hand heater hose away from the heater blower by loosening the retaining clamp. This allows you to unscrew the plug to the timing mark. Then, using a wrench on the crankshaft, turn the engine clockwise until a black notch on the pulley aligns with the V-shaped notch in the blower housing. Now you need the static light. Attach one lead of the static light to the coil-to-distributor terminal on the coil or distributor and the other one to a ground.

Next, loosen the distributor hold down clamp and turn the distributor clockwise until the light goes out and the points are closed. Now turn the distributor counterclockwise until the light comes on and the points begin to open. Tighten the hold down clamp. Replace rotor and distributor cap.

Next you need a regular stroboscopic timing light—any type will do. Remove both vacuum hoses from the distributor and install the timing light. Run the engine to normal temperature. On most 914 models the engine must be revved up to 3500 rpm for an instant—but not longer, and that's important. So you need someone to step on the gas, while you aim the strobe timing light into the inspection hole. The red notch on the crankshaft pulley should line up with the V notch in the blower housing. If they do not, again loosen the distributor and rotate it until they do.

On 911 models you do something similar, except that the high speed timing with the strobe light should be done at 6000 rpm's. Also, you don't use the static light for low speed timing, but the strobe light at idle should hit the 5 degree ATDC notch, which is to the left of a ZI notch (which is TDC), a 30 degree BTDC and 35 degree BTDC notch.

The first step is to attach the timing light to the No. 1 spark plug, start the engine at slow idle (with connected vacuum advance hose at the distributor). The light should pick out the 5 degree ATDC notch in the pulley in alignment with the notch in the blower housing. If not, make the usual adjustment to the distributor, by loosening the hold down clamp and turning it slowly. Next, you have someone rev the engine to 6000 rpm's for an instant as you check dynamic timing. It should fall between 32 and 38 degrees. If it doesn't, move the distributor slightly. Warning: be very careful of the fan belt and pulley, and make sure that the fan belt is in good condition and in correct adjustment. A frayed fan belt that isn't adjusted properly is dangerous. (Note: early 911 models—up to 1971—also require static timing.)

Timing on 914/6 models requires static adjustment with a static timing light, as above, and dynamic timing falls into the 35 degree alignment mark at 6,000 rpm's. In all cases, don't hold the engine at 6,000 rpm's for longer than it takes to see the alignment relationships under the strobe light—which should be a matter of a few seconds only, never more. If you don't catch it in that period, instruct whoever is "gunning" the engine to bring it down instantly. And we emphasize again: never work on an engine running at high speed unless you are certain that everything is safely away from the belts, and the belts themselves are in perfect adjustment and condition—they are extremely dangerous. The same caveat pertains to the fan itself, which should be inspected carefully for nicks, breaks, and misalignment of blades, any of which can lead to disaster, whether or not you are in its path. A fan and belt gone berserk because of flaws can destroy anything in the vicinity. And electrically driven fans which don't have belts, can be the worst of all, if you turn the ignition on and forget it. The fan, which may not be running one moment, can suddenly turn on the next, because of the thermostatic switch. None of these warnings should be interpreted as indications that car work is dangerous. It is not, except to the foolish and the reckless.

Toyota tuning

Toyota's Celica and other sporty cars all follow standard tuneup processes. Toyota recommends replacing spark plugs every 12,000 miles. It also recommends cleaning and adjusting them every 6,000 miles. Because most Toyota engine heads are aluminum, tighten the plugs securely but not drastically—11 to 14 foot pounds on a torque wrench. That's not much; just a light tug.

Toyota also recommends putting a thin film of oil over the plug threads before replacing them in the engine, and if the threads have rust on them cleaning it off with a 14 mm plug tap. A wire brush will do just as well, if you don't have the tap.

Be particularly careful with spark plugs and aluminum blocks. The best procedure is to put the plug in the spark plug socket where it should be held snugly and firmly by the inner gasket of the socket. Then, holding socket and plug, start it carefully, probing the threads until you can feel the plug entering smoothly and without any resistance. If there is resistance, remove the plug and clean it off again, noting anything on the threads that might interfere with correct fit. This language may make it seem touchy; not a bit of it, just precise. If the spark plug opening in the block is easily accessible—few of them are—you can start the plug with your fingers, then switch to the socket.

Points and condenser on Toyotas can be replaced with the distributor in the engine.

Point gap is .018 in most distributors (that's almost universally true—when in doubt use that setting in any car).

In Toyotas with electronic ignition, though you don't have to worry about points, you may find it necessary to check dwell setting. Attach the dwell meter to the negative side of the coil (the wire going from the coil to a ground) instead of to the primary lead as in previous instructions. This is an exception and if you get it wrong you can ruin the coil. This is only on electronic distributors. Engine timing follows procedures already described.

Toyota has one unusual feature on its distributors—the octane selector. It's an adjustment to mate gasoline grade with engine timing. It is near the vacuum control unit beneath a plastic dust cover. It does not get routine adjustment. Not all Toyotas have these devices and they have been discontinued in some models recently.

Datsun "Z" cars

Datsun "Z" cars have two different timing settings for automatic transmissions; one is an advanced setting for temperatures below 30 degrees F, the other is a retarded setting for temperatures above 50 degrees F. Timing marks are on the crankshaft pulley with a pointer on the engine front cover. TDC or 0 is at the left, next is either 5 or 10 before TDC. Succeeding marks are 5 degrees apart. Datsun suggests disconnecting the vacuum advance tube from the distributor. Timing is set as described above. It will probably be necessary to use a piece of chalk to brighten the timing marks, especially if you use a neon strobe light.

It isn't necessary to remove the distributor from the engine for timing.

Mazda rotaries

Mazda rotary engines, used in the Mazda sports cars, differ radically from other engines. However, their maintenance and servicing are remarkably similar to the cars discussed already, and to those that follow. The rotary engine has points, plugs, distributors, and emission control equipment, all similar to familiar reciprocating engine usage. That is because the rotary engine is an internal combustion engine. It just doesn't have the reciprocating systems—valves, pistons, crankshaft, etc.—of the customary engine.

Spark plugs should be cleaned and adjusted every 4,000 miles or four months. Plugs are Japanese NKG B-7EM or B-7EJ; also Nippondenso W-22EA. U.S. plugs are Champion N-80B. These are standard plugs. For cold heat range plugs use NKG B-8EM or B-8EJ; Nippondenso W-25EA; Champion N-78B.

Plugs should be gapped to .031-.035 inches. If electrodes are burning or show signs of white burning at the regular inspection periods, replace them with the cold range plugs. But all plugs should be the same heat range and, if possible, by the same manufacturer, according to Toyo Kogyo Co., the car's manufacturer.

RX-2 and RX-3 rotary engines have two distributors, one for the leading plugs, the other for the trailing set. Both distributors should be inspected and serviced together. Do to the one what you do to the other. Some Mazda rotaries have two sets of points in the leading distributors. Others have three.

Service to these distributors follows the same procedures as above; point gap is .018, adjusted with the screwdriver in the slot provided on the point plate. To rotate the engine in order to get the points open and on the high point of the rubbing cam, flick the ignition key on and off. Note that inside the distributor containing three sets of points the lower sets can be adjusted through access holes in the base plate of the upper point set.

To adjust dual point distributors you can either use a dwell meter, which is the most accurate method, or the old fashioned feeler gauge, which will yield good results if done carefully and with a wire feeler gauge. (Don't use a flat metal gauge.)

Mazda specifies new points and condenser every 12,000 miles or once a year. Replace distributor caps and rotors only when flaws appear.

Engine timing on Mazda rotaries has some things in common with other engine timing procedures, but it has a few details that are not shared.

Rotary timing up to 1975 was more or less similar to ordinary engine timing. The timing light was connected to the leading distributor spark plug cable going to the front (No. 1) rotor. A timing indicator point at the front housing (a pin) and a yellow TDC mark should line up under the flashing light. If not, make the usual correction by loosening the hold down clamp and turning the distributor bowl slightly until the two marks line up.

Then time the trailing distributor the same way, except that the timing light is connected to the spark plug cable which goes to the No. 1 rotor. Point the timing light to the eccentric shaft pulley—an orange mark which signifies 10 degrees ATDC. The pointer and orange mark must coincide; if not make the usual correction.

Beginning with 1975 rotaries you connect the timing light to the leading (lower) spark plug on the front rotor housing and aim it at the indicator pin below, making corrections if needed.

Now, with the timing light connected, (the engine off) use a paper clip to jump between the yellow and blue wires on the distributor connector. Don't disconnect the connector. Start the engine; aim the light at the indicator pin. You are timing for retarded timing—the engine is designed to retard the spark during warmup, otherwise poor performance results. Mazda color-codes timing marks; orange is the retarded timing color. But 10 degrees BTDC is the value you want in retarded timing. You get that setting, if you don't already have it, by finding the timing adjusting screw which is located in the spot where you would expect the vacuum advance device to be.

Now turn off the engine and remove the paper clip. Put the timing light connection on the trailing (top) spark plug at the front rotor housing, and aim it at the indicator pin—the motor is again running. This time, if you need to make an adjustment, rotate the screw on the square plate below the retarded timing adjustment. It all sounds terribly complicated, compared with other timing adjustments, but it isn't. The screw that you use to adjust the retarded timing is the point adjuster. Changing the gap changes the timing.

Fiat tuning

Fiat has made sports cars with unusual power train placement, and configuration, including especially the 124 Spyder, Sport Spyder and the Sport Coupe, all with double overhead camshafts. Though they are identical with the more common overhead valve engines in all other respects, the two overhead camshafts and timing belt (instead of timing chain) set these engines apart. The X 1/9 sports car by Fiat is a mid-engine (actually rear) model, which is responsible for a whole new set of problems of access, or at least orientation. In the U.S. the only rear engine was the G.M. Corvair (1960-1969). It was air-cooled; Fiat uses only water-cooling. Spyder engines are in front.

Tuneup procedures for all Fiat engines are much alike. Nor do they differ from standard procedures for other cars. Fiat sports car engines are inline 4-cylinder engines, whether of the overhead camshaft or overhead valve design. For purposes of tuneup, the location of the camshaft changes valve lash adjustment—when mechanical lifters are used. But nothing else is changed. Only engine overhaul is changed. (Spark plug location differs, but the plugs are still available.)

Spark plugs should be changed at the usual intervals.

Fiat distributor shows two points sets (1 and 3) and two condensers (2).

Engine timing on Fiat shows (1) 10 degree mark (2) 5 degree and (3) 0 degree or TDC.

Points, condenser and other distributor maintenance should begin with a decision as to whether to remove the distributor. It isn't necessary in most models; however, in early models of some cars (mostly 124s), it is necessary. Recent sports cars don't require it.

If, after the necessary tests, you have to replace the distributor (worn gears, etc.), remove the cap (it's held by two attached screws which remain in the cap once they are loosened). Now, make a mark with a screwdriver to indicate the position of the rotor and distributor housing—scratch a mark on the engine somewhere. Disconnect the distributor wires, push the cap off to the side (but don't disconnect the cables unless you have to—tape any disconnected cables with a note indicating where they go). Remove the distributor hold down clamp and pull the distributor out.

Fiat's X 1/9 shares engines with the 128, but the X 1/9 is, as we noted, an engine unable to decide whether it is in the center of the car or at the rear. That complicates distributor work. Some X 1/9s make it almost impossible to change points and condenser and adjust the points without removing the distributor. But most of them, though reluctant to yield their contents, will respond to anyone determined enough, without removing the distributor. (It isn't that difficult to remove or replace.)

Distributors of recent sport coupes and Spyders have dual point distributors. They do different things. One set is for starting, the other for the rest of the time. The starting set is to produce 10 extra degrees of spark advance during starter operation.

The running set maintains top dead center timing. (On early models this was also the case, but the early models—up to 1974—had a complicating switch called a thermoswitch.) When normal oil pressure builds up, the first point set is taken out of the operation. Point gap differs for the two sets, but they are set in the usual way—a screwdriver in the adjusting slot, turned until the desired gap is reached, when the rubbing block rests on a high cam lobe point. The gap for running points is .016; for the starting points it's .012-.019. Note: dual points mean dual condensers, and you must always replace condensers when you replace points, in this case both sets. Condensers are, of course, outside the distributor in all dual point systems.

You tell the two-point sets apart by wiring color; the wire lead for the starting points is green with a black stripe, for the running points it's green.

To check dwell or not to check depends on (1) whether you have a dwell meter and (2) whether the car runs properly, accelerates, and gets proper gas mileage, once you put the points in and check timing and get it adjusted. Dwell is a setting that determines the number of degrees of distributor rotation when the points remain closed. If you set the point gap very precisely, feeling a slight tug on the feeler gauge as you pull it through the gap, and set the timing right on the nose, you can usually forget dwell. It's basically a refinement of point gap setting, but not so essential as gap or timing, if you get them right. Also, a good dwell meter is required, and it's costly. A feeler gauge costs a couple of dollars at most. After you've done it a few times you'll be surprised at how accurate your results will be, without the dwell meter.

Symptoms of failure to get dwell and timing right are poor accleration, engine ping, poor gas mileage—the things you set out to correct with an engine tuneup.

Note that on X 1/9 models (and 128) you should take off the hose connector at the distributor (the vacuum) and stick a pencil in it (the hose), during timing.

If you have a dwell meter and wish to check dwell on cars with dual points, it isn't quite as easy as on other cars. You check each point set separately.

Running points are checked for dwell by locating something called the ignition mode selector relay. That's a switch over on the passenger side of the fender well. Trace it from the distributor—wires go between the two components, and are plugged into the relay switch. Pull the plug off; connect the power and running slots of the relay with a jumper wire. Any solid wire will do. The slots to connect are the middle slot and the slot that faces it at 90 degrees (not the slot that runs parallel to it). Connect the dwell meter positive lead to the green distributor lead, start the engine and check for dwell. If it's off, adjust the point gap.

To check dwell on the starting points, move the center jump wire over to the next (parallel) notch, leaving the other jumper where it is. The dwell meter positive lead goes to the green and black lead on the distributor. Now check dwell and if it is off, adjust the right point set—but you check by cranking the engine, not by running it.

Elsewhere in the Fiat repertory, the dwell meter is connected to the distributor lead in the center of the post that is the primary wire to the coil.

In theory, if you change dwell (point gap) you must once again set timing; it's a little like a circular argument, and it could go on forever. But, as we note above, the proof of this pudding is always in the car's performance. It should run like new, more or less, and drastically better than it did.

Ignition timing on Fiat 124, Sports Coupe and the Spyder, goes like this (first single point distributors):

Fiat usually has two kinds of timing marks, one on the bell housing cover, the other inside on the flywheel, which you can see through the rectangular opening. As with Rabbit and other cars using the enclosed flywheel for timing mark locations, you have to turn the engine over patiently, until you find them. The easy way is, of course, to flick the ignition key on and off, if the distributor is in the engine. Whenever there is an easy-to-reach nut or bolt on the harmonic balance wheel, as with the Rabbit, you can get the same results sometimes more quickly. In any case, once you find it, mark the advance degree that you need and the reference mark on the fan belt pulley, or wherever it will be (harmonic balance wheel or the pulley), with white chalk (or white paint, so it will be there the next time). The white color enables the timing light to pick up the marks clearly and unambiguously.

Always get idle speed in approximately correct limits. A tachometer is the only instrument for the precisely calibrated purpose. But, unless you already have one, it isn't essential. The Fiat sports cars all call for about 850 revolutions per minute (rpm's). If you worry about accuracy, get a tachometer. First try without it.

An rpm of 850 is a common idle speed, slow enough to keep the advance mechanisms from affecting timing, fast enough to keep the engine idling accurately. The engine should always be at normal operating temperature, during timing.

Timing on all recent 124 Sports Coupe and Spider models is TDC ("top dead center"). But, when you disconnect the vacuum line (which is a retard not an advance) you are aiming at 10 degrees "BTDC" (before top dead center), and when you take the pencil out of the vacuum hose and reconnect the hose, the timing will shift over to top dead center, or

0. Do it both ways; line up the marks at 10 BTDC, with the hose off and plugged, then reconnect the hose and line up the marks at 0 or TDC. Adjusting is done in the usual way—loosen the hold down clamp and turn the distributor slightly in the engine.

Again, after you've done it a few times you can forget all the complexities and time the engine by ear—turning the distributor left, then right, until you get the most perfect idle.

Timing on dual point distributors in the 124 Sports Coupe and the Spider models requires using a jumper wire on the ignition mode selector relay, as before—in checking dwell and point gap.

Connect a wire between the power and running terminals (as you did on the running points gap and dwell setting). Now connect the timing light as usual, to the No. 1 spark plug and the No. 1 spark plug cable (in other words, between the cable and the plug) if it's a neon light, or to the No. 1 spark plug and battery, if it's a D.C. timing light. Timing lights always come with instructions, so follow them if you're confused.

With the engine running at 850 rpm's, aim the light at the chalk marks you've made on the front cover and the pulley at TDC. They must coincide. If not, make the usual correction of the distributor bowl.

Next—on dual point cars—move the jumper wire to the starting and power terminals. The starting is on the left, as before, but the power terminal is opposite it on the right. Start the engine and the timing should now be 10 degrees BTDC. If not, adjust by resetting the points. If timing is less than 10, increase the gap slightly; if more than 10, decrease it.

General Motors tuneup

General Motors' Firebird and Camaro (Pontiac and Chevrolet) are sporty cars with power trains that are shared with other G.M. cars. Corvette engines also are standard G.M. engines. Tuneup in all these cars follows General Motors practice, which differs somewhat from the cars discussed above.

Firebird, Camaro, and such cars as the X-Body Citation, have electronic distributors. G.M. says their spark plugs should last 22,000 miles or more. But don't count on it.

Normal operation is defined by G.M. as a spark plug whose electrodes have brown to grayish-tan deposits and with only slight electrode wear. These may be cleaned, gapped, and re-installed, but if they continue to misfire they must be replaced. If re-installed, G.M. urges that new gaskets be used in those cases requiring it (not all do).

Red, brown, yellow and white colored coatings

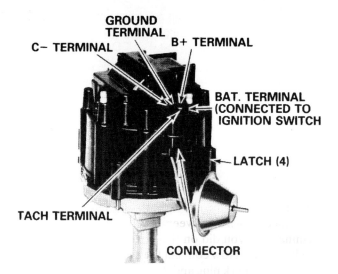

Terminal connections on a G.M. High Energy Ignition distributor.

mean that while the engine may be operating normally under such powdery formations, it is best to replace these plugs. They can cause missing.

If powdery formations turn into a shiny yellow glaze coating on the insulator, the plug must be replaced.

Dry, fluffy black carbon formations, from too rich a carburetor setting, from too much hand choking, faulty automatic choke, or a sticking manifold heat valve, should also be cause for replacing the plug. Note that a clogged air cleaner can restrict air flow into the carburetor, thus causing too much gas in the mix, hence too rich a mix. Faulty points in mechanical distributors, weak coil, condenser, defective cables, all can cause spark plug fouling.

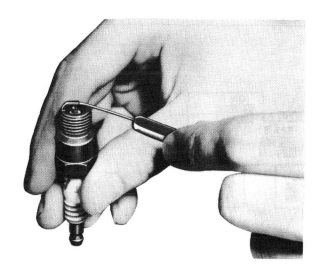

Spark plug gapping.

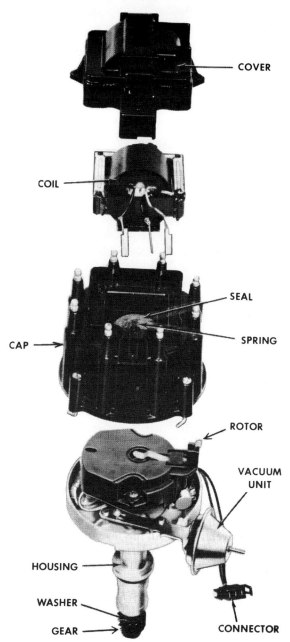

Photo of an 8-cylinder H.E.I. system distributor with coil.

These symptoms, which G.M. lists as specific to their cars, are the same for all other cars.

Beginning in 1975, all G.M. cars use electronic "high energy" ignition systems, with electronic modules inside the distributor, and special coils, some of them mounted on the engine block, others integrated into the distributor. On these cars, engine tuneup consists mostly of changing the spark plugs, whenever engine performance shows they need it. Distributor work is not required, in theory. However, the spark plug cables can crack and arc, like any others, as the distributor cap itself can destruct, along with the electronic module. G.M. claims that statistically this doesn't happen often enough to worry about, but the replacement of electronic modules is unfortunately all too common. The trouble with the module is that when it conks out the car will not start or run, whereas with the mechanical distributor some performance is always possible. There is no need to set engine timing with an electronic distributor, (unless timing has been set incorrectly), even if you replace the module, the cap or the spark plugs and cables.

If you have reason to believe that any G.M. engine since 1975 requires timing, the procedure is exactly like the mechanical distributor timing.

Corvette, Camaro, Firebird or any other G.M. car before 1975 has an easy mechanical distributor (there were a few electronic distributors before 1975, including Corvette and Pontiac, but the numbers were insignificant). Most V-8 engines prior to 1975 had a small window on the side of the distributor into which you stuck an Allen wrench and adjusted timing and dwell with the engine running. Other engines—4s and 6s—had the usual adjustments inside the distributor.

Firebird through 1974 was usually the 350 or larger V-8 engine. To change spark plugs requires no special instructions, except that some models with air conditioning made at least one plug difficult to remove without loosening the air conditioner—the compressor—and pushing it up as far as possible. This entails loosening as many as five nuts and bolts on the compressor clamps. It further entails using a double jointed or universal spark plug wrench extension to curve the wrench around the bottom of the compressor. Also, it isn't easy to get the spark plug cable off with the usual prying technique. But don't just grab the cable and pull; use something with a hook on the end of it such as a slide hammer. It is helpful, in extricating difficult spark plug cables, to twist them back and forth, slowly, thus breaking their hold.

Replacing points and condenser requires some body contortion on those engines with the distributor at the rear. The distributor isn't easy to reach if your arms are short. You can sprawl across the fender and reach it that way, or remove the distributor if that seems easier. If you remove the distributor, mark the direction of the rotor on a stationary point so you can replace the distributor in the same position.

The distributor cap is held in place by two keepers under spring tension. With a thin screwdriver—thin enough so that when you push down on the keeper you don't damage or break the keeper's slot—turn the keepers around to release each side of the cap. There is a built-in warning here; when you return the cap, guide the keeper back with one hand, making sure that it turns into its correct spot below the

distributor. A loose distributor cap will result if you don't get the keepers back where they belong.

The rotor, held by two screws, fits in only one way. When you remove it (and the dust shield), notice the fit—a notch and groove.

Examine the condition of the rotor. If the tip is corroded the contact spring tension may be insufficient. Usually the new point set will contain a new rotor and condenser. If so, replace the rotor. Look at the inside of the distributor cap carefully. The inside terminals should not be worn off or corroded. Make a careful inspection for cracks and signs of carbon tracing. Lift each cable off in turn, looking for burned towers. Corrosion can be cleaned out, but a burned tower condemns the cap. Any crack also means replacement of the cap as does any erosion or burning of the inside terminals.

If you replace the cap, line up the new one and replace the cables one at a time, cleaning any corrosion from them.

Suppose you have removed the distributor for one reason or another and didn't mark the rotor's position or the mark got rubbed off (use a screwdriver and make a scratch in metal, then chalk the scratch if you want to avoid the situation). To find the firing position, remove the No. 1 spark plug and get someone to turn the engine over for you, using a wrench on the harmonic balance wheel below the radiator. When you feel air pressure coming out of the spark plug hole, stop the turning. Now put the rotor pointing in the direction of that spark plug, put everything else back together and the engine should be ready for timing—should start. The No. 1 spark plug is usually marked on the engine—look at the intake manifold above the rocker arm panel.

To disassemble the points and condenser, use a screwdriver to push in the tension springs that hold the two wire clips. Remove the clips and wires, one of which goes to the condenser. Next, loosen but do not remove the jacket surrounding the condenser. We want to re-use the jacket in order to avoid the ticklish problem of getting the screw replaced in a new jacket. The jacket doesn't wear out; your patience might because of the awkward position involved in working with the distributor inside the engine. If you remove the distributor from the engine, you needn't worry about the jacket. With the distributor out it is easy to remove the old one and use the new one, if you wish. However, some point sets combine points and condenser, eliminating the problem.

Before removing the point set, put a cloth around the inside of the distributor to cover the holes where something might fall. Unscrew the point set screw, but don't remove it, and unscrew the other holding screw, which you may have to remove. Some point sets have open ends for both screws so the points slide in and out. Others don't. Incidentally, some people tighten point set screws so ferociously that thier removal becomes difficult. To avoid damaging the head of a too-tightened screw, use a screwdriver whose blade fills the entire screw slot. Don't take chances. If, by some remote stroke of bad luck you do ruin the screw head, remove the distributor (marking the rotor and its relation to some point directly opposite it), file off the ruined head, remove the points and unscrew the exposed ruined screw. You will obviously have to track down a new set screw.

Before replacing the points with the new set and condenser, clean everything out, including the vacuum advance mechanism on top of the distributor. Examine the two curving vacuum advance links for smoothness of operation. If they're rusty, clean and grease them. Don't lose the two springs that hold them.

Now install the new points and condenser, and if you bought a set that combines them in one package, forget the instructions on the condenser jacket (above). Tighten the screws lightly.

Notice that the points fit into a slot and cannot fit in any other way. Do not try to be innovative; there will be no rewards for it. In replacing the leads, the two clips must back up to each other on their smooth sides, and the wires should go back in their original positions, so as to avoid all moving parts and rubbing surfaces. Before installing the points, use your finger to grease the rubbing cam on the distributor center pole. Grease is usually provided with the point set, but if it isn't use a light Lubriplate or something similar, and use very little—just a film. So when you go shopping for points, check the grease. If none comes with the set, buy a small container. It will be useful in many other places—door hinges, hood locks and latches, and elsewhere. If your distributor has a cam lubricator, put the grease on it. (It's a little brush.)

Before replacing the wire leads, look at them for corrosion. It will help to sandpaper them off a bit. Use a screwdriver to push in the spring tension that holds the leads, and get them all the way into their slot. This can be ticklish in a distributor at the rear of the engine, if you are not a basketball player.

Now check each step: (1) leads where they belong, not touching anything, the clips firmly in their slot, back to back; (2) the points tightened loosely, awaiting adjustment, the dust shield or radio interference shield (it can be either or both) not yet reinstalled; (3) the grease on the cam lobes or the wick; (4) the condenser, if separate, back in place, centered so as not to interfere with the distributor cap, and tightened in its jacket.

Now for the engine timing.

If the rubbing lip of the point set is not resting on

Corvette timing marks.

one of the high cam lobes, turn the engine until it does—flick the ignition switch on and off once or twice until you get it right. Right means in the center so that what little play there is in the distributor shaft will when it is turned move the rubbing lip equally off center right or left, depending on which way you turn. Now, using a hex wrench ("allen wrench") turn the adjusting screw in the point set until you get a gap of .019. Tighten the two screws on the point plate securely—but not excessively. Put the plastic cover back in place, making sure it doesn't touch anything. Replace the distributor cap and check the cables for fit in the posts.

Push down on the latch keepers with the screwdriver, guiding each keeper into its correct channel below. You push and turn and the spring has a good deal of tension. When they are correct, you can feel them in place. Also, pull up on the distributor cap, as a test, once you think you have it right.

Locate the timing marks below the radiator on the harmonic balance wheel pulley and chalk the mark and the mark opposite it, once you line them up. Check the correct timing setting you want on engine decal listing specifications. Connect the timing light and start the engine. The timing light goes between the No. 1 spark plug and its disconnected cable. The engine must idle slowly. Disconnect the rubber tube to the vacuum advance on the distributor. If you need to reset the idle speed of the carburetor to get it down, turn the set screw controlling throttle action counterclockwise. Put a pencil or any plug into the tube of the vacuum advance.

If, as is likely, engine timing is not correct, put the hex wrench back into the contact point set screw, only this time with the distributor cap in place it goes

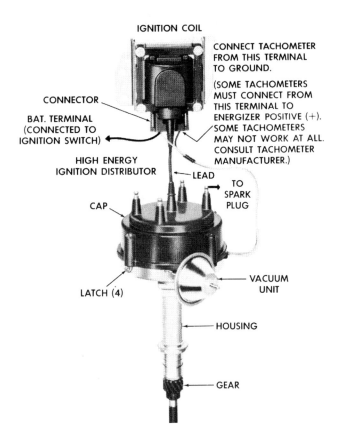

IGNITION COIL

CONNECT TACHOMETER FROM THIS TERMINAL TO GROUND.

(SOME TACHOMETERS MUST CONNECT FROM THIS TERMINAL TO ENERGIZER POSITIVE (+). SOME TACHOMETERS MAY NOT WORK AT ALL. CONSULT TACHOMETER MANUFACTURER.)

CONNECTOR

BAT. TERMINAL (CONNECTED TO IGNITION SWITCH)

HIGH ENERGY IGNITION DISTRIBUTOR

LEAD

TO SPARK PLUG

CAP

VACUUM UNIT

LATCH (4)

HOUSING

GEAR

Photo of 4-cylinder H.E.I. system.

through the small metal window in the cap. It's not easy to reach, either. An extension tool, worthy of purchase, eases the job and costs a dollar or two. Loosen the hold down clamp below the distributor, which is also out of the way but will yield to an extension on the socket wrench. Turn the distributor slightly, with the timing light shining down, until the two chalk marks line up. Note that you musn't loosen the hold down clamp too much, otherwise the distributor is apt to turn simply from engine vibration, upsetting timing. Turn the hex wrench until the motor almost dies; turn it back to a correct idle. Once you get it right, stop the engine and tighten the clamp as it was before. Replace the spark plug cable.

We've been talking about the V-8 engine. The 6-cylinder is the same except that it has no window on the distributor. You set the points inside with a screwdriver that pushes them apart or closer, then check the timing as above. Set it by moving the distributor bowl.

The differences are that the hex wrench is needed in V-8 distributors, and the hex wrench adjustment (external) should agree with correct timing. That is, the rough adjustment with the hex wrench through the window is a dwell adjustment, to achieve maximum smoothness of idle, whereas the timing adjustment at the pulley is for firing versus piston

stroke and valve opening. They should coincide, but the timing adjustment should be done last.

Camaro engines are identical to the above, insofar as tuneup is concerned.

Beginning in 1975, all General Motors cars, including Corvette, Camaro, and any other sporty models, have electronic distributors ("H. E. I." which means High Energy Ignition).

Tuneup consists basically of changing spark plugs, and any of the supporting but separate procedures in other systems, such as PCV valve, canister, and so on.

The H.E.I. system prolongs the life of spark plugs, from 10,000 to over 20,000 miles, in some cases. But you still have to take them out periodically, clean and gap them, and put them back. Your time might be better spent putting new ones in, especially if you buy them on sale, which isn't hard to do—it may be harder to avoid, since stores use spark plugs as "loss leaders" hoping to entice you in thereby, and make a killing on something else.

Four-cylinder H.E.I. engines have separate coils mounted on the engine block somewhere, imitating the old fashioned coil in this respect. But the coils are different, behave differently, and look very different. They look like an old, homeless transformer, with an exposed, laminated, metal core—in the case of the 4-cylinder. The others—the V-6 and V-8 engine distributors—have the coil inside the distributor. The first thing you notice about the distributors is that they are larger. The caps are bigger so that the higher voltages in the wiring have less chance of cross-firing and shorting out the cylinder

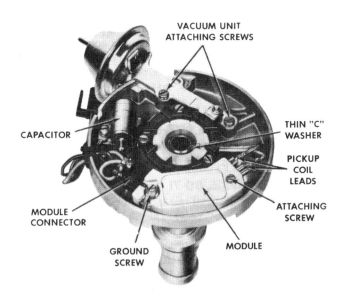

VACUUM UNIT ATTACHING SCREWS

THIN "C" WASHER

PICKUP COIL LEADS

CAPACITOR

MODULE CONNECTOR

ATTACHING SCREW

GROUND SCREW

MODULE

Vacuum module at bottom, and other H.E.I. details.

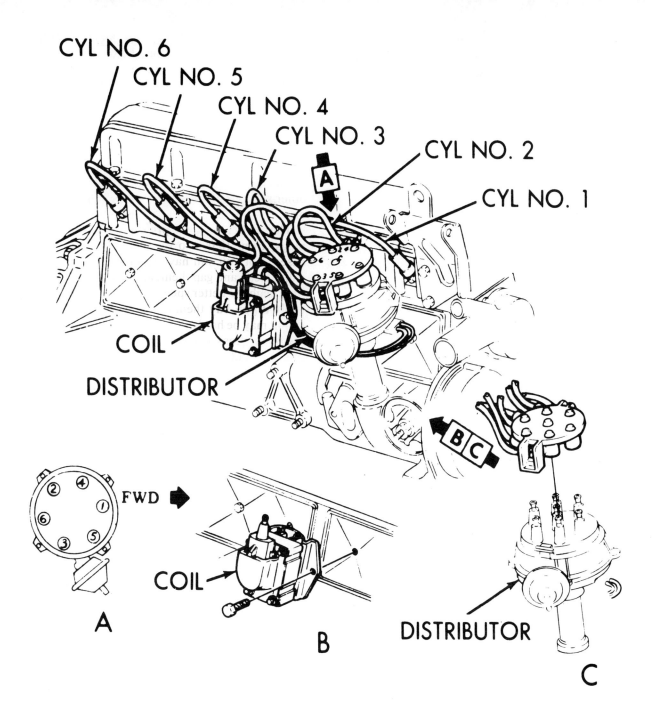

CYL NO. 6
CYL NO. 5
CYL NO. 4
CYL NO. 3
CYL NO. 2
CYL NO. 1

A

COIL

DISTRIBUTOR

B|C

2 4
1
6
3 5

FWD ➡

COIL

A

COIL

B

DISTRIBUTOR

C

Correct routing of 6-cylinder H.E.I. spark plug cables.

or firing the wrong one. You may also notice that cables appear to be different. They are. The new materials used in distributor caps and cables will, it is hoped, last longer and be more efficient. Don't count on it. Distributor caps crack just like old ones, and when they do their behavior is no less eccentric. Cables, which cost a lot more, also are subject to the ills that cables are heir to, though it is true that they do seem to last longer (but this judgment is anecdotal and based on personal experience only).

H.E.I. problems, in addition to wires and distri-

butor cap, center mostly on the electronic module, since coil breakdown is very rare. The electronic module, which is mounted inside the distributor, has these tasks to perform: to limit and control the ignition coil current; to break the current at ignition time, and to withstand the high voltage, about 350 volts; to control dwell time of the coil current so that full output is present at the right time; and to do all that even in the coldest weather when cranking voltages sometimes drop off to a third of normal starting voltages. The module, which is a small rectangular chip of a thing, has to perform these almost bewildering tasks in split-second timing. No wonder that it sometimes breaks down. As we've noted, when this happens the car cannot be started. In the past, when this situation developed suddenly, one suspected a broken timing chain or fuel pump, less often a cracked distributor cap—that is, when the car had been running, then suddenly stopped even though the cranking system seemed okay, and you hadn't run out of gas. Hence one must add the electronic module to the "sudden death" components of past cars—basically cars up to 1975.

Electronic modules do not have a mileage expectancy. They are designed for the life of the car, so it is somewhat pointless to keep a spare on hand. Still, if you do much driving on long trips, it might not be a bad idea, especially since you can buy them from the catalogs for about $25 to $35 whereas if one conks out on the road you will have to pay a heavy towing charge and the usual high rate for labor and the part itself, which would bring the total bill to something well over $100. Also, it's something you could do in an emergency, since it requires very few tools and little time.

As to the other radical breakdown systems, the timing chain and fuel pump are designed for the life of the car and replacement of either one is a rather extended garage procedure and not to be done on a highway.

To replace an electronic module requires merely that you remove the distributor cap, unscrew the module and pull off the wire clips, noting which one goes where. They're color coded. To replace the new one, follow instructions on greasing—it is vital that you grease the new one on the bottom side exactly as instructions explain, otherwise the new one will soon follow the old one into oblivion. Grease should come with the new module.

Note that the H.E.I. distributor cable posts differ from the old ones. Cables are fastened more securely, as you will notice when you extract them. Pry them off carefully. In some cases, a separate cover must be removed before the cables come off. This cover is held by plastic fasteners or clips.

It is important that cables be routed correctly. When removing them for any reason, tag them so you can return them in the correct order through the separators that hold them on their paths to the spark plugs.

Before you decide that the module needs replacing, make sure the coil is functioning by removing the center lead to the distributor from the coil and, with ignition turned on, hold it just above its connecting point. If there is a spark between the cable and its connecting point, the coil is probably okay. Needless to say, you replace the module only when you have checked out all other breakdown components,

including the fuel pump, battery lug connections, and the timing chain, though on some cars no easy test for timing chain failure exists. (It's a vicious cycle; to eliminate the timing chain from suspicion you test everything else. But unless you have a special tester for the module, you have no way of eliminating it from suspicion.) You can test for a timing chain that may be in need of replacement in the near future. But you need a tachometer, unless you can hear an engine running at about 2,000 revolutions per minute. The test requires that you hook up your timing light and test engine timing, at 2,000 r.p.m.s. With the engine warmed up, and running steadily at that speed, the alignment marks should hold steadily and without movement. If there is movement, the timing chain and gears have worn sufficiently to warrant replacement. In some cars, a worn timing chain shows up as distributor shaft wobble; you shouldn't be able to turn the distributor pole much in either direction. If it wobbles, (and there is no undue wear on the distributor shaft gear itself), that probably indicates a worn timing gear. But, this test, as noted, depends on a normal distributor.

Car manufacturers stress that statistics show high reliability for electronic distributors. Little comfort will be derived from these statistics if yours fails on the highway, but the module is the only component with a significant rate of failure. Distributor caps and cables have normal wear and can be expected to fail in due time, hence should be inspected regularly.

It may seem excessively annoying to have to pull off the distributor cap from an electronic distributor—a slightly more complex task than its mechanical forbear—merely to check for cracks and corrosion. But the point isn't to annoy you, it's to prevent breakdown. Not all future breakdowns are prefigured inside the distributor cap and its cables, however. Any hairline crack is such an omen, and you can prevent others by clearing away corrosion. But the disaster inviting cracks can happen suddenly and may or may not begin as tiny, innocent cracks. This may seem to contradict the admonition to make regular inspections, but some disasters can be prevented by regular inspection—say every six months after the car (or component) is a year old.

G.M. Citation and other X-body sporty models all use the H.E.I. distributor. Both the newer 4-cylinder and 6-cylinder engines have the coil integrated into the distributor assembly. There are no differences between these cars and the G.M. cars discussed above as to ignition system tuneup and repair. Remember that in removing and replacing spark plugs be precise about routing details of the cables. Wires must go below cruise control (if equipped) and above the throttle cable. It goes without saying that cables should not be routed so as to contact rubbing sur-

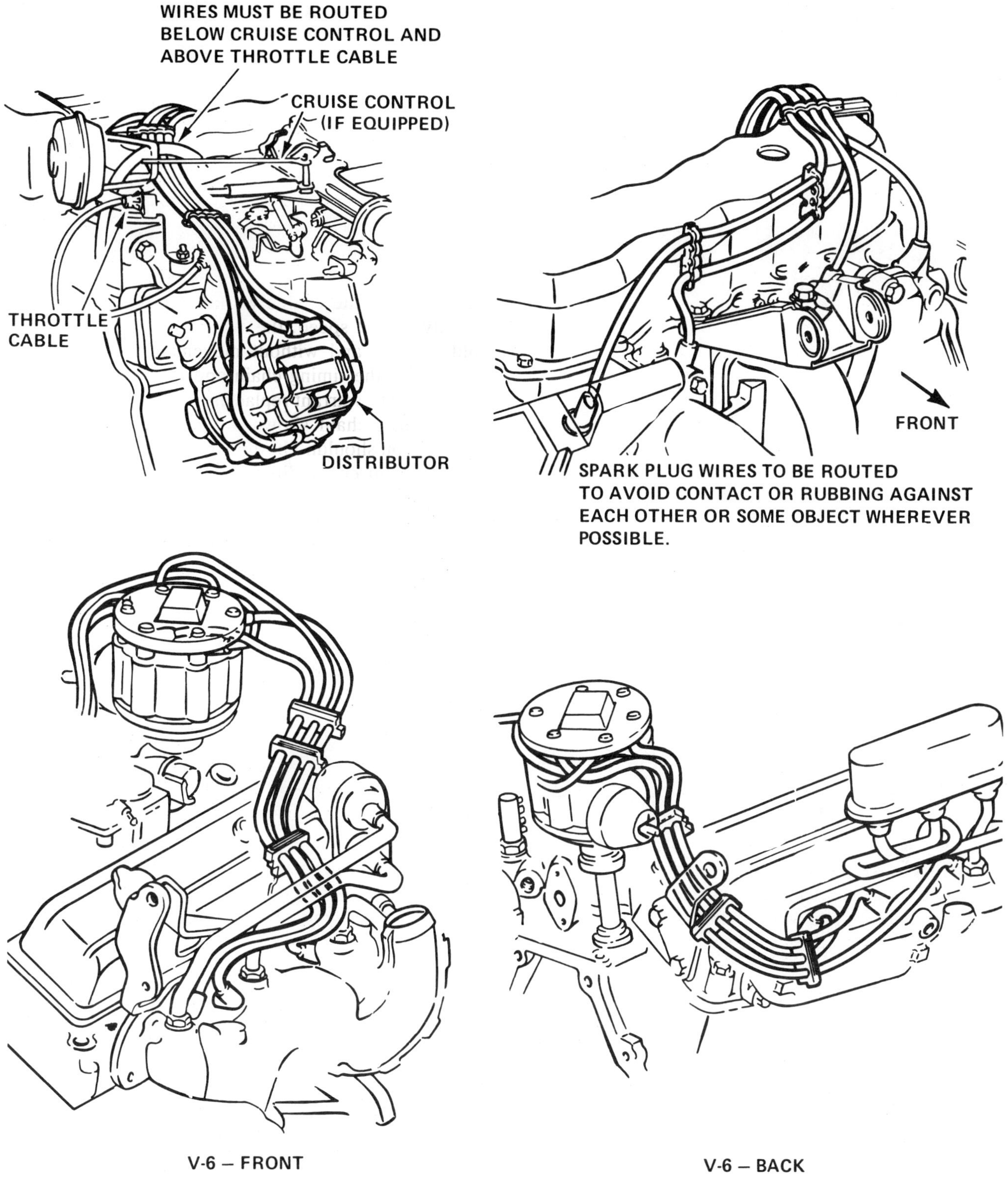

WIRES MUST BE ROUTED
BELOW CRUISE CONTROL AND
ABOVE THROTTLE CABLE

CRUISE CONTROL
(IF EQUIPPED)

THROTTLE
CABLE

DISTRIBUTOR

FRONT

SPARK PLUG WIRES TO BE ROUTED
TO AVOID CONTACT OR RUBBING AGAINST
EACH OTHER OR SOME OBJECT WHEREVER
POSSIBLE.

V-6 — FRONT

V-6 — BACK

G.M. High Energy Ignition system cable routing in both 4 and 6-cylinder engines.

faces, nor should they touch each other unless it cannot be avoided. If you don't get them properly routed and in their retainers your radio reception may suffer from noises. Plugs can be cross-fired.

Electronic systems incorporate coils into their distributors. When no spark is received at the plugs, either the module or the coil can be at fault. Coil testing requires an ohmmeter; follow instructions that come with the meter. If the coil tests well, the module must then be replaced.

Chapter Three

Brakes

Most brake systems nowadays are dual diagonals. Dual chamber master cylinders control the right front wheel/left rear wheel, and left front/right rear. Leaks, which used to send the brake pedal to the floor and the driver into powerless hysterics, now affect only half the system. The other half is easily able to stop the car. In Scirocco (Rabbit, Audi Fox and all other VW products) the most recent systems are front disc, rear drum. Also, recent VWs have warning lights which indicate low hydraulic pressure in the lines, even though you may not notice the usual symptom—flabby pedal going almost to the floor, requiring that you pump it to stop effectively. Needless to say, when the warning light goes on it is time to examine the system without delay.

Brake work is specialized, as you can judge by the proliferation of shops devoted almost exclusively to it and other wheel problems.

What are the symptoms which require attention at various levels?

We have mentioned the worst—the pedal going to the floor. This means at least worn linings that must be replaced. It means also a leak in one of the systems (leaks in both systems aren't likely unless there has been an accident or sabotage). The leak can be at the wheel cylinders, the master cylinder, or in the lines themselves. Visual inspection will settle it. Correction is something else.

Sometimes you make the correction and the pedal is still too far down at the end of the stroke. Usually that's a sign of something wrong with the master cylinder. We'll tackle that. But it can be nothing more than failure to bleed the air out of the system—a fairly simple correction, as we'll see.

Oil or grease on a lining or linings can cause the brakes to lose effectiveness. This warning is to the effect that you must assume the habit of cleanliness around brake work, if you have it not. Any oil or grease on linings, rotor or drums, must be carefully cleaned off with a lot of rubbing and clean rags or paper towels.

Overheating is possible when springs don't pull the shoes back on release, or (less often) the pedal push rod is out of adjustment.

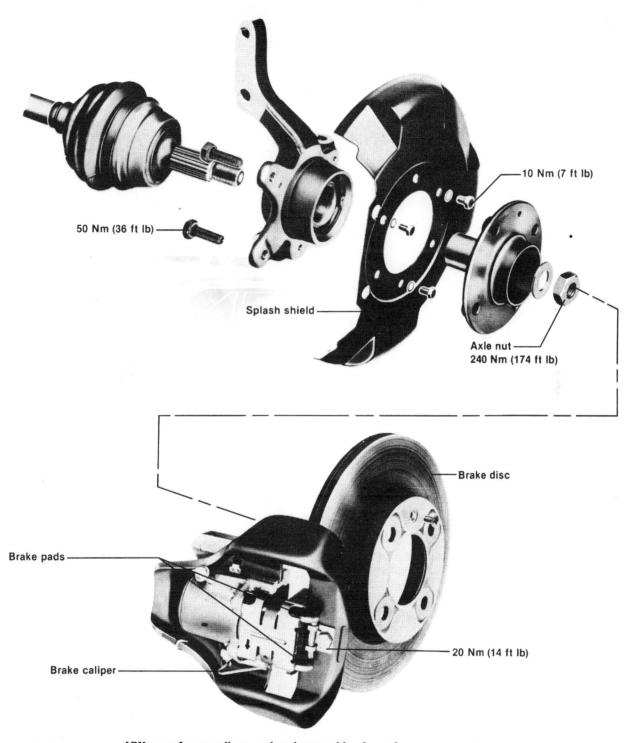

10 Nm (7 ft lb)

50 Nm (36 ft lb)

Splash shield

Axle nut
240 Nm (174 ft lb)

Brake disc

Brake pads

Brake caliper

20 Nm (14 ft lb)

VW type front caliper and pad assembly plus other components.

Binding, chattering, squeaking and squealing are more common faults. In drum brakes (rear) look for dirty, worn linings, worn drums, wrong (incorrectly fitted) linings, weak springs, or distorted backing plates—from damage of some sort, for example, a wreck. In disc brakes, the pads probably need replacing. Look for loose pads or lining, rusty surfaces, missing spring (spreader), or glazed pads.

CALIPERS DIFFER

VW has used different disc brake calipers—a single piston made by Teves (ATE), another by Girling has opposing pistons that move through opposite ends of the same cylinder. There are others.

In troubleshooting parking brakes, which are operated by cable from the hand lever between the front seats, a tightening adjustment will usually restore sufficient tension.

When working on brakes, block a wheel diagonally opposite to the wheel you're working on with wooden blocks. Jack the car up with the car jack. Then use a jack stand or a second jack, preferably a small hydraulic jack under the front suspension system, so that you support both the body and the suspension system.

DISC BRAKES

To get at front disc brakes, remove the wheel as if changing a tire. Usually it is recommended that you loosen the wheel lugs while the car is on the ground in order to avoid pushing the car off the jack when or if one of the lugs has been tightened too much. Impact wrenches, in universal use, cause over-tightening. But if the lugs are too tight, it may be necessary to use a hammer and the large extension rod of a ½-inch drive socket. A blow or two on the end of the rod will free such an over-tightened lug, and it can be done safely with the car on jacks or stands.

Girling caliper pad removal requires that you remove the so-called spreader spring, which is a tension fit metal plate across the caliper. Pry it off with a screwdriver. Next, notice that the pads are held in a U-shaped retainer bolted to the caliper. Unbolt the pad retainer, pull it out with a pliers, and now you can remove the pads. You will have to fish them out with screwdrivers, and if they are insufficiently loose in their places, force the pistons back to give them more room. You will have to do that in any case, when installing new pads, and when you exert

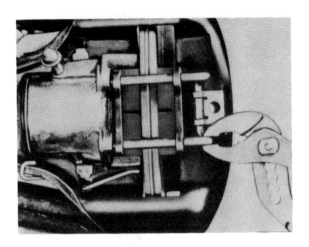

Removing pad retainer on Girling caliper, after unbolting the retainer.

pressure on the pistons, oil will be forced back up into the master cylinder. The oil will overflow. So, it is best to remove the cap and take a bit of the oil out, or simply put a rag underneath to catch the oil. It isn't any good, anyway, once it spills out. Remember to replace it, up to the level mark on the master cylinder, using only prescribed oil—don't mix brands and buy the oil at the VW dealer. You may pay a little more, but you will save yourself a ton of grief and expense later on.

When the pads are out, examine the disc surfaces, the spreader spring and retainer, and the pad seating and sliding surfaces. These must be clean and the caliper must move easily and smoothly—the moving part of it. The piston dust seals should not be cracked or deteriorated, or (above all) leaking. If they are, you'll have to remove the caliper and replace the seals.

Removing Girling spreader spring.

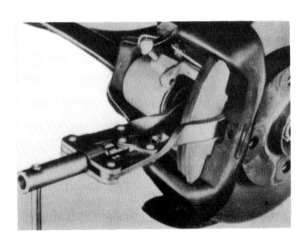

A special tool for pushing in the pad; but you can force it back with a heavy screwdriver or bar.

46

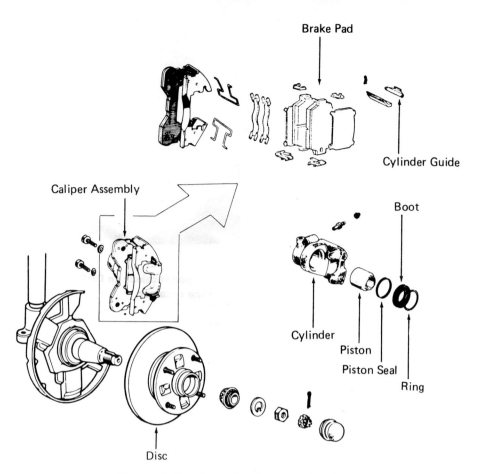

Brake Pad

Cylinder Guide

Caliper Assembly

Boot

Cylinder

Piston

Piston Seal

Ring

Disc

Toyota Celica front disc brake and caliper assembly.

To remove calipers, once the pads are out, remove the two retaining bolts—15 mm size. Notice that these bolts are heavily torqued. Put them back that way—torque is 43 ft. lb. (6.0 mkg). Do not let the caliper dangle from the oil hose; it can weaken and distort the joint coupling. Tie it up and away with a piece of wire or cord. If you have to replace the dust seals, remove the cylinder assembly from the caliper frame before tying it out of the way. You may find it necessary to unbolt the oil line to do the work thus far. If so, unscrew it and plug it.

The Girling cylinder assembly comes out of the caliper frame easily enough. Fish out the retaining rings that hold the dust seal, then pull the dust seals

Caliper retaining bolt on Girling disc.

Girling pad removal.

47

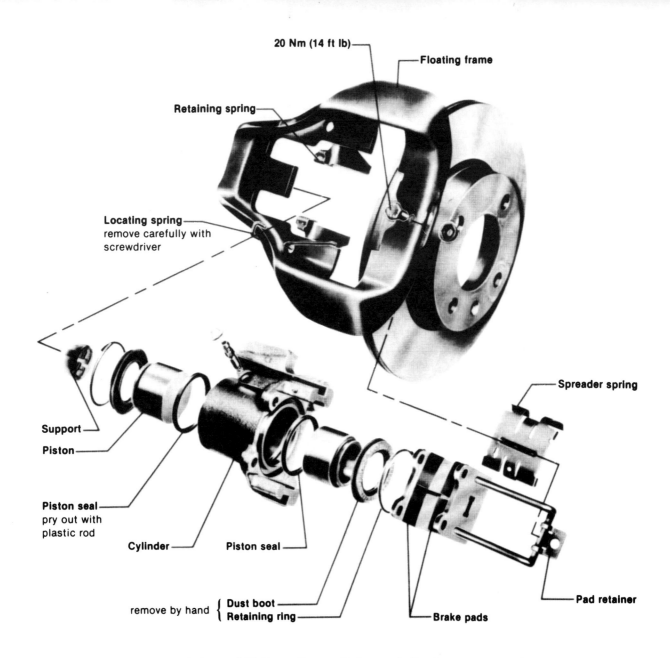

20 Nm (14 ft lb)

Floating frame

Retaining spring

Locating spring
remove carefully with
screwdriver

Support

Piston

Piston seal
pry out with
plastic rod

Cylinder   Piston seal

remove by hand { Dust boot
                 Retaining ring

Spreader spring

Pad retainer

Brake pads

Exploded photo of Girling caliper, cylinder, and all related components.

out. If there is oil at these seals you must get the pistons out of the cylinder in order to replace the piston seals. To do this, put the cylinder in a heavy cloth, exposing the bleeder valve. Use compressed air, if you have it, through the bleeder valve, to force the pistons out. Or push on the brake pedal. That will force at least one piston out and you can push the other one. You may need nothing more than your finger to push it out—once one of the pistons is out.

Look for rust, dirt and corrosion in the cylinder and on the pistons. Clean everything off. Buy new piston and dust seals and any other worn parts. Buy some brake cylinder paste to coat the pistons and seals, as well as the cylinder bore. Push all the parts back in the order they came out.

To install the cylinder assembly back into the caliper frame of the Girling caliper, requires that you get it between the retaining tension springs and the locating spring. The locating spring should push against the upper edge of the cylinder assembly; the retaining springs are between the sliding surfaces of the frame and cylinder. If these surfaces are corroded, clean them off and use a light grease on them—a fine film barely visible. VW recommends using only Plastilube, which you can buy at the VW parts counter. Replace the caliper on the car, and replace the brake hose, if you removed it. Girling hoses have a left-hand thread, (like a bicycle pedal or knock-off hub).

Incidentally, if you took the pads out not to re-

48

Pressing pistons and seals into cylinder.

Using compressed air to remove pistons.

Removing caliper assembly.

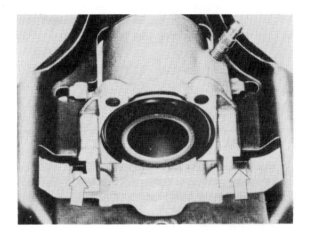

Sliding cylinder into its frame.

place them but to get at the seals, and you want to re-use the pads, they must go back as they were—don't mix them up. That means marking them, when removed. Generally, you will be replacing the pads.

Before replacing the caliper over the rotor surfaces, examine these surfaces. If they've been scuffed and worn, with ridges on the surfaces, they'll have to be ground off ("turned") at a machine shop. Don't worry about ridges at the edges—that's normal wear and doesn't interfere with braking surfaces. These ridges might interfere with getting the new pads and caliper back in place. File them off, if they do. Remember that you'll have to push the pistons into their cylinder if you are installing new pads, because the pads will be much thicker than the old ones and to the extent that they are, that is the amount of extra space you need—and can only obtain by pushing the pistons in. Oil forced out of the master cylinder in this process, as we've noted, must

be replaced. Push hard on the pistons to get them where you want them. Generally, a heavy screwdriver will do the job, but if not, use something sturdier. VW makes a special tool or spreader, but that isn't necessary.

Once the caliper and pad retainer, clip and bolt, spreader spring, and the caliper's two 15 mm bolts are back, check out all the parts, and visually check the moving part of the caliper.

If you removed and replaced the brake line hose to the caliper, you must now bleed the lines.

Bleeding

For that process you need a rubber hose about 15 inches long that will fit over the bleeder valve on the caliper. You will also need a small kitchen glass, a

Bleeding brakes: (1) open valve with (2) appropriate wrench, and (3) have helper push pedal so pad is forced against disc.

Reversing bleeding process: as helper holds pedal down, (1) close valve with wrench, then signal helper to release pedal and pad.

can of VW brake fluid, and a wrench that will fit over the bleeder valve when the hose is attached to it. You will also need an assistant smart enough to push down on the brake pedal in the car and hold it, when you issue these instructions. If you are going on to do a job on the other wheels, don't bleed the lines until you've done the complete job.

But if the wheel you've just re-assembled is all you're doing, either because you don't have the time to do more, or more isn't needed, you have to bleed the lines now.

Incidentally, VW recommends that you change brake fluid in the lines every two years—regardless of what else you do to the brakes. That is because brake fluid absorbs moisture which causes corrosion and can even cause the fluid to boil, ruining hoses and other components. This seems a super cautious instruction, and is that if you're not experiencing any brake problem.

If you want to change fluid, here's the way to go about it. Attach hoses to the bleeder valves on the left rear and right front bleeder valves. Open these valves (counter-clockwise), with the other end of the hoses pointing into a glass or other container. Pump the brake pedal until all the fluid is out of the lines. The bleeder valves are temperamental customers. Before doing anything with them, splash penetrating oil over them. Then take a socket wrench to them— each one in turn—and see whether they are willing to loosen easily. Don't, under any circumstance, use much force. They break; you must then either buy an entire new unit or do a difficult job of extraction, which might not succeed, on the broken valve. So, slip a socket wrench over the valve—or use an ad-

justable open end wrench on it (a "crescent" wrench)—and see how willing it is to loosen. Most such valves will loosen with a little urging. Then attach the rubber hose over the valve, and put the open end in a container (if you're draining all the oil out). Turn the valve until oil starts to flow—it will take several extra turns, once you "crack" it open.

But to bleed the lines is a somewhat different task. Do the same routine on the bleeder valve with the open end wrench. Then attach the hose as before. But this time the other end of it must go to a glass with a small amount of brake fluid (it can be old) on the bottom, enough to cover the open hose end. If the hose isn't long enough to reach the glass, put the glass on a block of wood, or a can. Open the bleeder valve until fluid flows out, turning the wrench while the hose is attached. The hose must remain submerged while the valve is open, to prevent air from stealing back in.

Now you need an assistant. That creature must, on your signal—that is, when you have gotten the valve open—push the brake pedal slowly down to the floor and hold it there until you close the valve, turning the valve back in until the flow stops. Then instruct your helper to release the brake pedal. Again, slowly, the hose submerged.

Then, repeat this process—and it might be half a dozen times or more—until the flow into the glass has no more bubbles coming out, only fluid. That's at the wheel you have just worked on. Now, check fluid levels in the master cylinder and replace all the oil that gushed into the glass. Use fresh oil. Try out the brakes. If the pedal is doing its duty, you're home free. But if it is not, you have to do the opposite

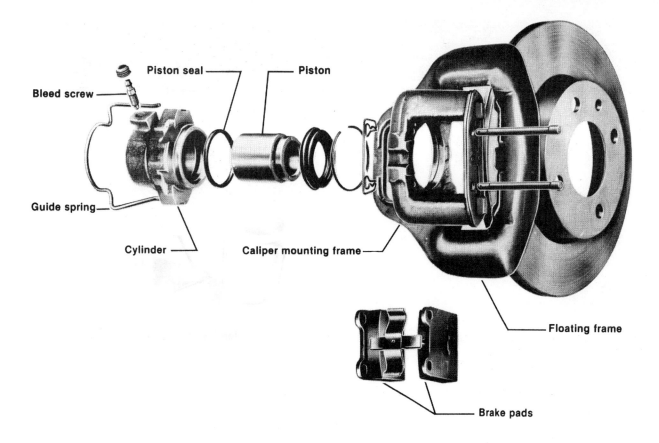

Exploded view of Teves brake assembly, including the floating frame, piston, cylinder, pads and rotor.

diagonal wheel. Note that only one well in the master cylinder is depleted of oil in this process. If you do the other disc brake wheel you have the same process.

Brake fluid is poisonous and will ruin paint. Govern it accordingly.

If you have an accident and ruin or twist off a bleeder valve, all is not lost—don't rush out to buy an entire new caliper at some astronomical cost. If the line must be bled, for whatever reason, and the bleeder valve has broken off in the closed position, unbolt the caliper's fluid hose, put it into the glass with oil at the bottom, treating it as the rubber tube you used before. When your helper releases the brake pedal, however, during the entire period of release—you must block the hose opening to prevent air from going back in. Use a finger or some kind of plug. If you use a finger, wash it off with soap, when you finish. The brake pedal must be held in at the end when you bolt the hose back.

One other rescue operation is possible—extract the remnant of the bleeder valve in the usual way, by drilling into it with a metal bit and cutting a new thread or extracting the remnant with an extracting tool. But this kind of operation is chancy and not terribly successful. Though the solution above might be condemned by an ultra fastidious type, (bleeding

the caliper hose), it has two merits; it works and avoids the price of a new caliper. If you remember to use penetrating oil, letting the oil soak in, and tap briskly on the valve before putting a wrench to it, you shouldn't have such troubles.

All these instructions apply to the Girling VW front disc. They also apply to all disc/drum brake

Use of wood block to force cylinder assembly from Teves frame.

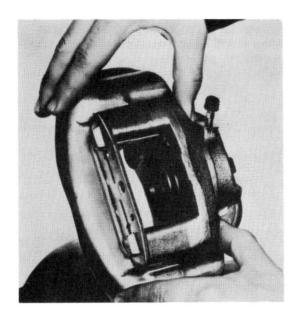

Removing piston seal from its groove.

Pushing mounting frame of Teves brake away from cylinder.

combinations insofar as they involve such general considerations as flushing brake lines and bleeding them.

Let us return to specifics—the Teves caliper.

Teves pads are interchangeable with Girling, but few of the servicing details are the same. To change pads, remove the tire as before, using two jacks. Put wood blocks in front and behind a wheel (tire) diagonally opposite the raised wheel you're working on.

Pull off the retaining pin spring clip, then knock out the two pad retaining pins with anything that will fit—a nail or a punch of some sort. The spreader spring will pull out now. The inner pad now can be extracted, using anything you can grab it with. The brake pad remaining is notched. To get it out you must push the caliper frame and cylinder away from you; so tap it with a rubber hammer, then fish the pad out. Don't just push; you could push the car off the jacks. If you intend to use the old pads—say you're working on the cylinder because of leaks—mark them so you can return them to their original positions.

If it is necessary to remove the caliper and cylinder, follow the procedures for the Girling component. The piston can be blown out with compressed air or pushed out with the pedal. A seal inside the cylinder should be taken out and replaced. So too the dust seal and any metal parts that show signs of wear. Examine the cylinder and piston for wear, rust and corrosion. Clean carefully, using steel wool and brake oil.

Use VW brake paste on the components when you button up the caliper. Force the piston in the cylinder

carefully. You can tap it in with a rubber hammer (and a wood block) or force it in using wood blocks to protect its edges in a bench vise.

The cylinder is a force fit in the floating frame of the caliper. First, push the guide spring on the cylinder, then tap the cylinder into the mounting frame. The mounting frame and cylinder now go into the floating frame.

Disc brakes malfunction because of leaks (rarely), worn pads (most commonly) or dirt and corrosion in the piston and cylinder (rarely). Nowadays pads have warning devices when they need replacement and that's usually all you need to do to them. If so, it's a simple operation, basically, if you follow the few rules. Complications set in only when the cylinder and caliper require attention.

If the brake rotor is allowed to wear—when you don't replace the pads in time—you must remove the

Pushing cylinder into its floating frame. Hit the drift alternately on the surfaces indicated by arrows.

Installing mounting frame into floating frame in grooves noted by arrows.

Installing brake pad with special tool (which you don't need) in Teves brake.

rotor and have it machined ("turned"). The rotor on the front wheel hub is held by a flat-head screw located between the wheel bolt holes. Unscrew that and pull the rotor off the hub. If it is rusted, use great care in prying it off. Use penetrating oil and a rubber hammer or a wood block. There are many ways to skin this particular cat; always think first of prying with a wood block or pounding with a rubber hammer or hitting the wood block with a heavier hammer. In the scale of force, the lowest is the wood block, next the rubber hammer, then a lead hammer, finally a steel hammer. Brake components call for the lowest possible force level. Once the rotor is off, take it to a machine shop for turning. They may tell you it can't be done. The statistics are these; a new rotor is .472-inches in thickness (12.00 mm). The least acceptable thickness after turning is .413-inches (10.50 mm). Also, both sides of the rotor must be ground off to a maximum of .020-inch (0.50 mm). If rotor wear is confined to superficial ridges, forget it. The worst that will happen is that the new pads won't last as long. However, if other symptoms show up—noise, uneven braking, etc.—the rotors will have to be shaped up or replaced. Replacement is very costly. You can buy used ones at a junk shop, but if you do, measure them to the specifications above.

DRUM BRAKES

Drum brakes once constituted the entire braking fraternity (parking brakes are not for braking but for holding). Drum brakes now are relegated to the rear wheels, which do only a marginal part of the stopping. In some cars—Corvette, for example—they

have disappeared altogether. They are not gaining new adherents, for the usual reason; they're not as good as the disc.

But (like women or men) they remain half the population and must be dealt with accordingly.

Most drum brakes are self-adjusting. However, the VW drum brake isn't; it requires adjustment. Adjustment is accomplished at the back of the wheel using a screwdriver. A brake adjusting hole, on the brake backing plate containing a rubber plug that you remove, will give you a "reading" on lining thickness. It also contains the star wheel adjuster. Adjustment procedure must be accomplished with the car on a jack, the parking brake released. Also, it helps to push the brake pedal in a couple of times before starting, thus centering the brake shoes.

Turn the star wheel upward until the shoes grab the drum; and the wheel turns with difficulty. Then back it off three or four notches. The wheel must turn freely.

Adjust both rear wheels. Note; though you can peek at the brake linings through the adjusting hole, the only adequate assessment of their condition is to remove the wheel and examine them. Linings sometimes wear unevenly.

Drum linings on rear wheels should last virtually the life of the car, with any luck, since they don't do much work. However, there is no assurance. (It should be noted that some VW products from 1975-76 also had front drum brakes.)

Symptoms of a need for relining drum brakes are soft pedal, the noise of metal against metal (rivets of the linings rubbing—and ruining—the drum) heard especially in an enclosed area, brake noises such as squealing, and brake grabbing in wet weather. These symptoms must be distinguished from front wheel disc symptoms, which are similar. The point is, you

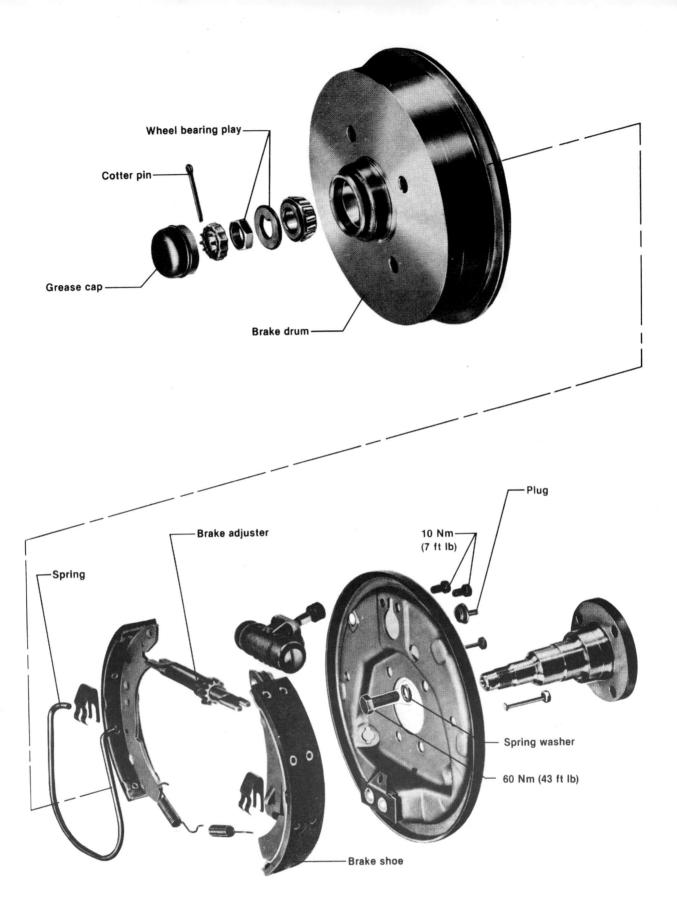

Wheel bearing play

Cotter pin

Grease cap

Brake drum

Plug

Brake adjuster

10 Nm
(7 ft lb)

Spring

Spring washer

60 Nm (43 ft lb)

Brake shoe

An exploded view of a VW drum brake system, with components and fastening torque specifications.

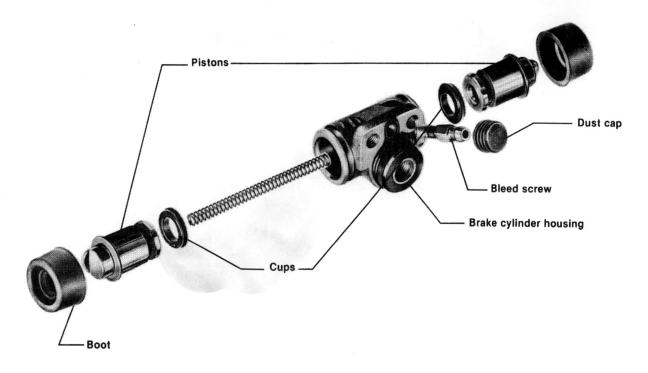

A VW brake cylinder. Points of wear include all rubber cups, caps and gaskets.

Labels on figure: Pistons, Dust cap, Bleed screw, Brake cylinder housing, Cups, Boot

have to check brake linings and pads periodically, once you get past about 20,000 miles. The first such check will give you a clue as to probable life expectancy. If much lining remains, the next check can be postponed. Those cars with disc warning signals require the checking of the drum brakes only.

Remove the tire and brake drum by removing the dust cover, cotter pin, nut lock, the wheel nut and its large washer. That will enable you to pull off the bearing and hub—if the drum hasn't become so deeply ridged that it catches in the lining frame. If that is the case, back off the star wheel to gain added clearance. Also, make sure the parking brake is fully released.

When you remove the brake drum assembly, look at the bearings and bearing races for adequate grease supply. (Don't let the bearing fall out.) It isn't necessary to repack the grease supply if you don't get dirt in it, and it is an adequate, uncontaminated amount. Undoubtedly you will get dirt on the axle, so it will have to be cleaned before you re-install the hub.

The parts to any rear drum brake are, in addition to the shoes and their linings, the brake adjuster, the parking brake lever, the shoe return spring or springs, the wheel cylinder, and the various fasteners, including the fastener-spring at the bottom where the two shoes are joined.

Anyone familiar with U.S. type drum brakes will be pleased to learn that VW's are similar and simpler—easier to overhaul.

All these parts must be inspected. The wheel cylinder should be checked for leaks and for incipient leaks. Poke around the rubber boot for leaks, but don't poke a hole in it. If oil is there you will have to rebuild the cylinder, replacing the boot and the inner seal. VW uses two different kinds of wheel cylinder. If yours leaks, take it apart and take the parts and the cylinder to the parts counter for a cylinder rebuilding kit. There is nothing to it—clean out the cylinder of any rust, corrosion or other debris and replace the rubber or plastic parts with new ones the kit will contain. To remove the wheel cylinder, unbolt the two bolts that hold it to the backing plate, and unbolt the hose. Warning: follow the same procedure with these cylinder bolts that you followed with the bleeder valve; douse the bolts on the cylinder with penetrating oil, also put penetrating oil on the coupling joint of the hose and tap the bolts with a small hammer before putting a wrench to them. They break. Sometimes the cylinder surfaces have been worn to the point of no return. If the metal piston rattles around in the cylinder you have to decide what part is at fault—the piston or the cylinder. If it's the cylinder, there is no fixing it, only replacement. But if there is no oil around the cylinder boots, let sleeping cylinder boots lie.

The only disassembly on wheel cylinders is to pull off the boots and push out the inside components— the spring, rubber cups and pistons, noting their sequence. Sometimes the rubber boots must be pried out. When installing the new parts, lubricate them

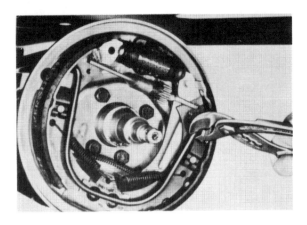

Starting to disassemble drum brake by removing anchor spring.

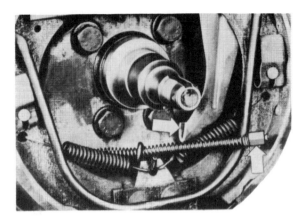

Parking brake cable must be removed.

with either fresh brake fluid or VW brake cylinder paste.

To get the brake shoes out requires that you disconnect the parking brake cable from the lever. Pull the lever forward and you can remove the cable, if the parking brake is fully released and there is no tension on the cable. Take out the clips and pins that hold the brake shoes with pliers. The return spring can also be removed with pliers. Pull the shoes out and remove the star wheel adjuster. The coil return springs can be removed without trouble by pulling the hoses off and disengaging them from the lower anchor.

Examine the drum for ridges and wear. If the lining rivets have worn through you probably will have to have the drums smoothed out. When this happens, take the drum or drums to a machine shop and they will also tell you whether or not you need oversize linings. It depends on how much they take off.

When you install the new linings, clean off the axle and put some axle grease on it—but only a light film. VW warns against mixing different greases, and if you don't have original VW brake hub grease, just

Brake adjuster—a screwdriver that fits.

finger a little bit of the uncontaminated supply in the hub on the axle. You need very little.

When you install the drum assembly do it carefully so that you don't damage the grease seal or the bearing and races. The brake adjuster, which it is well to clean and grease, must be all the way in. The shoe that contains the parking brake lever is installed to the rear. Shoes go on before the adjuster.

When the job is done, adjust the brakes as described above. If you removed the brake line hose you'll have to bleed the lines as described above.

Sometimes brake drums appear to be in need of machining, but if the ridges aren't deep and the wear on the drums is not too bad, don't bother getting them turned down. The new linings will soon enough adjust to the territory. Obviously they won't last as long as with a new drum but they'll do.

PARKING BRAKES

To adjust parking brakes, locate the cable distributor underneath the car which contains the adjusting nuts. Each adjusting nut has a lock nut with it. Loosen the lock nut and tighten the adjusting nuts. To be precise about it requires that the two rear wheels be off the ground so you can tell when the tightness is sufficient—when you can turn the wheels by hand with the brake lever pulled up several clicks. But you can also tell by the amount of slack in the two cables. Before adjusting, push on the cables and judge how much slack there is. Then adjust until most of the slack is gone. Now pull up on the brake handle in the car and judge whether it takes effect after two or three clicks. Don't get it too tight. Tighten the lock nuts.

Brakes, from model to model, make to make, do

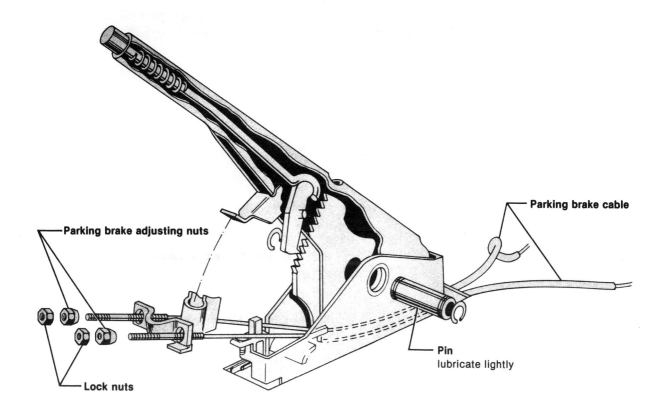

Parking brake adjusting nuts

Lock nuts

Parking brake cable

Pin
lubricate lightly

Two drawings of parking brake assembly (top) showing the control lever assembly and (bottom) the cable adjuster, equalizer and pathways.

not vary a great deal. Nevertheless, details vary. Also power brakes have the power booster between the brake pedal and the master cylinder. Fortunately it's an extraordinarily durable component, rarely re-

quiring attention. About all that goes wrong with it is an occasional hose.

Corvette brakes differ in that there are four disc brakes. Rear discs require a parking brake installa-

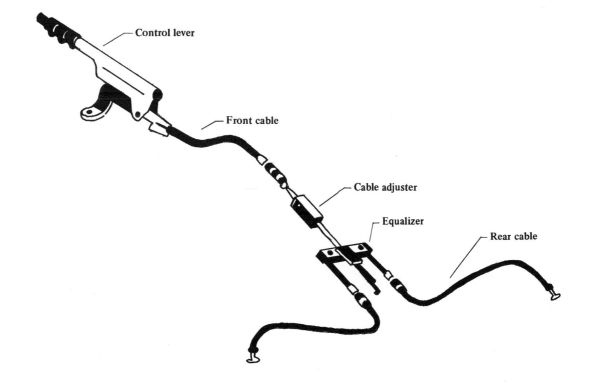

Control lever

Front cable

Cable adjuster

Equalizer

Rear cable

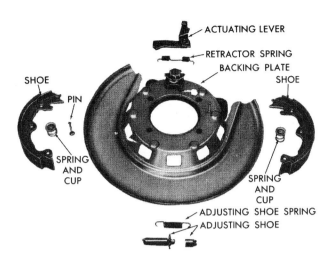

Corvette parking brake assembly.

Adjusting parking brakes on Corvette rear discs.

tion of some sort. This turns out to be a small set of brake shoes as in drum brakes that behave pretty much as you would expect—they expand against drums and they have retractor springs, shoe adjusters with star wheel, and the various fasteners. These shoes should never require replacement but once in a great while it might be necessary to adjust them. There is an adjusting hole in the front that can be reached once you remove the wheel and turn the brake rotor until you can see the star wheel. To tighten, turn the adjuster by moving the screwdriver upward (away from the floor). Turn until you can't move the rotor, then back off six or eight notches. This should be done with the brake on. Test the results by turning the wheels. There should be no "drag," turning by hand. Turn the wheels both di-

rections. Incidentally, this is not the approved G.M. method of adjustment, but I have found it to be as effective as theirs. In the G.M. method you loosen the brake cables at the equalizer check nuts (where the cables come together) until the parking brake levers move freely to the "off" position with slack in the cables. Adjust as above, then place the brake handle in the normal position of braking—13 notches. Tighten the check nuts at the equalizer until an 80 pound pull is obtained when you put the brake handle into the 14th notch. Then tighten the check nuts. But this method requires that you have some way of gauging the 80 pound pull.

Corvette pads

To replace the disc brake pads on Corvette (recent models) raise the wheel you're working on with the usual two jacks—say the right front. G.M. recommends removing about two thirds of the brake fluid from the master cylinder—the front reservoir in this case—by opening the front line connection and bleeding it out there. But you can also forget that and put a rag underneath the master cylinder and let the oil drip on the rag. Less sweat. G.M.'s recommendations are for professional mechanics, and it is conceivable that they are right as a super cautionary procedure involving all the Corvettes (and other G.M. cars) in existence. In theory, if you let the oil, which is corrosive and poisonous, splash out over the top of the master cylinder it will do some damage if it gets on something. Well, amateurs and slobs can rest assured that if you put a big enough rag below, nothing fatal or even corrosive will happen.

Parking brake installation on Corvette rear disc.

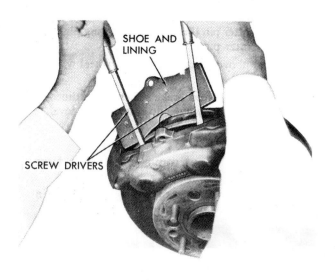

Corvette pad removal using two screwdrivers.

We amateurs have to look out for our time, unlike the professionals—who look out for theirs.

Take the wheel off and the cotter pin that holds the retaining pin on the inboard end of the shoe, and slide the retaining pin out. It may not slide; you may have to take a pliers to it. Once the pin is out, you can pull up the inboard shoe. Mark it ("inboard") if you're putting it back. If not, put the new one in. Pull the other shoe out, marking it if you intend to put it back. To install new pads it will be necessary to press the pistons back into their cylinders. Use two heavy screwdrivers on them, but first open the master cylinder top so the oil can flow out if it wants to. Replace the retaining pin and cotter pin. Fill up the master cylinder.

It is probable that you will have no other service on these brakes.

If there is any sign of leaking at the pistons you can rebuild these four-piston calipers. Rebuilding kits are available and a few special problems will be encountered in replacing the seals and boots. In cleaning out the cylinders use clean brake fluid and nothing else. Gasoline, kerosene, carbon tetrachloride, acetone, paint thinner or any solvent containing these chemicals will ruin rubber parts quickly.

Remove the caliper assembly by taking out the two hex head bolts. (Hex head wrenches are needed increasingly in sports car work.) Pull out the cotter

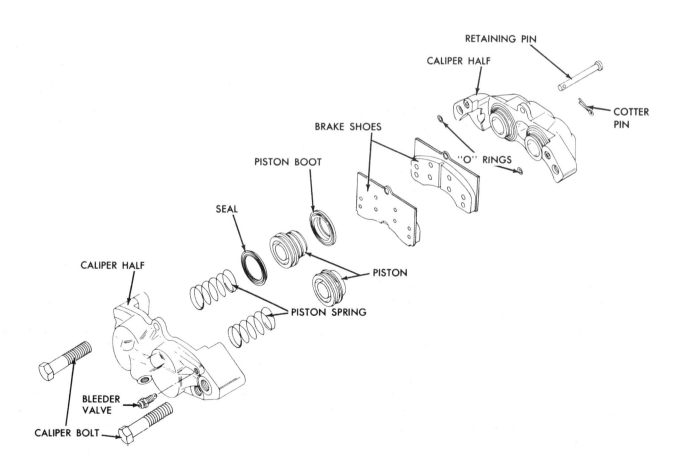

Exploded drawing of caliper, pistons, and all other braking components of the caliper in Corvette brake.

PISTON —

Repairing piston assemblies in Corvette caliper.

pin from the shoe retaining pin, remove the pin and shoe assembly from the caliper. Tag the shoe pads for re-use. Separate the caliper by removing the two large caliper bolts. Remove the two small "o" rings from the two ends of the caliper halves. Push the piston down into the caliper as far as you can and with a screwdriver blade push under the inner edge of the steel ring in the boot and pry it out. Remove pistons and piston springs, and boots and seals from their grooves in the piston. If the piston cylinders are dirty, rusty or otherwise corroded, clean them out with brake fluid. But if there are pits and other damages you'll probably be unable to prevent new leaks from developing, even with the new parts. Polish the

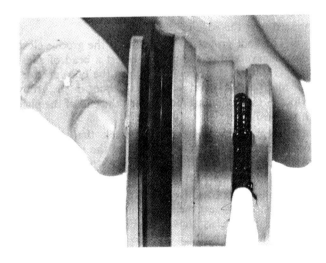

G.M. sealant must be placed on the outer diameter of the retaining ring.

surface with a fine crocus cloth, to remove such imperfections.

Reassemble the components beginning with the seal in the piston groove closest to the flat end of the piston. The lip on the seal faces toward the large end of the piston. Put the spring in the bottom of the piston cylinder. Lubricate the seal with brake fluid. Install the piston assembly and it will take some doing because of the seal lip. To get everything back isn't as easy as taking it out, as you will discover. The seals are easily pulled out of place as you push the piston in. Also, the scenario of installation requires that you put G.M. sealant on the outer diameter of the boot retaining ring, to form a sealed barrier between the boot retainer ring and the cylinder housing. To do this you have to depress the pistons—no great trick—then apply the sealant to the rim of the boot retaining ring.

Many possible brake malfunctions can occur. They include excessive pedal effort, brake grabbing, roughness, and pulling to one side. However, these and other problems such as noisy brakes, are almost invariably caused by the basic malfunctions we've been discussing. One other class of problems arises with brake lines, which can burst or get contaminated. Brake fluid contamination occurs when the wrong oil is used, either after flushing the system or in additions to the fluid. It can also happen after prolonged use whether or not there are additions. Eccentric patterns of wear on pads sometimes can cause odd symptoms—roughness of braking, for example. But new pads will cure the situation, and most others. If existing pads have plenty of life left in them, try filing them off or better yet have them machined.

Some squeaks are almost impossible to track down. Dirt is often the culprit and it is always good policy to clean off brake components whenever you inspect them. Brush off all components such as fasteners and springs, as well as the backing plate. A steel brush and vacuum cleaner are the best tools.

Fiat brakes

Fiat X 1/9 is one of the most widely accepted sports cars in the world, thanks to its advanced engineering, and the Italian genius for design.

The brake system of the Fiat X 1/9 is four-wheel disc, floating caliper, single cylinder. Front calipers are easily accessible for purposes of pad removal and replacement. Front calipers differ from rear inevitably, because of the rear parking brake. The parking brake has a special caliper attachment lever that activates the pads, mechanically.

As with most Fiat systems, maintenance and

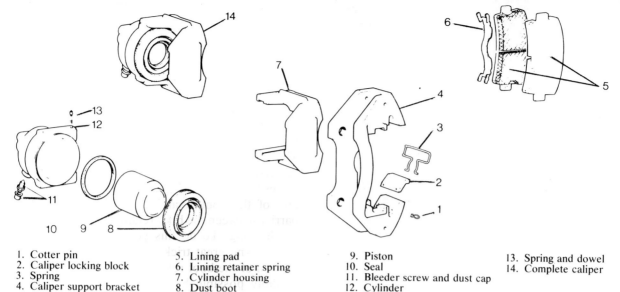

1. Cotter pin
2. Caliper locking block
3. Spring
4. Caliper support bracket
5. Lining pad
6. Lining retainer spring
7. Cylinder housing
8. Dust boot
9. Piston
10. Seal
11. Bleeder screw and dust cap
12. Cylinder
13. Spring and dowel
14. Complete caliper

Details of Fiat X 1/9 disc. brakes.

service on the brakes follows simple procedures using a minimum of unusual tools.

With the front calipers, remove the cotter pins from locking blocks. These blocks come out and once out allow the removal of the caliper, the pad linings and springs. On the front brakes, a bolt holds the bracket to the caliper. It should be removed, if you're doing more than replacing pads. Check the pad lining for minimum thickness. Fiat says you should replace pads when the lining gets down to .079 inches (2 mm). However, uneven wear could make that figure risky. It means that's the measurement at its least thickness, and it means further that

you must inspect the pads carefully. Uneven wear is more common than not.

Rear brakes involve identical components excepting the parking brake lever. There are inevitable differences of design that relate to the parking brake, but to change pads the routines are similar. Remove the cotter pins, locking blocks, spring and then the pads.

If it ever becomes necessary to disassemble the calipers because of oil leaks or piston corrosion, that isn't too difficult.

The front caliper requires that you separate the cylinder from its frame support, and remove the dust boot, the piston and oil seal. Fiat recommends using compressed air to blow out the piston. That means removing the oil line from the caliper so the compressed air can go through the bleeder valve. But all you need to do whenever compressed air is specified is simply to push on the brake pedal with the caliper removed. That will push out most cylinders. To repair the rear caliper imposes the additional task of disconnecting the hand brake shaft and the easier problem with the piston—it merely unscrews from its plunger, thanks to the hand brake shaft and plunger.

It should be noted that the chief service you can expect to perform with these and other disc brakes is pad replacement. If that is neglected, you then must attend to the rotors. When they become sufficiently scoured as to require grinding off, you are faced with added disassembly tasks.

Master cylinder repair on the Fiat X 1/9 is a major job which, unfortunately, requires removal of the steering column just to start the job. This is not a job for an amateur.

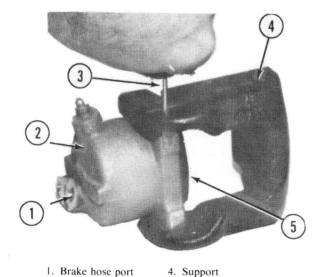

1. Brake hose port
2. Cylinder
3. Thin rod
4. Support
5. Cover

Fiat brakes require separation of cylinder from its frame support.

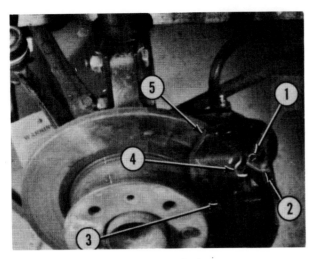

1. Cotter pins   4. Spring
2. Locking blocks 5. Support bracket
3. Caliper

Fiat Caliper and disc.

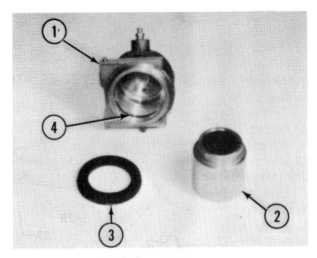

1. Cylinder   3. Cover
2. Piston   4. Seal

Component parts of Fiat caliper.

The Fiat 131, which is interchangeable in power train and suspension systems with the Fiat Spyder, uses a front disc/rear drum combination.

Front disc brakes are similar to the X 1/9 discs.

They are single piston with cotter pin and locking blocks. To change pads you must remove the cotter pins from the locking blocks and force them out. The caliper will now come out; so will the pads and

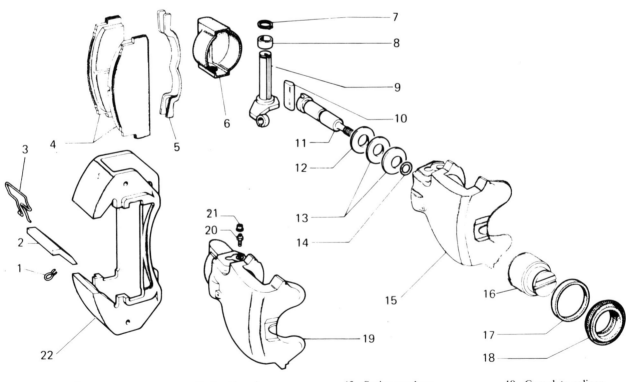

1. Cotter pin
2. Caliper locking block
3. Spring
4. Lining pads
5. Lining retainer spring
6. Rubber boot
7. Locking ring
8. Spacer
9. Hand brake shaft
10. Pawl
11. Plunger
12. Spring washers
13. Spring washers
14. Seal
15. Caliper cylinder
16. Piston
17. Seal
18. Dust boot
19. Complete caliper
20. Bleeder screw
21. Bleeder boot
22. Support bracket

Exploded view of Fiat rear brake caliper and bracket components.

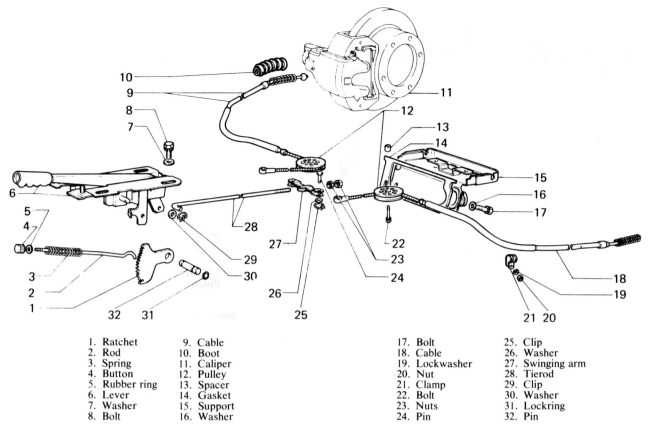

Fiat parking brake lever, cables and attaching components.

1. Ratchet	9. Cable	17. Bolt	25. Clip
2. Rod	10. Boot	18. Cable	26. Washer
3. Spring	11. Caliper	19. Lockwasher	27. Swinging arm
4. Button	12. Pulley	20. Nut	28. Tierod
5. Rubber ring	13. Spacer	21. Clamp	29. Clip
6. Lever	14. Gasket	22. Bolt	30. Washer
7. Washer	15. Support	23. Nuts	31. Lockring
8. Bolt	16. Washer	24. Pin	32. Pin

springs. Note the position of the springs. If the rotors have scouring and ridges you can remove them only if you have some type of puller. They are held by two bolts and tension. A large diameter puller is required. But disc removal is only called for when there is radical wear caused by pads that are worn down to the metal surfaces or rivets, depending on pad types. So long as you replace the pads before such wear sets in it isn't necessary to grind off the rotors (or discs, as they are also called). Some wear is inevitable.

To replace piston seals and dust covers (because

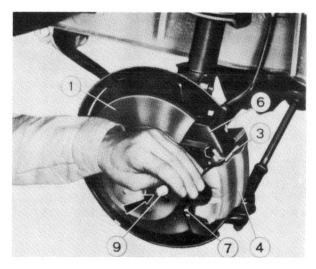

1. Brake disc	3. Locking block	5. Pliers	7. Lining retainer spring
2. Cotter pin	4. Caliper	6. Support bracket	8. Lining pad
			9. Drift pin

Fiat disc removal begins with wheel off, and removal of spring, liner retaining spring, cotter pin, caliper locking block, and pads.

1. Brake disc	4. Caliper
	6. Support bracket

7. Lining retainer spring	10. Spring
8. Lining pad	11. Brake shield

With caliper off, don't let it dangle; tie it up and away so that you can work on the brake without risk of damaging the oil line into the caliper.

of leaks or improper performance of the piston) you will need to push the piston out. If you don't have access to compressed air (and to an attachment that will fit the oil inlet connector), simply push it out with the brake pedal. Professionals might squirm at such advice; let them. Put a rag below the caliper to catch oil that squirts out.

Rear brakes are drum. To get at them, remove the wheels as if changing a tire. Release the hand brake and the two bolts that hold the drum. Pull the drum

off. Fiat drum brakes have the wheel cylinders at the top, the hand brake cable at the bottom, with the lever on the side. The usual springs, clips and retainers will be encountered. Use caution when removing the linings from the wheel cylinder. Fiat recommends putting a retaining tool over the ends of the cylinder to prevent the pistons from pushing out, thus splashing oil and making a bleeding job necessary. You don't need a special tool, but any improvised holder will work—for example, a couple of small clamps. Most wheel cylinders are sufficiently stuck so that there is no danger of them pushing out.

Disconnect the wheel spring from the shoes at the top. Then push the side retaining spring into the backing plate using anything that will work (Fiat

1. Shoe and lining	7. Dust cap
2. Caliper support bracket	8. Bleeder screw
3. Spring	9. Caliper body
4. Piston	10. Cotter pin
5. Seal	11. Block
6. Piston dust boot	12. Lining spring

Details of Fiat caliper, piston, pads, and fasteners.

1. Caliper	5. Bracket
2. Cover	6. Brake hose
3. Piston	7. Brake fluid inlet
4. Bolt and washer	8. Bleeder fitting

Fiat caliper and piston with bleeder valve and fluid coupling.

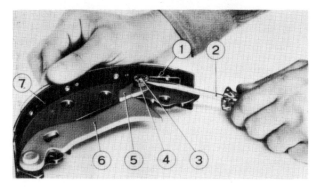

1. Spring
2. Screw driver
3. Pin
4. Spring retainer
5. Adjuster lever
6. Lever
7. Brake shoe

Drum brake disassembly on Fiat involves many small parts, as on any similar brake.

suggests a special tool; but you can get by without it). Then remove the lower spring from the shoes and turn it to disconnect it from the clip. The hand brake cable comes out from its link; the shoes come out next.

The self-adjuster can be pried out if necessary; it shouldn't be. The wheel cylinder can be removed by disconnecting the fluid line at the back, and removing the two bolts that hold it to the rear of the backing plate. There should be no reason to remove the wheel cylinder unless inspection reveals it to be in need of replacement. That would be rare. If it leaks,

you merely replace the rubber grommets and the boot, then bleed the lines, as explained above. Sometimes, because of brake fluid contamination, the cylinder may become so pitted that it has to be replaced. That shouldn't happen in the normal course of events.

The hand brake has an unusual adjustment. It's at the hand lever. To adjust you pull up the lever three clicks, and turn the adjusting nut underneath the hand brake lever until the wheels cannot be turned by hand. The spring underneath the adjusting nut should rest flatly on one side of the nut. The adjustment obviously requires that both rear wheels be off the ground.

Horizon and Omni

Plymouth Horizon and Dodge Omni brakes are front disc/rear drum combination. They are Chrysler brakes—single piston, floating caliper. To change lining pads, remove front wheel and tire. Two caliper guide pin bolts, removed from the rear, and the anti-rattle spring from the top, are all that keep the caliper in place. Next, pull the caliper off slowly. Calipers may often need persuasion. Use a rubber hammer to tap them at opposite sides. If the caliper assembly doesn't slide readily, clean the rubbing surfaces with

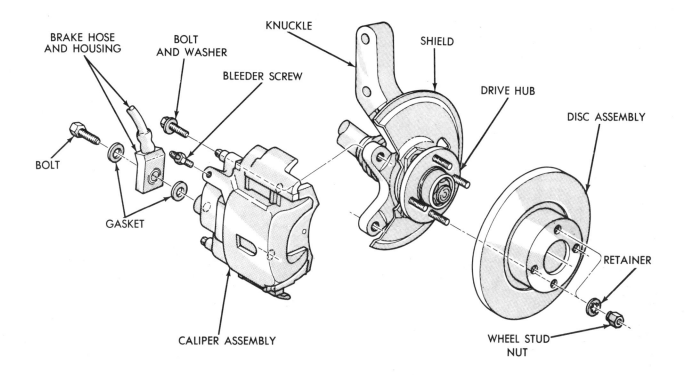

Components of Omni and Horizon disc brake and wheel hub.

65

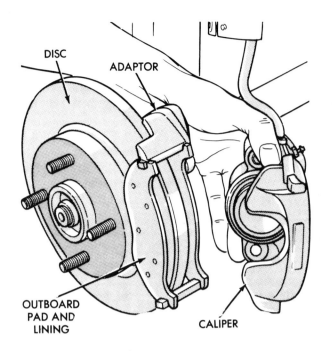

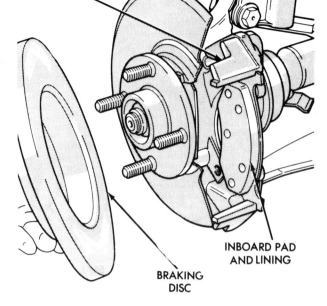

Removal of caliper from Omni/Horizon disc adaptor.

Disc removal on Omni/Horizon disc brake.

a wire brush or some other abrasive, then put grease on them—but just a light film.

Slide the outboard shoe out. Notice that the frame into which the pads fit separates from the caliper and piston. That frame is called the adaptor and in order to get the inboard pad out (the pad inside the rotor, facing in to the suspension) you have to get

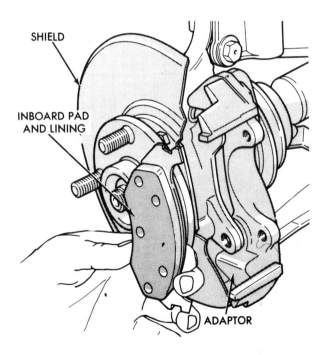

Inboard pad removal.

the adaptor out. If you didn't take it out with the caliper—which is the frame around the adaptor—take it out now, and the inner shoe will slide out. The rotor (braking disc) also comes off. Examine it for severe wear. It can be machined for a few dollars if it has been badly ridged. If it has a rough, rusty edge but is otherwise smooth or fairly smooth, buff off the edge with anything that will do the job, taking care to avoid scuffing the smooth disc area.

An excessively worn disc (rotor) can cause these symptoms: inadequate lining contact hence weakened braking; an increase in pedal travel; increased seal bushing wear; pedal pulsation, chatter and surge (or none of the above). If the rotor has some irregular wear, but shows no unusual symptoms once you install the new pads, the only effect ultimately will be slightly accelerated pad wear. You can live with that.

To rebuild a caliper, (because of leaks or a sticking piston), push on the brake pedal to force the piston out of its cylinder. Do that over a rag to catch the oil that will follow. Prop up the brake pedal with a piece of two-by-four or anything else to prevent further loss of fluid. It doesn't have to be propped all the way up—a couple of inches up from the floor is adequate.

Be very careful with the cylinder bore, once the piston is out of it. Treat the piston carefully also. You have to pry out the oil seal which circles the cylinder. Use your fingers or some kind of wooden instrument. Use a screwdriver to remove the dust boot, which is usually stuck. Push the bushing out of the caliper with a wooden stick of some sort, or

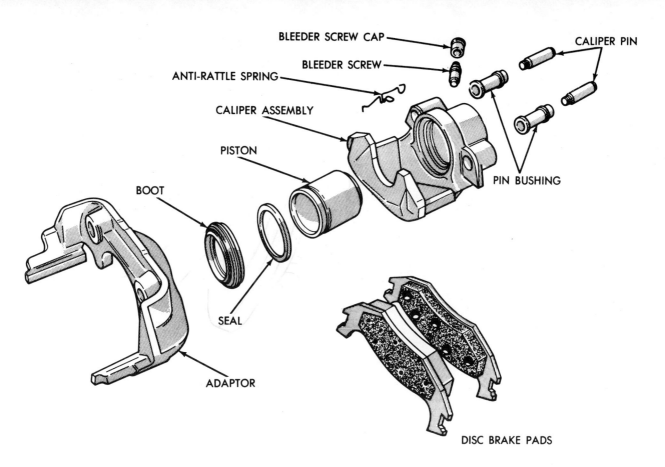

BLEEDER SCREW CAP

BLEEDER SCREW

ANTI-RATTLE SPRING

CALIPER PIN

CALIPER ASSEMBLY

PISTON

BOOT

PIN BUSHING

SEAL

ADAPTOR

DISC BRAKE PADS

Exploded view showing all components on Omni/Horizon front discs.

whatever fits. Check out the piston and the cylinder groove for defects, rust, and unusual wear. Slight defects can be cleaned up with a crocus cloth.

Replace all the soft parts—the seals and bushings.

Dip all parts in fresh brake fluid before putting them back.

To get the new dust boot into its groove, use a small steel plate of some sort over the seal and pound on it with a hammer and wooden block or dowel. A small "C" clamp can also work. Push the piston through the boot using your fingers. Apply oil to it, generously. It is well to plug the inlets to the caliper, if you took off the oil hose and the bleeder screw. That traps air below the piston which in turn forces the boot around the piston and into its groove as you force the piston down. Apply force uniformly to the piston by using a circular tool—say a large enough socket. Push in the new guide pin bushings.

It will be necessary to force in the piston before you can get the caliper over the rotor.

Once everything is back in place, bleed the lines as described above.

Drum brakes on the Horizon/Omni should be inspected periodically. Whenever you grease the rear bearings—say every 20,000 miles—or whenever the brakes misbehave, take a good look at the linings. Brake adjustment should be made whenever pedal

travel increases and there are no other symptoms—say a fluid level decrease in the master cylinder,

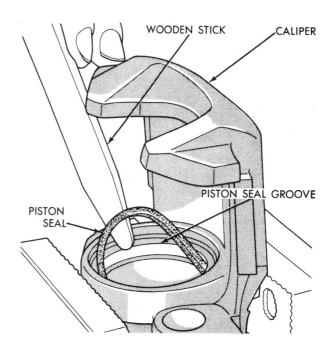

WOODEN STICK

CALIPER

PISTON SEAL GROOVE

PISTON SEAL

Removal of piston seal.

67

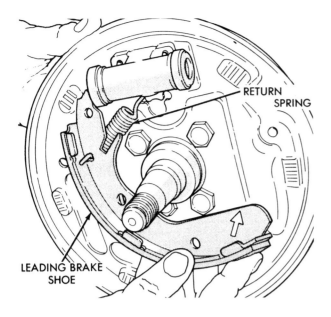

Installing leading brake shoe and return spring.

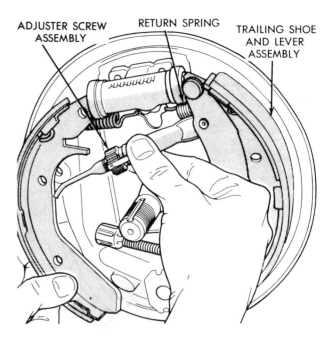

Putting adjuster wheel assembly into place.

which would indicate leaking. Brake adjustment on these drums is done through the adjusting hole which is at the top rear of the brake. It has a rubber plug, which you fish out with a screwdriver. Look inside the hole at the star adjuster wheel. Use a screwdriver with a thin blade and tighten the shoes by moving the screwdriver up on the right side, down on the left side.

If you find it necessary to reline the brakes, you may have to turn the star wheel adjustment all the way in (reverse directions for expanding the shoes).

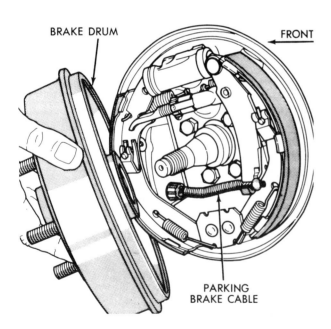

If the drum doesn't go back it means the shoes are not positioned correctly. If it doesn't come off, it means the parking brake is on.

Then remove the wheel. Force off the grease cap covering the wheel axle. If you can't get a screwdriver between the cap and the wheel, drive it in with a rubber hammer. Remove the cotter pin, lock, retaining nut, washer, wheel nut and bearing. Pull off the drum—straight off so as not to scuff the inner bearing and race.

The sequel for removing shoes is: remove parking brake cable, shoe-to-anchor springs, and adjuster star wheel assembly (force shoes apart; wheel nut must be fully backed off). Then raise the parking brake lever, pull the shoe away from its support so as to release spring tension. Remove the shoe and hold-down spring, which isn't a spring but a tension clip. Follow the same procedure with the other shoe. When you take the shoes off, place them so that you can get the new ones on correctly; the shoes are different. Compare the new ones with the old so that you get the leading shoe facing the front of the car, the trailing shoe to the rear. It isn't self-evident.

Clean off the backing plate and put grease on all contacting surfaces as well as on all the threaded areas of the adjusting assembly. Dirt is an enemy of good braking performance, but so is grease. Don't get grease on the linings or the drum. If you do, clean it off completely. But do get all the dirt off, and put a thin film of grease where it belongs—the contact areas involving the hand brake lever and its coupling, the adjustment assembly, and the six contact areas of the brake shoes. These will all be marked by signs of wear.

Installation of the parts follows the disassembly procedure, but it doesn't have to be an exact reverse.

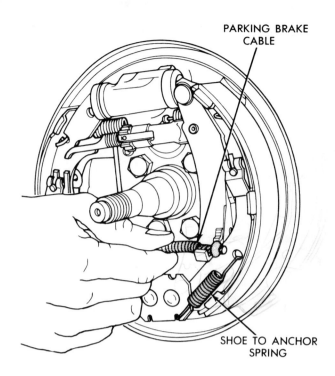

PARKING BRAKE
CABLE

SHOE TO ANCHOR
SPRING

Installing the parking brake cable.

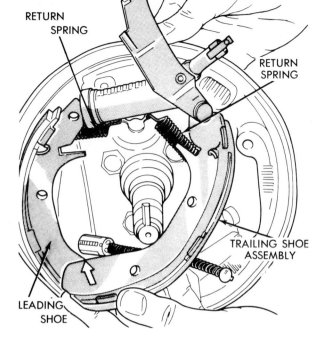

RETURN
SPRING

RETURN
SPRING

TRAILING SHOE
ASSEMBLY

LEADING
SHOE

**Putting the trailing shoe assembly in place, with
return spring installed.**

The trick is to get everything back. One thing to
remember; the adjusting assembly finger points
down. Getting the springs in place at the same time
that you position the linings is the main trick. Trial
and error will guide you. You have to position the
shoe so that it contacts the cylinder push rod surface,
and still lets you attach the return spring. Then you
can force the shoe back where it belongs. Next put
the adjuster assembly in place, with the forked end
curving down. Make sure the adjuster screw is at the
adjusting hole. The hold down clips and pins go in
easily enough. Use pliers to force the bottom anchor
springs where they belong. Push the parking brake
cable spring in a little, exposing the cable end sufficiently to allow its installation in the parking brake
lever.

Put the drum on. If it won't go on that means you
haven't turned the adjusting screw all the way in. If
the grease needs changing, clean the old grease out
completely before putting the new supply in. Don't
over-grease. The bearing should be greased generously. Put grease in the palm of your hand and
push the bearing into it, again and again, until you
can see grease all through the bearings. Put the large
washer over the bearing and tighten the drum retaining nut securely. Turn the drum by hand to make
sure that it's seated properly and turning, though the
new linings may scrape a bit until they are seated by
wheel movement and braking action. Sometimes the
springs lose their tension and if the brakes drag it

means they aren't being pulled back where they belong by the springs. That means you have to replace
the springs. Anyway, don't tighten the outer nut
excessively. Bring it up so there is no wobble, then
back it off so that you can turn it with your finger. But
don't loosen it—turn it a tiny bit one way or the other

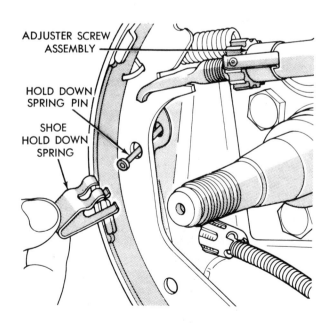

ADJUSTER SCREW
ASSEMBLY

HOLD DOWN
SPRING PIN

SHOE
HOLD DOWN
SPRING

**Installing the shoe hold down spring. Hold the pin
from the back.**

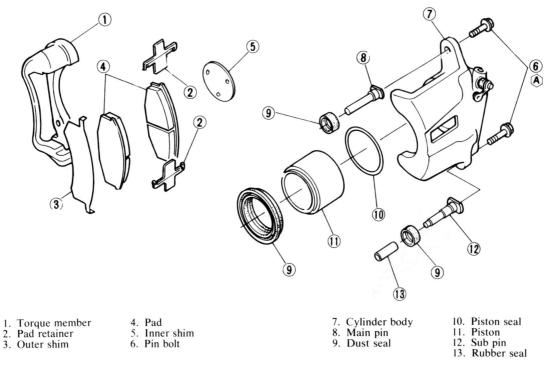

1. Torque member	4. Pad	7. Cylinder body	10. Piston seal
2. Pad retainer	5. Inner shim	8. Main pin	11. Piston
3. Outer shim	6. Pin bolt	9. Dust seal	12. Sub pin
			13. Rubber seal

Exploded drawing of a Datsun disc brake showing components and fasteners.

to expose the cotter pin slot. Put the lock nut on and install a new cotter pin (don't take chances with an old one).

Put the wheel and tire back, and turn it. It should turn but not wobble. Shake it back and forth. It shouldn't shake at all.

When replacing tires and wheels on the Omni/Horizon, or any other 4-lug wheel, it is essential to observe the rule that you tighten lugs across from each other in sequence, and tighten them pretty much according to torque. It's pretty high. Four-lug wheels can come loose much more readily than 6-lug, so don't risk botching the job and courting danger. Tighten the lugs. Usually we warn against over-tightening. Now we issue the opposite warning—plenty of torque on these wheels.

Datsun

Datsun 280ZX cars (Model S130 series) use 4-wheel discs with easy pad removal. The calipers are single piston. To replace pads, put the car on two jacks or a jack and stand and remove the wheel. Look behind the wheel hub on back of the caliper for two bolts and remove the lower one of them. Loosen the upper bolt, then pull the cylinder body up, block it there and pull off the pad retainers—small metal clips at the top and bottom of the pads. They pry out. Inner and outer shims hold the pads. They now come

out. Minimum thickness of pads—if you plan to re-use them—is .08-inches (2mm). If you are using new pads, force the piston in with the usual attention to the master cylinder (put a rag below it or remove some of the oil). In some cases, pads may have adequate thickness but may have oil or grease on them. Needless to say, they must be replaced, and the cause of the oil corrected. Undoubtedly it will be a leak at the piston cylinder.

To correct such a leak requires disassembly of the caliper. Remove both pin bolts from the caliper and separate the cylinder body from the rest of it. Take out pad retainers and pads, and force out the piston and dust seal by pushing slowly on the brake pedal (or using compressed air—the approved way). Take out the seals and examine piston and cylinder surfaces. Clean off rust or hardened grease in the cylinder with fine emery cloth. Be careful with the piston; its surface is plated and an abrasive rubdown could ruin it. If metal surfaces are heavily scored or damaged in other ways the component must be replaced. It isn't likely. Lubricate new seals with brake fluid and use rubber grease on the inside of the dust seal. Use brake grease on metal wear points before assembling the caliper and cylinder. These points are shown nearby—they are the metal rubbing surfaces.

Pin bolts are not heavily torqued—about 20 ft lbs. The caliper mounting bolt is—between 53 and 72 ft lbs.

Rear disc brakes on the Datsun are much more complicated because of the parking brake assembly.

70

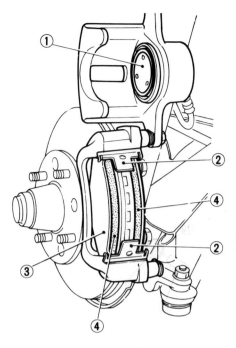

1. Inner shim
2. Pad retainer
3. Outer shim
4. Pads

Caliper pulls up for easy removal of pads and replacement of them.

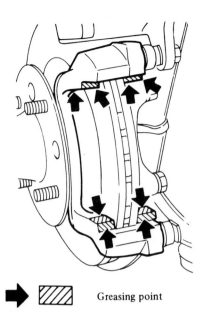

➡ ▨ Greasing point

Greasing points on Datsun disc brakes. Grease very lightly.

However, if you are only replacing pads the procedures are more or less identical with the front pads. It's only the parking device that complicates matters, and since the parking brake shouldn't wear out—it gets little wear—you needn't worry about it. If something goes wrong with it you have a major disassembly job which you may or may not wish to undertake.

Installation of new pads on rear brakes has several minor differences, despite the identical disassembly. It involves the piston, which is both turned and pushed in order to make room for new pads. Use a screwdriver to turn the piston clockwise while pushing it in. Its surface is notched to allow turning with a screwdriver.

The hand brake has its own piston and pushrod with brake lever. There are several dozen small parts including springs, washers, snap rings, seals and gaskets. Any disassembly would require that all soft parts be replaced—possibly springs and other parts. You would only disassemble the hand brake in some unusual situation.

MASTER CYLINDERS

Master cylinders wear out because they have rubber parts that wear sufficiently to fail, or they de-velop leaks at the tubing inlets and outlets, or the springs lose tension, or so much corrosion is built up inside that they cannot go through their motions.

Master cylinder kits are fairly easily installed.

VW Scirocco and other VW master cylinders are typical but they don't exhaust all the possibilities of detail found in other cars. Master cylinders are positioned in front of the driver on the other side of the firewall and are part of the brake pedal-to-master cylinder combination. The pedal you push down on to stop the car is attached to either a power booster that gets its power from engine vacuum via a hose, or to the master cylinder itself via a push rod that forces the piston assembly to move forward. That movement expels fluid forcefully into the lines, the calipers and wheel cylinders, which in turn force the car to stop by pushing against the rotors and drums. This rough explanation conceals a lot of little parts.

To discover a faulty master cylinder requires that you eliminate all other possible culprits, beginning with the wheel cylinders. That means you must examine the four wheel cylinders for signs of leaks. Either they leak or they don't, however. There is no mystery. And you can tell it by visual inspection. Unfortunately, the leak is rarely at the back inlet coupling, which you can see easily enough by crawling under the car at the wheel. It is almost always inside on the brake backing plate, and requires wheel removal and pulling up on the end of the rubber boot to examine for oil. If you strike it there you know that the problem is not the master cylinder but the wheel cylinder.

Also, you must sort out the problem. Suppose you are not getting enough "pedal" in braking—the

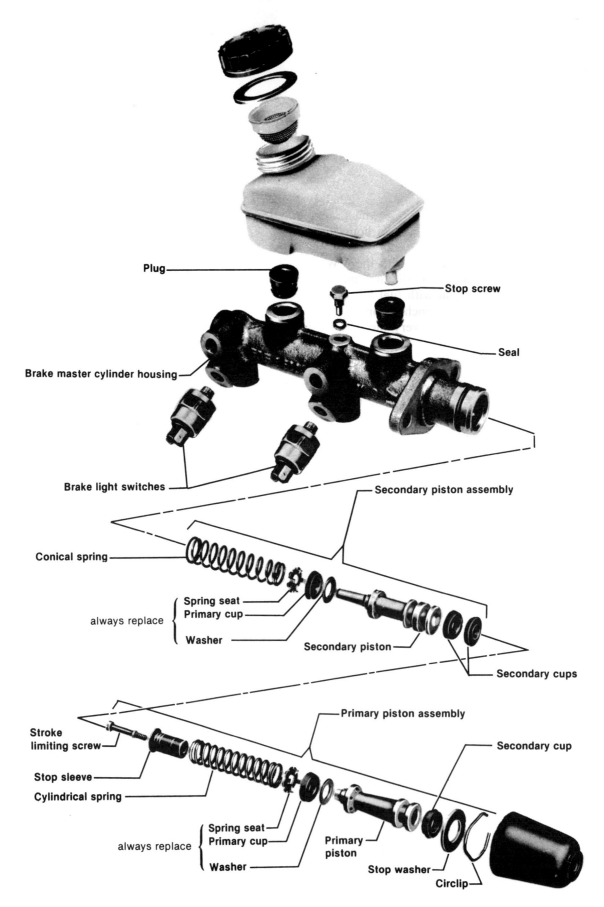

Plug

Stop screw

Seal

Brake master cylinder housing

Brake light switches

Secondary piston assembly

Conical spring

Spring seat
Primary cup
always replace
Washer

Secondary piston

Secondary cups

Primary piston assembly

Stroke
limiting screw

Secondary cup

Stop sleeve

Cylindrical spring

Spring seat
Primary cup
always replace
Washer

Primary
piston

Stop washer

Circlip

VW master cylinder showing all wear points. This job, which is very expensive professionally, can be yours for the cost of the kit.

pedal pushes down too far and you may even have to pump it for stopping. But are you adding oil? If you are, the leak can be in the lines, underneath the car somewhere, if it isn't at the master cylinder or the wheel cylinders (it usually is one or the other). If one of the lines leaks, only the line in question needs replacing. But if you are not adding oil, with the symptom above, the possibilities are that the lines need bleeding or the master cylinder is at fault and needs cleaning out and rebuilding. So first bleed the lines. It doesn't cost anything and takes only a half hour or so. Then buy a master cylinder kit, which can cost a fair amount and takes a couple of hours to install.

To rebuild a master cylinder, as with the VW, unbolt the brake light switches and the fuel lines—with care. Whenever you deal with fuel line couplings you always use two wrenches, or almost always (there are exceptions to every mechanical procedure). When the lines are unbolted, unbolt the front bolts that attach the master cylinder to the firewall, and the bolts that hold it elsewhere. It will then come out. It will be full of oil. Unbolt or unhook the oil container at the top, if it comes off—not all of them do, excepting the caps and cap holders, which come off for regular maintenance. Pour out the oil.

To rebuild, fish out the contents of the piston, starting with a steel circlip or retainer, then a washer

or two, and finally the primary piston. All these will come out, but you must also remove the stop screw, which will be either on top of the cylinder below the oil chamber as in the VW models, or on the bottom of the cylinder. It will be a bolt or screw. Take it out and then you can remove everything in the master cylinder—primary and secondary piston assemblies (remember, you are dealing with dual/diagonal brake systems which operate independently). Your kit will replace all these items. But first, clean out the cylinder housing—flush it out with brake oil and/or a toothbrush.

When you rebuild it with the new parts—all of them—put the master cylinder back, exactly as you found it, fill it with oil and bleed it. That means you don't put it back exactly, just yet. You want to bleed it first. The kit will have instructions but if it doesn't, a rough and ready bleeding can be done easily. Keep the fluid couplings loose; fill up the master cylinder and have someone push on the brake a little bit and hold it. Sop up the oil that comes out with a rag. Tighten the couplings first, however (you can always clean up oil). Do this once or twice with each coupling. You may escape having to bleed the individual brake lines altogether this way. But if when you finish the operation you still don't get a stiff enough pedal, you'll have to bleed all four wheels. Sorry about that.

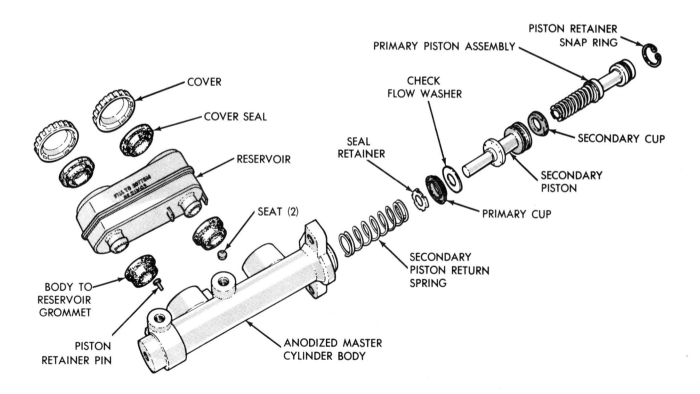

Omni/Horizon master cylinder in an exploded drawing.

Chapter Four

Electrical Systems

Electrical systems are the most complicated parts of the car in respect to troubleshooting, simply because so much can go wrong with them. But be of good cheer; we have already covered the key electrical system, ignition, and it was not such an ogre.

Let's look at the battery, cranking and starting, charging (alternator), and accessory electrical systems.

Battery service consists mostly of keeping corrosion off the terminals and cleaning the top occasionally with a solution of soda and water. Some cars have built-in testers or hydrometers. The G.M. Citation and its X-Body relatives in other G.M. divisions have such a device. There are three signals in this battery: Looking down on the built-in hyd-rometer on top of the battery, you may see the indicator darkened with a green dot; it may be darkened without a green dot; and may be light with a yellow or bright indicator. In the last case, the battery is simply dead and must be replaced. Also, you must not try to jump-start it, charge it or test it. If you do you can cause it to explode. In the darkened indicator case with no green dot, it may be jump-started; so too with the green dot indicator. Your battery in the last two cases has been cranked down or otherwise discharged, but remains serviceable, and you look elsewhere for problems (cranking system, ignition, and carburetion).

Always jump-start a car by hooking up cables with positive to positive, but negative on the starting car

BUILT-IN
HYDROMETER

Citation sealed battery with built-in hydrometer.

to frame on the car to be started—keep the negative away from the battery to be started. Otherwise you risk explosion of hydrogen gas. Always be wary of batteries. When the car is started, take off the negative jump cable from the car that was started, then remove the others.

CHARGING SYSTEMS

Scirocco and other VW charging systems consist of an alternator mounted down near the crankshaft pulley that drives it. The first check you make on an alternator that doesn't seem to be delivering the goods is its belt. A loose belt will lower or stop charging altogether. Tighten or replace the belt.

The next test you make on an alternator is a simple, "garage door" test. Drive your car up to a garage door, or any other surface, with the lights on. (It should be dark enough to allow you to make distinctions between lighting intensities of the headlights.) Turn the lights on to bright; then turn on the ignition key. The lights should not get very dim during the cranking. If they do, you have either battery trouble, alternator trouble or both. When the engine starts, accelerate in neutral. The lights should brighten. If they dim when you accelerate, and the belt is good, the chances are that an alternator diode is bad. Does the alternator warning light come on when you accelerate? If so, that probably means alternator trouble.

Wiring problems between the alternator and the warning light are about as probable as problems in the alternator. The signal that is meant to be a convenience can also be a big pain. Before condemning

the alternator, get the battery checked. If the battery is good, but discharged, look at some of your driving habits. Do you use all the possible accessory motors and electrical outlets during short city driving runs? That will discharge most batteries. But if your driving habits are not at fault, the battery is good, and charging is not taking place, it is time to believe the warning light.

Scirocco warning light signals should go out when engine speed increases slightly, as in most cars. When you turn on the ignition key, and before you start the engine, the alternator light should light up brightly. If engine speed does turn the light off, or if the light does not come on when the ignition key is turned on (engine not started yet), you have alternator trouble.

To test an alternator requires an ohmmeter and voltmeter. If you don't have such devices you have only one choice; remove the alternator and take it to a shop for testing. Usually you can watch the test. If the alternator fails the test, you have two alternatives—buy a rebuilt unit on the spot, or take it home and rebuild it. That's a big job. A rebuilt will cost less than half the price of a new one at a garage, where you drive in and simply complain about lack of charging. If you take the old one out, have it tested, buy a rebuilt and replace it yourself, you save half or more.

Before removing the alternator, either disconnect the leads to it or disconnect the battery negative cable, since electricity goes to the alternator even with ignition off. (That's why a shorted diode will cause the alternator warning light to stay on when ignition is turned off, in some cases.)

To remove an alternator is very easy. We've described belt removal; simply continue on and remove all the bolts and nuts that hold the alternator to its clamps and adjuster. There can be a half dozen of such fasteners. Some of them are available from the top of the engine; others may require that you remove them from below. For a small device, the alternator is fairly heavy, so don't drop it when you get it unbolted.

If you want to repair the alternator yourself, there is the simple repair in which you replace the brushes. That could save you the price of a new or a rebuilt alternator.

On a Scirocco (and other VWs), the alternator is held by three mounting bolts. If you remove it, one of the bolts is a socket head type, which requires a special socket.

To test the alternator yourself you must have a test light. You must also be willing to do some fairly touchy electrical work—not a bit dangerous, merely finicky and involving small parts and careful testing and soldering. Don't start the job if you don't like that challenge.

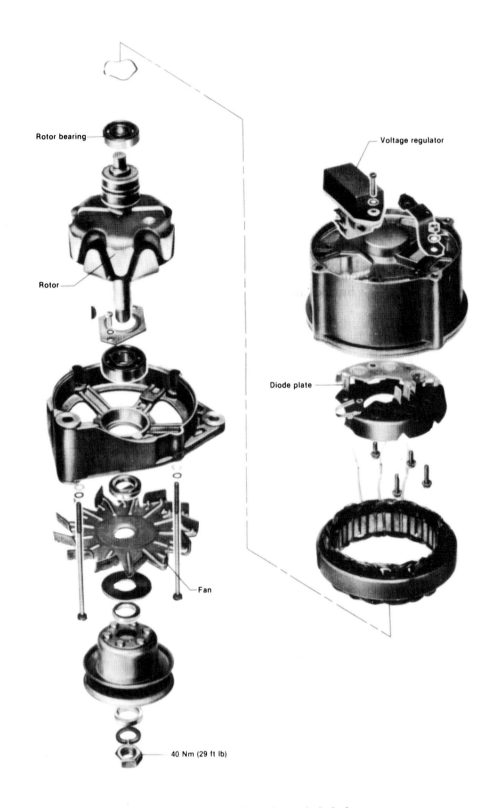

Rotor bearing

Rotor

Fan

40 Nm (29 ft lb)

Voltage regulator

Diode plate

Bosch alternator and regulator in exploded view.

VW uses both Bosch and Motorola alternators. But the Motorola admits of far fewer repairs, at least for the home mechanic. The first inspection to make on an alternator that isn't delivering sufficient charging voltage is of the brushes and brush holder. Brushes and voltage regulator come out together on the Bosch; Motorola brushes and regulators are also connected, though they don't come off as a unit.

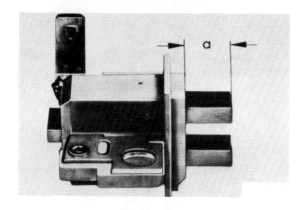

Motorola brushes—their wear limits.

Examine the brushes; replace them if they are worn to 7/32-inch or less (5 mm). New brushes are double that length.

If brushes were worn, replace them and put the alternator back on the car. It may now charge properly. If it does not, you'll have to take it off again—no big deal—and test the diodes and coils.

You can make all tests with a simple 12-volt test lamp and clips or probes. One warning: never run an alternator when the battery is disconnected—it will ruin diodes and regulator. Resist turning it when you take it off.

You could test an alternator on the car, as it is done in garages, if you had their equipment. A battery cutout switch, a variable resistance ammeter, and similar voltmeter, would be required. But unless you are going into the business, you'll have to make do as follows.

With the alternator off the engine, remove the through bolts and the brush and holder, which contains the regulator, brushes, and the diode carrier.

To test diodes (Bosch only), unsolder the wires from stator (stationary field coil) to the diode carrier, avoiding too much heat. Attach a pair of needle-nose pliers as a heat sink to the wire nearest the diode you are unsoldering, to dissipate some heat. It is essential to do this; diodes are easily ruined by heat.

Use a 12-volt test lamp to test the rotor coil; there should be no light when you touch the slip rings of the rotor and the rotor poles. If the light goes on, the coil of the rotor is grounded; the rotor must be replaced. The stator (stationary) field coil lead also can be tested, once unsoldered. Again, there should be no light when you touch coil winding lead and the iron frame. If there is, replace the coil. You need an ohmmeter to test between two slip rings—the resistance should be around 3.40 to 3.75 ohms (Bosch 55-amp unit). If resistance is less, the field coil is shorted. You can use the test lamp and if the light is dim, the coil is probably okay; the meter confirms or denies it.

Now go to the diodes. There are three groups of three diodes each. Each group must first be tested in isolation, hence unsoldered. (You've already unsoldered the lead to the stator.)

To test diodes you need either a 1.5-volt battery test lamp or an ohmmeter. Put one test lead on the diode lead wire, the other test lead to the diode case. Then reverse the two test probes. The light should go on in one direction but not in the other. If the light does not go on in either direction, the diode is open and the entire carrier must be replaced. If the diode goes on in both directions, it is also defective and the entire unit needs replacement. You have to test each diode individually, since it is possible that if you test them in groups, as we've just done, you will miss a faulty diode. Unsolder connections between individual diodes (always using the pliers as a heat sink) and test them as before.

Assuming that you discover a defective diode, you have to replace the diode carrier. You must also install a suppression condenser in either Bosch or Motorola alternator, if there was no such device as original equipment. It forestalls voltage surge, which ruins diodes.

If you don't find any defective diodes, and the coils test out to be good, replace the regulator.

Before you replace anything, and in fact when the alternator is still on the car and operating, listen carefully to it for noises. Any unusual noise such as bearing noise—a grinding noise—means you will have to do a bearing job as well as an electrical rebuild. That requires pressing off and pressing on new sets of bearings and races. You may have to pay for this service, if you don't have any puller that will do the job of removal, or a vise or other pressure to install the races and bearings. If so, any shop will do it for very few dollars, if they have a slow few minutes and the inclination.

Other noises are squeaks (belts and pulleys) and whistles. These can be a diode or stator that is shorted, but whistles can also be normal operating sounds, oddly enough.

Corvette

General Motors also uses an integral regulator-alternator, in Corvette, its X-Body cars and others.

G.M. notes that trouble in the charging system (alternator) will show up as one or more of these: faulty indicator light operation (the dash light doesn't behave); undercharged battery, indicated by slow cranking or by the hydrometer sign noted above; an overcharged battery, indicated by spewing of electrolyte from the battery vent.

The light malfunction shows up as the ignition

Marking end frames of an alternator.

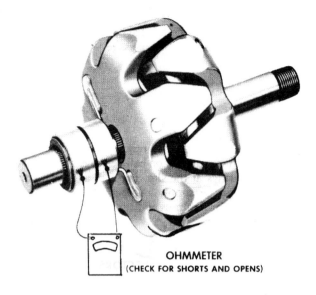

OHMMETER
(CHECK FOR SHORTS AND OPENS)

Checking a rotor for shorts and opens.

switch being off, the light on. Unplug the connector from the alternator's No. 1 and No. 2 terminals (they are marked nearby). If the dash light remains on there is a short somewhere between these two leads. If the light goes out, replace the rectifier bridge, which is a device underneath the slip rings and fairly easily replaced.

If the ignition switch is on, the light is off, the engine is stopped, it is caused by the same conditions as above, but also by an open circuit—a blown fuse, burned out bulb or bad bulb socket, or an open line in the No. 1 lead between the generator (alternator) and the ignition switch.

If the ignition switch is on, the dash light out while the engine is running, look for a blown fuse between the light and the switch, and also (if present) in the air conditioning circuit.

If the battery is undercharging, though the dash light operation is normal, and it isn't caused by something outside the alternator, look first at the wiring, especially the connections at the alternator, the firewall, the starter, the engine ground, and the battery cable connections at the battery lugs.

Many tests are possible, using a voltmeter, ammeter, and a specialized meter, an alternator meter. But most engine analyzers will do the job. Follow the instructions with the tester, if you have such a device, since all have their own methods.

If the battery is overcharging, use the tester if you have it, or you'll have to test the diodes and rotor windings.

To remove the alternator, remove the usual bolts and the belt. The alternator through bolts—four of them—come out next. Make a mark across the frame with a pencil or a scratching tool so you can get the two halves back in the same position. Pry the two frames apart with a screwdriver.

If you have to remove the drive end of the frame (for bearing work), you'll have to remove the shaft nut—which has much torque. You can put the rotor in a vise, but if you do you must not tighten the vise too much or too little, otherwise you can damage the rotor. Once the shaft nut is off, the other components come off. It is possible to loosen the shaft nut by holding the pulley and/or the fan, but be careful not to distort the fan.

Testing the coils is very similar to testing on any other alternator. G.M. suggests using an ohmmeter rather than a test light. Either will do.

With an ohmmeter, if the reading is high (infinite), the winding is open, if low the rotor winding is grounded. To check for short circuits or excessive resistance, use the ohmmeter on the two slip rings and readings should be 2.4 to 3 ohms. Below that value means short circuits, above means excessive resistance. If the rotor is good, go next to other components.

Diode testing is similar but simpler. Remove the diode trio from the frame by removing the three nuts and attaching screw. Also, remove the stator (stationary field coil) assembly.

Ohmmeter readings on the diode trio must be done with a 1.5 volt battery meter. Use the lowest range setting. Check the reading, reverse the leads to the same two connectors. If both readings are the same, the trio must be replaced. Good diodes should have one high and one low reading. Repeat the test between the single connector and each of the other two connectors. Then connect the meter to each pair of the three connectors, and if any reading is zero, which means shorting between the diodes, replace the diode trio. It is important to get all insulating washers in place. Note that the insulating washer on

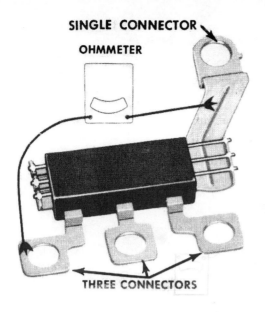

Testing diode trio.

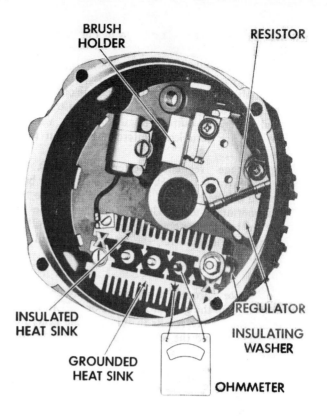

Checking rectifier bridge of an alternator.

the diode attaching screw goes over the top of the diode trio connector.

The rectifier bridge check should be next. Connect the meter to the grounded heat sink, which is a comb-like device, and one of the three terminals. Then reverse the connections. If readings are the same, replace the rectifier bridge. It should have one high and one low reading.

Stator windings should also be checked by ohmmeter. If the reading is low connected to any stator lead and the frame, the winding is grounded and must be replaced. If the meter has a high reading when connected between each pair of stator leads, the windings are open. Note that this applies to the

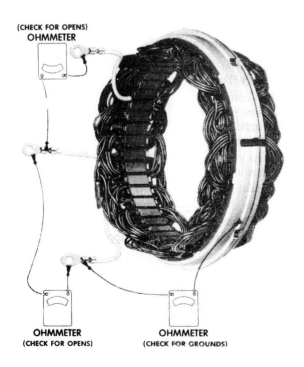

Testing field coils with ohmmeter.

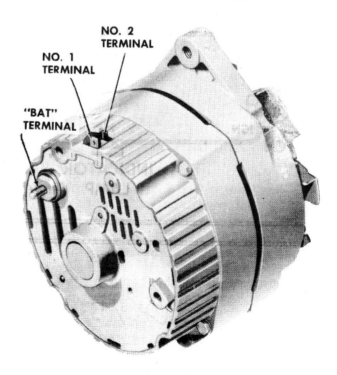

The G.M. Model 10SI alternator terminal connectors.

79

model 10-SI alternator. The larger 15-SI cannot be checked in this way.

If all other checks are normal and the alternator still fails to produce the rated output, that means shorted windings and replacement.

Clean the slip rings, if they need it, with a 400 grain or finer polishing cloth.

To reassemble, put a pin through the holes in the brush holder to hold up the brushes when you install the shaft into the slip ring end frame assembly so as not to damage the seal. Match up the two frame halves according to the mark you made. Once the through bolts are tightened, pull out the brush retaining pin.

In all this, make sure that no dirt gets into any part of the alternator. Take special pains to clean off the bearing and shaft assembly (and keep bearings covered when alternator is taken apart).

Chrysler

The Omni/Horizon alternator-regulator has a pivot mounting bolt and an adjusting bracket to remove.

You must also remove the brush assemblies before taking the alternator apart. Brushes are mounted in plastic holders that keep them against the slip rings. Remove the brush screws. insulating washers, and pull out the brush assemblies. Remember where the insulating washers go. Examine the brushes for wear and clean off the slip rings if they need it. Replace brushes that appear worn (Chrysler makes brush replacement easy at any time, without removing the alternator).

Disassembly of the alternator follows usual paths. Remove the through bolts, mark across the housing and pry it apart with a screwdriver.

To test diodes, coils and slip rings, remove the nuts that hold the stator windings and the diodes (note: Chrysler calls diodes "rectifiers" which is what they are—they change direct current to alternating and back). Take out stator terminals and stator assembly—carefully.

Chrysler recommends using a 12-volt battery test light with a No. 67 bulb of 4 candle power. Connect one lead of the test light to the positive battery post; the other test light lead to the probe you're using and to the negative battery post (test lights have three leads, but one is, of course, simply an interrupted single lead).

Use one test probe on the rectifier heat sink; the other on the strap on top of the rectifier (diode). Reverse them, with the usual reading; if the light lights in one direction but not in the other, the rectifier is good. It is shorted (defective) if the light lights

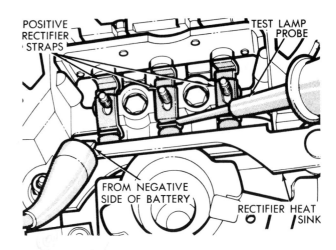

Testing positive rectifers with test lamp probe.

both ways; and it is also defective (open) if the light fails to light in either direction. Repeat the test for all diodes in both assemblies.

If you have to replace any of the rectifiers, make a precise note of the location of all washers and insulators.

To test the stator field coils for defects, scratch a bare spot in the varnish of the frame and hold the test probe on that spot. The other probe goes to each of the three stator terminals, one at a time. If the light turns on, the coil is grounded and defective.

Next, put one probe on one lead and the other on each of the remaining two leads—one at a time. The light should light with each contact. If it does not, the coil is broken. You need a new stator coil in either of the above cases.

To test the rotor, use an ohmmeter probe from

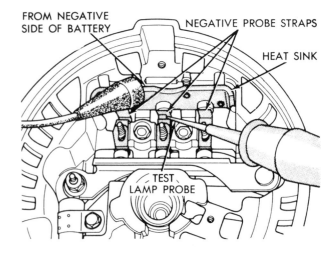

Negative rectifier testing with test lamp on Chrysler alternator.

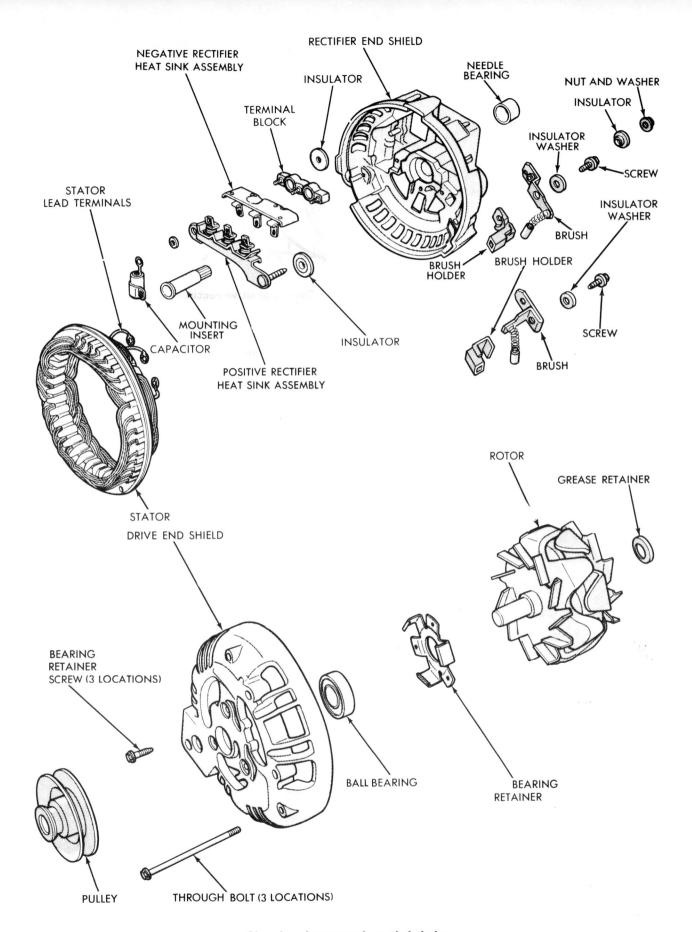

NEGATIVE RECTIFIER
HEAT SINK ASSEMBLY

RECTIFIER END SHIELD

INSULATOR

NEEDLE
BEARING

NUT AND WASHER

INSULATOR

TERMINAL
BLOCK

INSULATOR
WASHER

SCREW

STATOR
LEAD TERMINALS

INSULATOR
WASHER

BRUSH

SCREW

BRUSH
HOLDER

BRUSH HOLDER

MOUNTING
INSERT

INSULATOR

CAPACITOR

BRUSH

POSITIVE RECTIFIER
HEAT SINK ASSEMBLY

ROTOR

GREASE RETAINER

STATOR

DRIVE END SHIELD

BEARING
RETAINER
SCREW (3 LOCATIONS)

BALL BEARING

BEARING
RETAINER

PULLEY

THROUGH BOLT (3 LOCATIONS)

Chrysler alternator in exploded view.

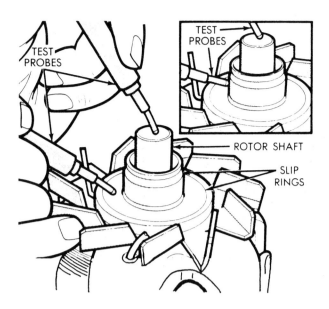

To test the rotor for ground use test probe on slip rings and shaft.

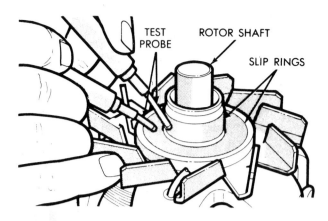

To test the rotor use lamp and probes on slip rings.

each slip ring to the shaft. You are testing for grounded, open or internally shorted field coils.

For a grounded coil, connect a probe from each slip ring to the rotor shaft. Set the ohmmeter for "infinite" reading when probes are separated and for zero when the probes are shorted. If the reading is zero or higher, the rotor is grounded.

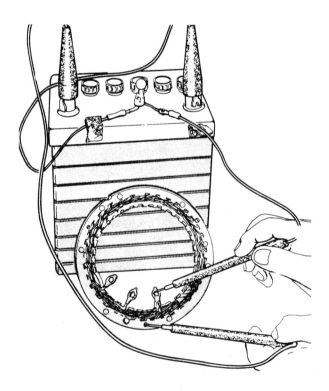

Testing the stator for ground using test lamp and probes.

To check rotor coils for an open coil, the ohmmeter reading should be between 1.5 and 2 ohms when probes are on the two slip rings (temperature is important; it should be about 70 F). The resistance will be between 2.5 and 3 ohms on rotors that are tested on cars operating at higher engine temperatures. Readings above 3.5 ohms indicate the possibility of a defective coil.

A shorted coil will yield an ohmmeter reading below 1.5 ohms.

If shorts or opens occur, the rotor must be replaced.

Bearings can only be serviced by you if you have a hub or bearing puller to remove the pully and the bearing from the rotor shaft. You will then have to get the bearing pressed on.

All the parts can be replaced, but as you can see in every case discussed, the work is tricky and finicky and if you have no stomach for it, simply buy a rebuilt alternator. It will cost a lot more, but will save a lot of time.

Fiat uses Marelli alternators, which are serviced like all others. The same is true of Japanese alternators, which are Japanese in origin. Alternators, like most other electrical components, are international. They speak the language of electricity, which knows no frontiers.

STARTERS

Starting motors have had little change for decades. Other than an occasional change of brushes and a few other parts, they are expected to last the life of the car. They are much simpler than alternators.

Solenoid coils, mounted piggyback on top of the starting motor, may sometimes require replacement without doing anything to the starter (other than removing it from the car). Mechanical problems

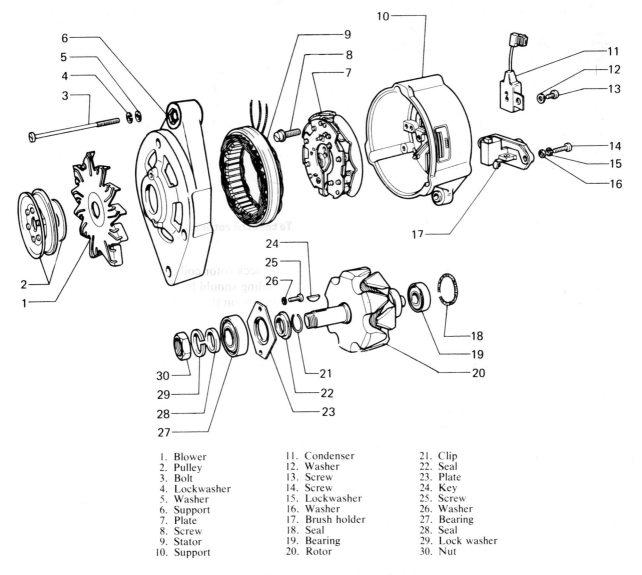

1. Blower	11. Condenser	21. Clip
2. Pulley	12. Washer	22. Seal
3. Bolt	13. Screw	23. Plate
4. Lockwasher	14. Screw	24. Key
5. Washer	15. Lockwasher	25. Screw
6. Support	16. Washer	26. Washer
7. Plate	17. Brush holder	27. Bearing
8. Screw	18. Seal	28. Seal
9. Stator	19. Bearing	29. Lock washer
10. Support	20. Rotor	30. Nut

A Marelli (Fiat) alternator in exploded view.

arise with the internal clutches and gears, as well as the solenoid's plunger mechanism, which activates the clutch, throwing it into the flywheel. Starters also have electrical problems, like any motor. In addition to brushes, their switches, coils, commutators, and wiring may fail. But failure rate isn't high.

Starters differ with manufacturers, but not much. All starters have brushes, solenoids, bearings, and other components that can be replaced, usually with less effort than is required to do an alternator overhaul. But you can also buy rebuilt starters, and if you bring in the old, the cost will be much less than simply driving the car in and saying "fix it." That is because you will quickly discover that the biggest job with any starter is getting it off the car, unlike the alternator, which goes quietly. The starter has to engage the flywheel, which is placed for the convenience of the engine not the mechanic. There is no

set of instructions that will govern starter removal, nor a set of tools that will make it all simple. Starter removal is a drag, like starter installation. The repairs are easy.

The chief complaints against starters are that (1) they don't turn over quickly enough or (2) they don't engage the flywheel but whine instead of doing their job. A whining starter is caused by failure of the drive pinion to engage the flywheel. (And that's often a solenoid failure). A slow moving starter is caused by worn brushes and other wear, and possibly short circuits in the coils. All these problems can only be addressed with the starter off the engine, and we are back to square one.

VW Scirocco and other VW cars allow you to remove one of two mounting bolts as well as the electrical leads from the top, while you complete the job from underneath. Some VWs have a support

Starter

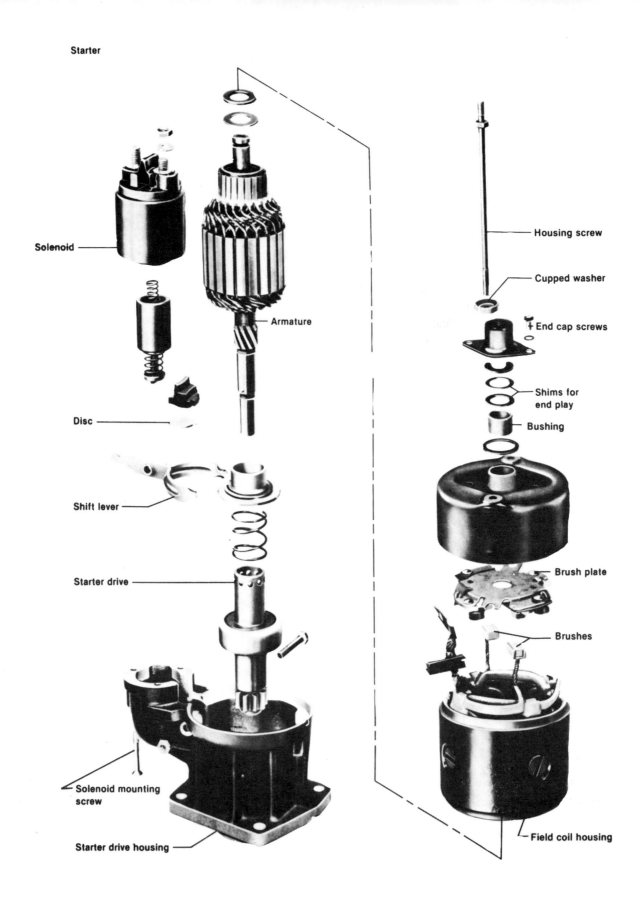

Solenoid

Armature

Disc

Shift lever

Starter drive

Solenoid mounting
screw

Starter drive housing

Housing screw

Cupped washer

End cap screws

Shims for
end play

Bushing

Brush plate

Brushes

Field coil housing

A VW starter in exploded view.

bracket that you remove from underneath; some do not.

It is wise to disconnect the negative post of the battery before starting removal of the unit. A hot (positive) lead to the center post of the solenoid from the battery is easily shorted when you work on the battery. It can cause tremors throughout the electrical system, with ruinous consequences.

In VW cars through 1974 (and others) a seat interlock belt can self destruct, making all electrical movement impossible. If you have such a car, the interlock belt has its own trouble spots, which recent cars have avoided. In case of an interlock failure, check the switch above the door for corrosion and wear.

Starters on VWs (and other cars, too) differ somewhat in the drive section between standard and automatic transmissions. If you deal with a VW automatic, the starter drive housing is more massive, with more bolts, but otherwise the starters are about the same. But then most starters are the same, with a few exceptions. (Chrysler large starters have small transmissions inside that make them more complicated.)

Once you remove the starter from the bell housing, and take out the through bolts or housing screws, remove the solenoid coil with its shift lever mechanism, the armature and the starter drive section, you have all the parts in front of you.

Brushes—typically four of them, but not invariably—can cause trouble getting them back in place. First, inspect them for wear, and if the starter hasn't been off the car for a long time, replace them. On VWs, minimum length is 1/2-inch (13 mm). Examine the commutator for wear. If it has much wear, with uneven spots and ridges, and it tests okay otherwise, it will have to be taken to an electrical shop where they "turn" commutators (grind them off on a lathe). If it is merely dirty, without ridges and deep abrasions, clean it off with some kind of polishing cloth, blow out any grains of copper from between the segments (otherwise they will short circuit), and put it back, after testing it electrically (see below).

If the starter "whines" instead of starting, it needs a new starter drive, or it needs the old one greased. First, inspect the drive gear, and if it doesn't appear to be cracked or worn, clean out the path it moves on and put some all purpose grease in the grooves of the gear and on the shaft. Now work it around until it moves freely. That could be the cure.

But if it is badly worn, it will have to be replaced. Remove the circlip and stop ring from the shaft, and the starter drive will come off. Examine the shift lever for wear, and test the solenoid coil with a couple of jumper cables from the battery. The coil arouses a magnet that operates the shift lever, but if

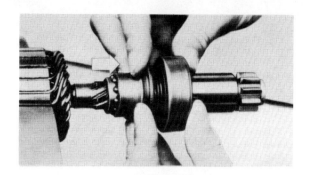

A starter drive on VW starter.

the coil doesn't operate, or the shift lever has worn off at the ends and doesn't engage the starter drive properly, the solenoid and/or the shift lever must be replaced, along with the starter drive. The solenoid, with current, should go in; without, it should drop out of the housing. Unless it does both it is defective.

Before you buy a new drive, take the old one along and compare it in detail with the new one, beginning with the gears. If you don't see any difference between new and old gears, the chances are that the problem is entirely in the solenoid or the shift lever. These can be replaced separately.

When replacing the gear, either with the new one or the old, the stop ring can give you some trouble. The stop ring groove faces outside and must be pressed down over the circlip. It must turn freely on the shaft. You can tap it down until you get it in the right place. The circlip is beneath the stop ring.

To check the various electrical components, first examine the commutator bars for burns. Burns are a sign of short circuits. A new (rebuilt) starter is the answer. This may be the answer all along, if you are willing to take the starter off and carry it to the starter store.

In general, a starter that needs only new brushes, a new solenoid, or a new drive gear, is worth fixing, because these three components are fairly inexpensive and fairly easy to install. Once past these three, it becomes a losing proposition. Each amateur mechanic may calculate these odds differently, however. You may decide that you are ahead of the game at the outset, when you get the critter off the car, and take it into the store to trade in on a rebuilt. In any case, the decision is yours.

G.M. starters

General Motors' starters, in Corvette, Citation, or many others, are familiar to anyone who has ever done anything to a starter. Removal is usually from below the car, and it is recommended that you get

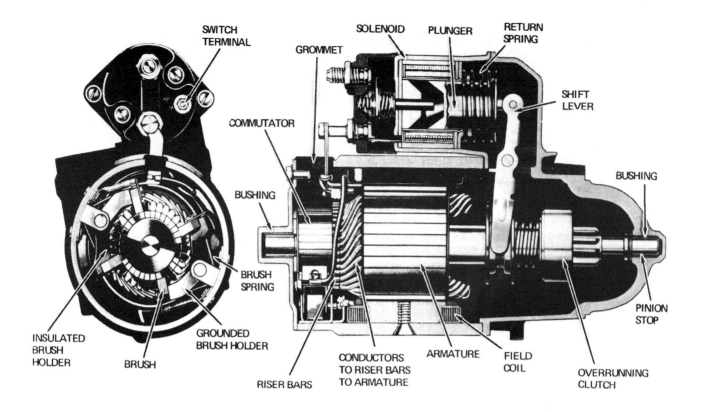

A Corvette starting motor in detail.

some kind of support for the starter, once it is loose and you begin the final process of removal. The motor is heavy and a wood block of some sort, or a small hydraulic jack—in addition to the other jacks and stands you are using on the body and engine—will help you manipulate the motor. Again, before you take it out, disconnect the battery negative lug.

The order of disassembly is to disconnect the coil connection from its solenoid terminal; remove the through bolts, commutator end frame and field frame assembly; the solenoid and shift lever from the housing and the armature. The thrust collar can be removed next. Remove the pinion gear from the armature by sliding a piece of 1/2-inch pipe or something similar over the shaft and hitting it with a hammer against the retainer. This drives the retainer toward the armature core and off the snap ring.

Visual inspection of brushes, springs, commutator, and coils, plus bearings (actually you usually hear bearing wear, but look for absence of grease), will tell you a great deal about the condition of the motor. If the commutator has burned spots, and heavy wear, it is probably shorted out. Noticeable wear of the commutator, with signs of shorts, is enough to condemn the motor entirely. But you can make a quick test with a test light. There should be no continuity between the copper segments of the commutator, and the metal surfaces of the armature.

If the light goes on with a test probe on the commutator and one of the armature metal frames, you need a new starter.

If you see nothing wrong with the solenoid, but suspect it, use two jumper wires. The solenoid should respond by pulling in the plunger instantly. Don't give it electricity for more than a few seconds. But that time should be enough; if it responds with force (and it has to push the plunger which pushes the shift lever which pushes the pinion gear) it is working.

The pinion gear must turn freely. If it doesn't move easily, try cleaning and greasing the track and the armature shaft. But don't put back gear assembly if the gear shows wear, no matter how freely it may work.

To install a new clutch and gear assembly requires only that you grease the shaft, slide the gear on, the retainer facing out, and force the snap ring into its groove. Note that it's ticklish. Using a screwdriver and pliers, force it across the first groove without going into it. When it is in its (second) groove, bring the collar on and snap the collar and ring together.

Omni/Horizon starters, whose location is similar to that of VW, are rather easy to get off. They use a Bosch starter, like the VW, on the manual transmission, and the Nippondenso starter on the automatic transmission.

CYLINDER
RETAINER

Removing the retainer from the snap ring.

The Bosch, which appears to be more or less identical with the model in use by VW, comes apart in this order; solenoid mounting screws, solenoid assembly, end shield bearing cap screws, "C" washer, through bolts, end shield, brush plate, both brushes, armature clutch and shift fork assembly (for automatic transmission; you've already done it on stick shift), press the stop collar off the snap ring with a socket that fits over, pull off the snap ring, remove

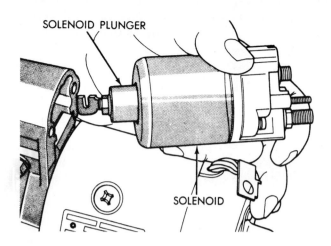

SOLENOID PLUNGER

SOLENOID

Nippondenso starter solenoid plunger.

the clutch and the drive end housing.

The Nippondenso starter has different details but is very similar. Disassembly goes in this order: the field coil wire, solenoid mounting screws, the solenoid, the rubber gasket and metal plate, bearing cover mounting screws, bearing end cap, spring, shaft lock, washer and seal, through bolts, end frame, brush plate, field frame, shift lever pivot bolt, armature assembly, snap ring and stop collar. All these parts come off easily.

Examine them all for wear, cracks, burrs, hangups of movement, and electrical flow. The armature, commutator and coils must be tested electrically. With a test lamp, touch the end of each copper commutator bar and the steel shaft. If the light goes on at any of the bars, the armature must be replaced. The coils can be tested with the lamp by touching the frame and the brushes. When you touch the field coil lead and frame the lamp does not light; if it does the coils are defective and must be replaced.

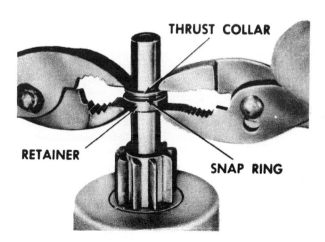

THRUST COLLAR

RETAINER

SNAP RING

Getting the retainer over the snap ring.

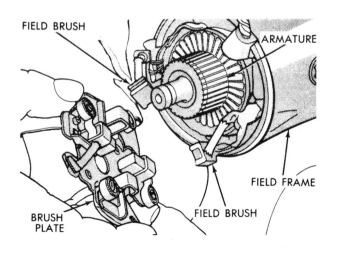

FIELD BRUSH

ARMATURE

FIELD FRAME

FIELD BRUSH

BRUSH PLATE

Brush plate details of Nippondenso starter.

Touch the brushes one at a time with one probe while holding the other against the brush plate. Two brush holders are grounded 180 degrees apart; with these the lamp lights. The other two should not cause the test light to go on. If the insulated brush holders cause the light to go on, the brush holders are grounded and the brush plate assembly must be replaced.

To assemble, reverse the order you followed above. The stop ring must be pulled over the snap ring with some kind of forcing tool. Any puller will do, but if you don't own a puller, you can improvise something.

Getting the brushes back should be done carefully, though it's not the ticklish problem it can be with the G.M. Delco starter.

Check out bearings for adequacy of grease, and for wear. New brushes should be installed if the old ones are less than half the length of the new ones. New brushes are 11/16-inches long.

OTHER ELECTRICAL COMPONENTS

Other electrical devices range from the doors to the windshield. If you have electric windows you have a motor assembly that may need attention on occasion. To avoid such problems, take off the door pad every two years or whenever the window slows up its performance and doesn't want to open and close quickly or completely. To get the door pad off can be puzzling, since it is designed cosmetically to make it seem impossible to remove. You must survey all the trinkets and gadgets on the door to discover where their fasteners are concealed. Handles and door openers generally have screws. Arm rests are bolted on from below, with bolts that sometimes have to be tunneled into with socket extensions. Sometimes a long phillips screwdriver will do the job.

Electrical switches on the door usually have plas-

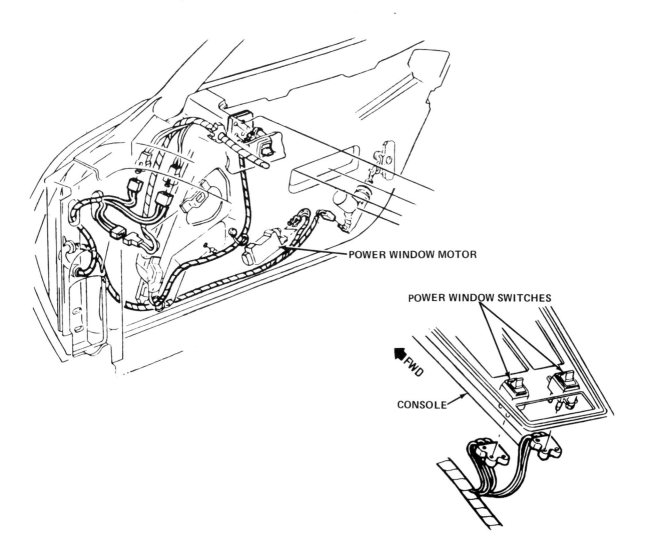

POWER WINDOW MOTOR

POWER WINDOW SWITCHES

FWD

CONSOLE

Corvette power window wiring.

88

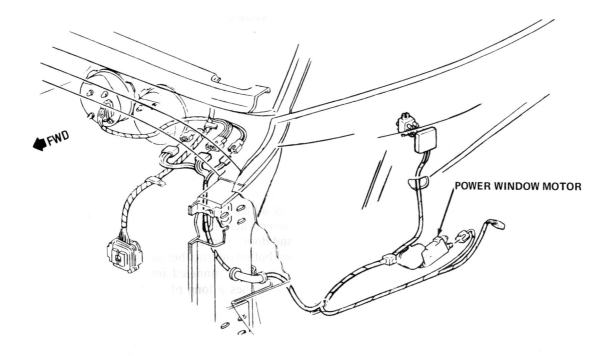

FWD

POWER WINDOW MOTOR

Added details of Corvette power window system.

tic tabs or metal keepers that can be exposed if you push the door pad in. Be careful with doors that have speakers—don't poke around the speaker. Also, keep a record of speaker fasteners and washers, so that you can get them all back in their original position.

Once you get the door handle and arm rest fasteners off, unscrew the push lock knob. Pry off the door pad carefully. Fasteners often are plastic pins of various configurations that press fit into other plastic devices. Electric switches may be push-in fit types or screw-on types that must be treated carefully. Use a screwdriver to pry off the pad, once you have all the retainers off. Some doors have plastic water seals inside the pad; don't poke holes in them.

You want to grease the motor inside without removing it. That's a big job, so be satisfied with greasing all the runners, gears, plastic wheel surfaces and metal surfaces that touch each other. With the pad off, you may have to install the switch temporarily in order to see what surfaces should be greased.

If the motor simply isn't working at all, use a test lamp to see whether voltage is arriving at the motor. It could fail. Then you have to trace wiring back to the dash area where the connectors probably originate (though they may also start inside the engine). If the motor is burned out—simply won't work at all—you have a replacement problem. Unless the motor is accessible to ordinary tools, don't try it. Fortunately, window motors are sturdy. If you grease everything that moves, you won't face the problem.

Windshield wiper/washer

Of all the convenience devices, the windshield wiper/washer system is the most ornery. That is because it combines the most intricate electrical system of switches, motors, and wiring, with a complex system of gears, arms and mechanical connectors that all combine to do what a human arm is designed to do. Nobody ever claimed the human arm was simple.

Nowadays, with rear installations as well as front, the problem is twice as ornery. You deal with heating, flushing, brushing and the separate signals that make them all come together.

The dash switches often fail. Switches inside the steering column, thanks to the "stalk" switch idea, are a special pain. The motors in the wiper arm system can fail, and the washer buzzer type motor and pump can have various failures.

The easiest failure of all is the broken washer hose or the clogged outlet in front of the windshield (or on top in back). If the outlets clog, stick a pin in them. If the hoses break, replace them. Motors and pumps at the washer well (or wherever it may be) can develop various ailments, both electrical and mechanical. They can develop leaks at the hose inlet and outlet, thanks to engine vibration. Some of these leaks can be fixed with the new glues on the market. Some can only be fixed with a new pump.

Hose replacement is easy in the engine; in the rear installation it isn't quite as easy. When replacing

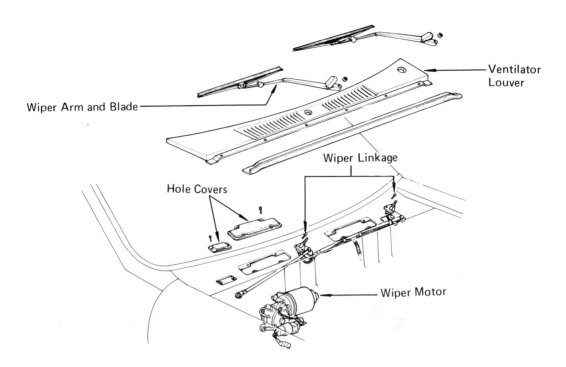

Details of a Toyota Celica windshield wiper motor and linkage in front mounting.

parts like these, always buy dealer counter parts, which are original equipment.

Wiper motors and their linkage which drive the front wipers are a story unto themselves. If the wipers stop altogether, but the motor runs, that means the ball joint or crank connection just outside the motor has failed. Wiper motors are powerful small motors located somewhere near the windshield.

VW Scirocco is considerate in its placement of the wiper motor—easily accessible in front of the windshield. Chrysler has the same placement in Omni/Horizon.

Motor linkage begins at the motor shaft, and through gears and links, and through the bearing-bushing that holds the wiper arms and turns them against the windshield. It can develop all kinds of binds and bad behavior. That is why an occasional lubrication of these cranks and links can postpone or eliminate total system breakdown. If the motor is forced to work harder than it likes, because of linkage binding, it will soon stop working altogether. Since people design these systems, it is not surprising that they behave like people.

No lubrication is needed or possible with the washer system, but the hoses can clog and jets clog or get out of adjustment so that the spray can't find the windshield. Spray adjustment usually is nothing more than loosening a screw or whatever holds the jet in place and moving it until you get it right. Sometimes it's less than that—stick a pin in it and move it. Clogged hoses can either be replaced or swabbed out with wire, if you have the patience for it. The washer

pump, below the container, can be tested if it stops pumping. Pull off the electrical connector and use jumper wires from the battery to give it a quick fix. Or first, clean off the contacts of the wires and trace them to their origin—their nearest connector. Clean those contacts and check for broken wires.

If the wiper motor turns but doesn't move the wipers, the problem obviously is in the linkage. Begin at the drive source and replace any broken or loose member of the chain of links.

What is more likely is an electrical failure somewhere along the line.

On VW Scirocco, pull off the harness connector on the wiper motor and use a couple of test probes from the battery. Connect the negative post to the connector lead you exposed by pulling off the harness that is in the center of the five terminals. Connect the positive battery post lead to the terminal on the left (facing the windshield). If the motor runs, the switch on the steering column needs testing and possibly replacing. If the motor doesn't run, it needs replacing.

Don't replace the switch until you can get it tested. I say "get it" tested because it is far too complex a series of tests to do it yourself. And the chances are that it won't be necessary to replace the costly switch. The chances also are that the trouble isn't very hard to find by someone trained in the troubleshooting at issue.

Rear window units have simpler systems because their motors have only one wiper to drive so they eliminate all the troublesome linkage. The motor

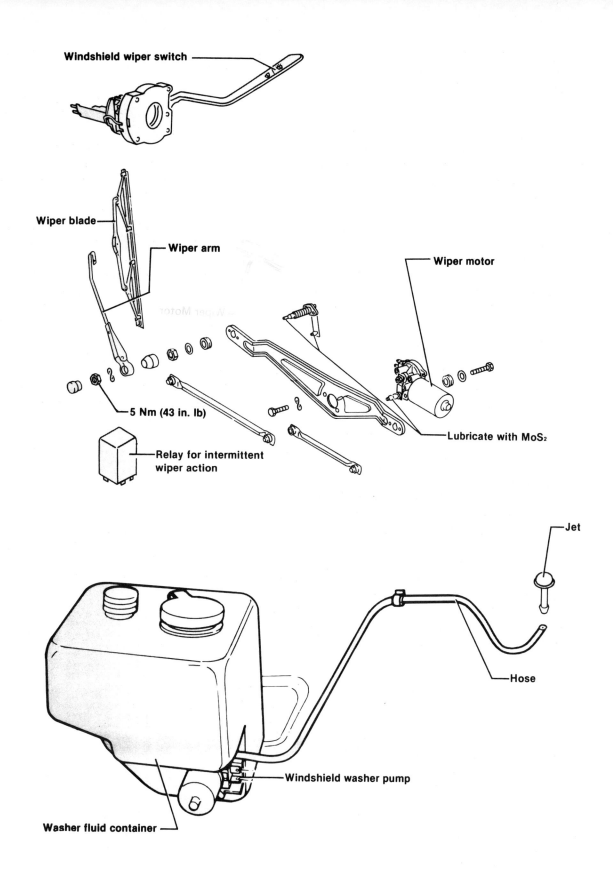

Windshield wiper switch

Wiper blade

Wiper arm

Wiper motor

5 Nm (43 in. lb)

Relay for intermittent wiper action

Lubricate with MoS₂

Jet

Hose

Windshield washer pump

Washer fluid container

VW windshield wiper and washer system.

usually is right under the bushing-bearing to which the wiper arm and wiper attach. So little trouble rises there. The washer, elsewhere, is subject to the same troubles as its cousin up front, and the same cures.

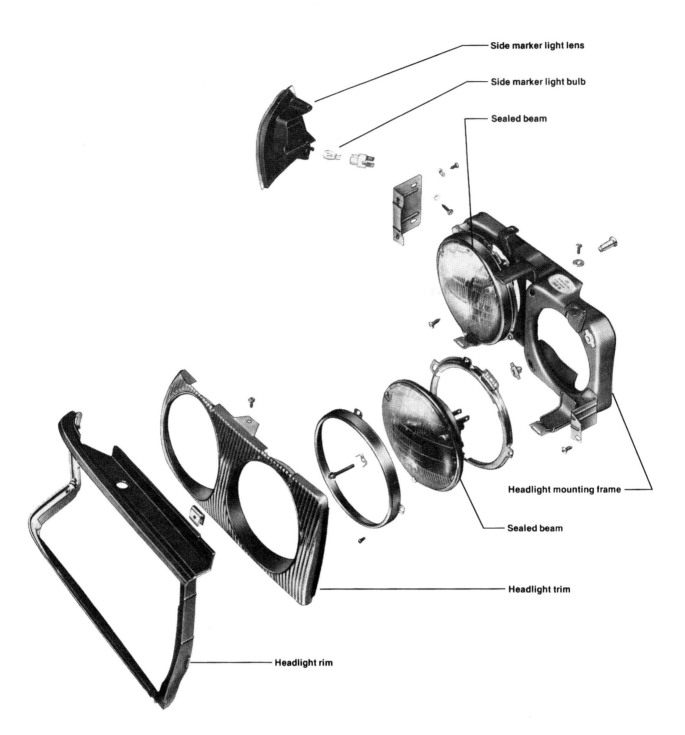

Side marker light lens

Side marker light bulb

Sealed beam

Sealed beam

Headlight mounting frame

Headlight trim

Headlight rim

Exploded view of Audi 5000 headlight system.

Lights

Replacing light bulbs outside or inside the car is never as easy as inside (or outside) the house. The sockets are different, because they have to be. They must withstand road vibration and a lot of other disagreeable conditions not faced by the bathroom light.

Headlights can be replaced by removing the surrounding frame, whatever it might be. It can be anything from the radiator grille, in the case of VW type cars, to single metal bezel plates in most other cars. In any case, they are all held by screws which usually are phillips type. The only thing to keep in mind in headlight replacement is that you get the right bulb. In a four-light system the inner and outer (or upper and lower) lights differ; in a two-light system they don't. So you order lights by car make, model, and

Corvette aiming screws for adjusting headlights on 4-light system.

light number. Bulbs are held by retaining rings. Unscrew the small screws that hold the rings in place, making sure you don't touch the adjusting screws. You can disconnect the plug in the back and the headlight will come out.

The new light will have to be adjusted, once it is installed. Back it off from a garage door, 20 or 25 feet. The car should be level. The left light (or lights) should be in a similar position to the right. Adjust, if necessary, on the low beams. If you live in a state where regular electronic inspection of beam adjustment is required, you may find it necessary to be

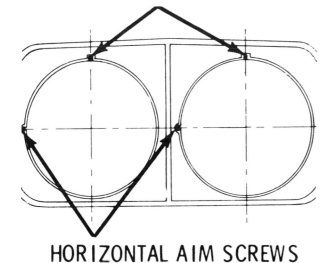

VERTICAL AIM SCREWS

HORIZONTAL AIM SCREWS

Headlight adjusting screws.

more precise. Actually the left beam is required to be slightly different than the right. The right beam, in effect, is closer in to the centerline of the car than is the left. But it is not much closer and doesn't affect vision or visibility.

Stop lights, dash lights, dome lights, and all the variety of car lights, are all fairly easy to replace, if the sockets aren't corroded or the wiring defective. That becomes a new ballgame. Sockets can often be cleaned with some kind of abrasive device or even a pocket knife. But sometimes they simply become defective and must be replaced. You cut off the wires and splice them to the replacement socket, using any splicing technique that appeals to you. Stop lights, turn signal lights, and other lights that affect driving, should be inspected regularly and replaced when burned out. Turn signal lights and other rear lights are bought by number. Look at the bottom of the bulb you replace; does it have one or two contact points? The new one must match.

Once in a while the brake and turn signal lights stop working and it isn't because the light is burned out or the socket is defective, but because the switches are defective.

Turn signal switches, in the steering column, can be repaired without major steeering column disassembly. On Scirocco and other cars with the turn signal switch lever on one side and the windshield wiper switch on the other, or both of them as part of a "stalk" switch, you pry off the steering wheel cover, or look underneath at the fasteners for the cover—some of them are bolted or screwed on. The cover usually operates the horn button. There will also be a locking nut below the wheel cover. Once these are removed you come to the horn button, or switch, if there is one. It may be nothing more than two contacting plates. Next in line will be the switches that you seek. Remove their fasteners and they come out. Cars with the ignition switch in the same area often keep that device separate. You don't have to remove it.

Stalk switches and wiper switches fall prey to wear and corrosion from dirt. But the contacts may not present themselves for either inspection and cleaning—replacement only. So it is important, before buying a new switch, to establish guilt; is it the switch, the wiring or the components involved? Diagnosis is always problematical in electrical matters. When motors are involved, as in the windshield wiper/washer system, always use jumper cables to test them. Then examine the wiring for breaks, corrosion at the connectors, insulation breaks, or disconnections. Then replace the defective component.

Can these motors be repaired? It isn't worth your trouble, but some shops do it. There you can buy a rebuilt if you bring your motor along. You save a lot of money that way.

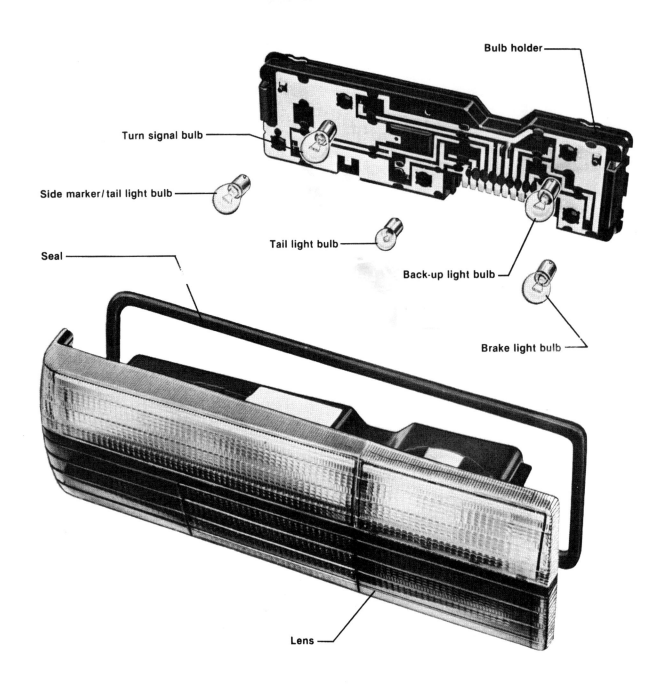

Turn signal bulb

Side marker/tail light bulb

Seal

Tail light bulb

Bulb holder

Back-up light bulb

Brake light bulb

Lens

Audi 4000 rear light assembly.

Switches

Switches are all over your car's electrical system. Switches range from simple off-on light switches for dome and accessory lights, to intermittent switches such as control flashers and turn signals, and to solenoid switches. Solenoid switches convert electrical energy into mechanical, by using magnetic force to push or pull something—for example, some Holley carburetors have solenoids that pull chokes closed, and most starting motors use them to activate the gears that turn the flywheel. So solenoids are half

way between motors and switches. In a sense, fuses are switches—they interrupt current when they sense something wrong, but they also burn out when something goes wrong with them.

Almost any switch can be tested for continuity, but some of them also must be tested for capacity. Very elaborate switches such as voltage regulators need several kinds of testing and require ohmmeters and voltage meters.

The ignition system, as we've seen, is loaded with various kinds of switches. But so are all the other electrical systems in the car, and mechanical systems also require them. Brakes have switches to turn

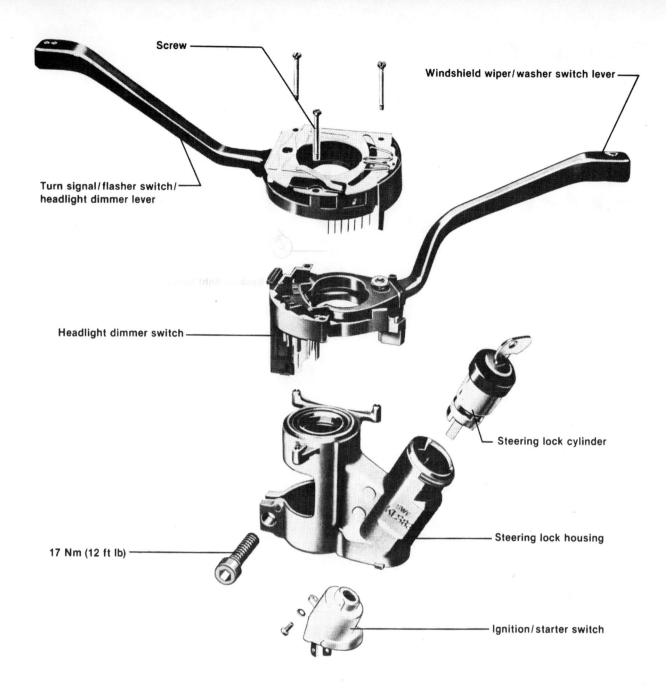

Screw

Windshield wiper/washer switch lever

Turn signal/flasher switch/
headlight dimmer lever

Headlight dimmer switch

Steering lock cylinder

Steering lock housing

17 Nm (12 ft lb)

Ignition/starter switch

Audi 4000 exploded view of steering column switches.

on brake lights. Brakes also have switches to regulate pressure in the lines.

Whenever you go troubleshooting in any system, think first of the switches involved. In some cases, such as electronic fuel injection, the switches are too complex for you to test them, excepting as you follow prescribed routines under the systems involved. But most switches can be tested for continuity with a simple continuity tester or low voltage lamp tester.

Blown fuses are also to be considered in any electrical troubleshooting. Fuse circuits are wired so that sometimes they don't disable the system they are supposed to protect but disable themselves from simple wear. Fuses protecting dash gauges can blow and cause the gauges not to stop functioning but to start warning—they may sometimes turn on with a red or yellow glow. That would normally cause anxiety about the component involved, but it could be merely a blown fuse, and that could be simply because of the fuse itself wearing out. So, always consider the possibility of a blown fuse in every electrical problem.

In those cases where the fuse blows repeatedly the problem is in the component or the wiring.

Chapter Five

Fuel Systems

FUEL PUMPS

Fuel systems in sports cars vary from standard carburetors to electronic fuel injectors. Fuel pumps are either mechanical or electrical, mounted in engine compartments or in fuel tanks.

Troubleshooting a fuel pump begins when you smell gasoline in the engine and can't see any sign of it around the carburetor. If the fuel pump is in the engine compartment it could be leaking either in the pump itself, around the gasket or at the hoses or tubing. Fuel pump failure can be sudden and complete unlike carburetors, which decline leisurely or develop as a partial loss of fuel pressure. That will interfere with starting, acceleration, and general performance, including idle. Obviously these symptoms overlap with carburetor and other symptoms, including ignition, and because fuel pumps often last the life of the car they should be

considered innocent until proven guilty, whereas carburetors are more likely to destruct early in the game and ignition systems are the earliest culprits of all. So, when faced with overlapping symptoms common to fuel and ignition, check out ignition first, then the carburetor, emission controls and lastly the fuel pump (unless you can see the pump leaking).

The easiest way to check the fuel pump is to disconnect the fuel line into the carburetor. Aim the disconnected line into a can in such a way that you can see what comes out of the line, from the driver's seat. Now, turn on the ignition. If a strong gush of gasoline spews into the can, the pump is probably doing its duty. A precise test: a half pint should be pumped in 15 seconds. But if the stream is weak or nonexistent the problem is clear; you need to replace a fuel pump. If the pump is located in the gas tank, rather than inside the engine compartment, you have a decision—replace it in the tank, or install it inside the engine, on the fender or in some other place

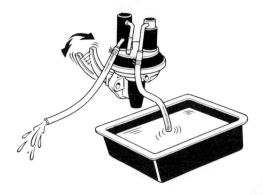

Checking a fuel pump, Toyota Celica.

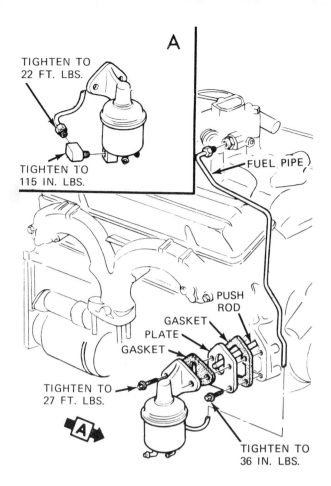

Corvette fuel pump details.

where there's room. To replace a broken fuel pump inside the tank is a major, difficult, dangerous operation. Any garage will charge you a large sum for the ticklish, specialized labor. Designers who put pumps in the tank should be sent to Siberia; perhaps that is where they do the designing at present. However, they can be foiled; buy an electric pump. You can buy an electric pump from the catalogs for about a fourth or fifth of the cost of a professional replacement job. You will also need some extra tubing and a mounting bracket, if the new pump doesn't have one. The tubing can be rubber rather than metal. You merely install the electric pump between the carburetor inlet feed line and the tubing that feeds it. Look along the tubing to the point where it enters the engine compartment. Look for a connector of some sort; disconnect the tubing there and replace it with the new line to the new pump, which you have mounted in an open area somewhere on or near the engine—a fender is an approved area. The inlet to the fuel pump goes to the line that runs back to the tank. The outlet from the fuel pump goes to the disconnected line that formerly served the carburetor inlet. In other words, both hoses from the new fuel pump go to the same place; one gets connected to the carburetor line; the other to the tank line. You also need an electrical connection, which you can take off any hot wire turned on by the ignition key. The new pump probably will have instructions. If not, trace the positive side of the battery to a line that lends itself to splicing and is turned on by the ignition key. The starting motor line is possible, but there are plenty of others.

Note: if there is no engine connecting point for the gas line, look under the car and trace it.

All this presupposes airtight fuel lines from tank to carburetor and that the lines themselves are open—free of clogging. It goes without saying that you examine the lines from tank to engine, before replacing anything. Look for leaks, holes, and worn spots.

Those electric fuel pumps that are mounted inside the engine are the most easily changed of all. Their electrical lead is disconnected, their inlet and outlet fuel lines are quickly unclasped, and their mounting brackets come open with a socket wrench. When such a pump fails the test, you have only to buy a replacement and put it on quickly enough. Note: always check electrical connections and fuses before replacing an electric pump.

Mechanical pumps are not so easy, and as noted the pumps in gas tanks are the worst of all. But, we take the easy way out with those. With mechanical pumps there may or may not be so easy a way, depending on their mounting site and method.

For example, Corvette's fuel pump is mounted at the front of the engine—actually alongside the harmonic balance wheel, water pump, and other low down components. It presents no particular problem of access from below the engine, and has two mounting bolts as well as the fuel lines. Take care with the fuel lines so as not to damage the connectors. Some pumps have a vapor line hose also—a vapor lock control component. Remove that. The Corvette has a push rod that activates a rocker arm and diaphragm. The key to proper installation is the fitting that goes to the carburetor. The best way to avoid stripping it is to disconnect the upper end from the carburetor (using two wrenches—one to hold, one to turn). Tighten the fitting in the pump to which the carburetor line goes. Then hold that line in place and finger tighten it at first. Next, with an open end wrench holding the fitting in place, tighten the carburetor line connection, securely. These are soft metals so don't over-tighten. Then replace the line into the carburetor inlet coupling.

The Omni/Horizon fuel pump is similar to Corvette's. On the left side of the engine, it has a vapor separator line. It can leak oil because of loose mounting bolts, defective oil seal, or simply a defective pump gasket. It can become noisy due to loose mounting bolts, a stiff inlet hose, a worn rocker arm, or weak or broken rocker arm spring. All these are exotic difficulties. When fuel pumps fail, they fail to pump gas because of a ruined diaphragm, 99 times out of a 100.

There is always the possibility that the flow test using the pot and the opened line falsifies the condition of the pump. It may be that the lines either into the pump or between the pump and the carburetor are clogged. In winter they can freeze if the gas has become contaminated. Dirt sometimes makes its way into the lines. Clogging is very rare here. Freezeup usually takes place in the carburetor, where the small passages are easily frozen in extremely cold weather. But to test for a clogged line between the carburetor and the pump, remove the line at both ends and blow through it. You can unbolt the much longer line from the gas tank to the fuel pump and perform the same operation, if you suspect a clog in that part of it. The job becomes more difficult and the law of diminishing returns sets in; the most fragile element always is the plastic diaphragm. It's like human contraception; if birth occurs despite the use of the diaphragm one doesn't suspect something in the diet, however related diet might be.

CARBURETORS

The fuel pump is a simple device. Not so the carburetor, and since the age of emission control the carburetor has been staggered by a series of additions and deletions caused by the Kafkaesque maze of emission control technology. The once simple carburetor has lost its innocence. With computerized fuel dispensation slowly spreading through the industry, it will lose a lot more. Meanwhile, it sits nervously atop most engines, mixing the world's most precious liquid, gasoline, with its most common element, air. The complaint against the carburetor is that it can't do that job efficiently enough, and one reason is that it is too prone to dirt and wear. These failings are what concern us.

We are out to clean up its act. We do this by a literal cleaning of its vulnerable surfaces and by the replacement of its wearing parts. The carburetor is a mechanical device that has many murky catacombs and moving parts. The catacombs become congested; the parts simply wear out.

Carburetors, whether made in Europe, Japan, or the U.S., are more or less alike. That doesn't mean they have interchangeable parts. Mostly they have none. But they all do identical things, so it is not surprising that they have systems in common. The ingenuity with which carburetor manufacturers can defeat the possibility of sharing components between makes and models is one of the seven wonders of the industrial world, exceeded only by the rapacity with which they imagine they will be rewarded for it. Little financial gain results; nothing is changed in consequence. Confusion gains.

The key to carburetor malfunction is dirt. It changes the nature and flow of the fuel. Dirt, beginning with dirty air filters, clogs passageways. It also causes abrasive wear on moving parts. Engine vibration changes the settings of the needle valves over a period of time. That changes performance—inevitably for the worse.

The first thing to do about a carburetor that isn't doing its remembered duty is to sort out its problems. Hard starting in cold weather is probably the most common complaint ever heard. It is caused, basically, by the failure of the choke to close properly, and by a dirty filter which prevents the correct amount of air from entering. (We are excluding ignition here; but, of course, poor ignition is the biggest single cause of hard starting.) The easy part of the correction is to change air filters. A new one can have various impacts, from clearing up the problem completely to having no effect at all because the carburetor needs tearing apart—or adjusting.

Another common complaint is that the engine starts properly, but dies, and sometimes does this repeatedly. It may or may not be the choke, but it is the carburetor—unless it is a fuel pump that isn't forceful enough. If it is the carburetor (you've eliminated the fuel pump), you begin by checking out the choke. Is the choke closed correctly? If the engine starts and dies, you check the choke by taking off the air filter housing and filter and looking at the choke valve on top of the carburetor—it should be either tightly closed or almost. The key adjustment for this condition is the vacuum "kick" adjustment on the choke. It usually involves an allen or hex wrench adjustment on the choke vacuum pump. But it's a ticklish adjustment, easily botched and when it is you won't improve the condition.

The stall-start syndrome also is involved in an incorrect float assembly/needle valve setting, caused by wear, usually. Since the needle valve is the key replacement, it probably will correct the stalling-starting problem.

The vacuum adjustment, however, is also involved in producing black smoke. That's a sign of a too-tight adjustment. Again, don't touch the choke adjustment until you do the rest of the job, and especially the needle valve replacement.

If the choke valve is closing properly, and the engine still refuses to start—and you have exonerated ignition—it could also be caused by the needle valve not working properly. Engine flooding is a common symptom of this problem, when you can see gas going down into the carburetor and you then check out ignition—which is the proper thing to do. Spark is occurring; but nothing happens and the spark plugs develop a glaze that then interferes with starting. When that sequence happens—caused by the needle valve, probably—the cure is far removed. You have to take out each spark plug and sand off the glaze.

If the engine starts and dies, and none of the above causes or symptoms is the culprit, it could be a variety of minor malfunctions, including binding accelerator linkage, beginning at the gas pedal. It could also be incorrect idle adjustment, which requires nothing more than the turn of a screwdriver to correct.

Cold starting and running problems are the most common involving the carburetor. They are also the cause of warm engine problems—hesitation, stumble, surge. Ignition is the first suspect here too. Once eliminated, go to the carburetor. It could be the cause of these annoyances, beginning with the accelerator pump. That, with the needle valve, is one of the principal components you will replace in an overhaul, so you can expect the problems to be cleared up in the course of events.

Carburetors continue to be the most common method of injecting gas-air into an automobile engine combustion chamber. Carburetors fuel close to 99 percent of all cars on the road and all cars hitherto on the road. That percentage will change, but not drastically. Fuel injection is simply too expensive at present, despite its savings in fuel, which can amount to about 10 percent in some cases.

It is not quite true that if you've seen or fixed one carburetor you have seen and fixed them all, but it is close to the truth. This does not mean that someone who has worked only on a 1-barrel Carter carburetor from the 60s can tackle a complex Holley or Solex from the 80s. Though the Holley does the same thing as the early models, it also does a lot more. So it has many new features and systems. But it's still a carburetor.

We will examine several carburetors in detail, beginning with Corvette. We note that carburetor problems are caused by dirt, engine vibration and normal wear. Dirt is by far the most devastating culprit. It is what causes choke plates to stick (though carbon formation is the instigator there), and needle valve assemblies to wear prematurely, passageways to clog. The best cure is prevention, up to a point. If you change air filters often enough you can cut down on dirt damage.

Weak links

Carburetors are most vulnerable in two systems—the choke, which refuses to close for starting ("unload") because of binding from carbon and dirt, and the float/needle valve assembly, which wears and leaks and throws everything else out of whack. The accelerator pump is the next weak link in the chain. It wears and causes hesitation and stumble on acceleration.

Choke plates refuse to close, thus making cold starting almost impossible. The springs that are responsible for closing the choke are weak and any binding makes their task impossible. But if you oil the axles on the choke plate, thinking to avoid rebuilding, you only make matters worse; the oil hastens carbon formation and binding.

The float/needle valve assembly is critical. Wear changes the rate of flow and amount of gas-air mix being drawn into the intake manifold. That alters engine performance for the worse.

Why not strengthen the choke plate springs? That would upset the balance of power between the choke plate springs and choke housing spring—the coil spring that opens the plate. It's a no-win contest. Can't you make the needle valve assembly impervious to wear? That's why fuel injection was invented. It's not impervious to wear. We are back to square one, which is that every mechanical system will decay at its own set pace, indifferent to human wish, cunning or skill.

A carburetor operates from engine vacuum pressure. As the pistons go up and down they draw air from the intake manifold below the carburetor, which pulls air and gas from the carburetor. But the carburetor is not merely a passive instrument. It has a constant monitoring and supplying function, as well as a mixing and metering capability. In other words, it can do everything the fuel injection system can, all within that crammed, comparatively small, weird-looking box below the much bigger air filter housing, which is mostly wasted, showy space—a place for the air filter to hang its hat. Of course, the air filter housing in recent years has had new func-

WITH ENGINE RUNNING AT IDLE, CHOKE WIDE-OPEN, CAREFULLY INSERT GAUGE IN VENT SLOT OR VENT HOLE (NEXT TO AIR CLEANER MOUNTING STUD) IN AIR HORN. RELEASE GAUGE AND ALLOW IT TO FLOAT FREELY.

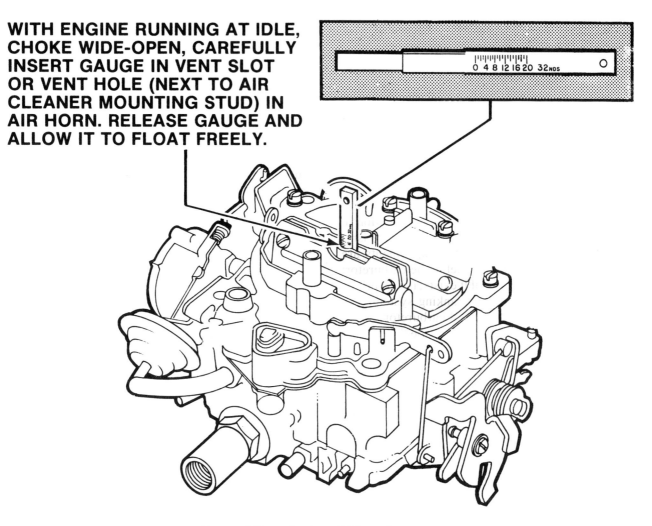

External float check on G.M. carburetor.

tions assigned to it, mostly involving emission controls, so that nowadays it has as many hoses going into it and coming out of it as a patient in extremis on some late night horror show.

Before taking any carburetor apart or even digging into it, make sure that the symptoms you are seeking to correct don't come from the ignition system or, possibly, the fuel pump, or even the valve train.

A General Motors Carburetor

The Corvette M4MC Carburetor is a standard General Motors component in use through various models of the G.M. line. It is tried and true and causes very little trouble. But you wouldn't guess that by the list of possible troubles G.M. lists for the mechanic to ponder.

Ten fault categories are listed by G.M.

1. Engine cranks normally but will not start.
2. Engine starts and stalls.
3. Engine is hard to start.
4. Engine idles abnormally and/or stalls.
5. Engine diesels (after-run) upon shut off.
6. Engine hesitates on acceleration.
7. Engine has less than normal power at low speeds.
8. Engine has less than normal power on heavy acceleration at high speeds.
9. Engine surges.
10. Poor gas mileage.

As to No. 1 (won't start) on this dubious parade, G.M. notes these possible causes: wrong starting procedure (read the owner's manual); choke valve not operating properly (that's the one we're betting on); no fuel in carburetor (in this day of shortages that's always a stunning possibility); engine flooded, to check for same remove the air cleaner with the engine immediately shut off and look into the carburetor bores—fuel will be dripping off the nozzles; and as to the basic correction, we're betting on a carburetor overhaul.

No. 2 (starts but stalls) in this dismal diary starts

with the fuel pump—is it working? See below. The choke heater system isn't working; the vacuum hose is lost, strayed or stolen; the choke valve is sticking and binding; and there isn't enough fuel in the carburetor. The basic correction will come down to overhaul, even though the chances are the chief malefactors will be the needle valve/float assembly and dirt.

No. 3 (hard starting) begins with loose, broken, or incorrect vacuum hose routing; you're also probably using the wrong starting procedure (what do you suppose they think you're doing—stepping on the brake instead of the gas?); there's a malfunction in the accelerator pump system; the choke valve isn't closing; the choke vacuum break adjustments are incorrect; there's not enough fuel in the carburetor; it's flooding; the vent valve, if it exists, isn't working or is out of adjustment; the cranking system isn't doing its thing. Again—overhaul carburetor.

No. 4 (abnormal idling) may simply be the result of the idle adjustment gone astray; air can leak into the carburetor; the PCV system is clogged; the carburetor is flooding; restricted air cleaner, plugged idle system; wrong idle adjustment; defective idle stop solenoid; throttle blades or linkage sticking.

No. 5 (diesels on after stopping) is caused by loose, broken, or improperly routed vacuum hoses; too fast an idle speed; malfunctioning idle solenoid, idle speed-up solenoid or dashpot; fast idle cam not fully off; excessively lean fuel caused by maladjusted carburetor idle mix; retarded ignition timing. These are mostly tuneup and carburetor external adjustments.

No. 6 (hesitation) can be caused by the vacuum hose; the accelerator pump (which you can test by turning off the engine, removing the air cleaner, and looking down into the carburetor bores—with choke plate open—while quickly opening the throttle lever, all of which should cause a quick, full stream of gas from each pump nozzle); accelerator pump clogged; float level too low; front vacuum break diaphragm not functioning; inoperative air cleaner heated air control; dirty fuel filter; advance mechanisms not operating; timing wrong; choke coil out of adjustment; EGR valve stuck open. It all adds up to an overhaul.

No. 7 (inadequate power) again starts with a vacuum hose inoperative; a defective PCV system; sticking choke; clogged power system, and probably a lot of dirt; air cleaner temperature regulation wrong; transmission, ignition, exhaust.

No. 8 (inadequate power—high speeds) begins with carburetor throttle valves not going to wide open position (you can check with engine off; push the pedal to the floor and look way down into the carburetor at the valve that looks like the carburetor valve on top); binding, sticking lockout throttle lever; ignition, especially spark plugs; dirty air cleaner; air valve malfunction; plugged fuel inlet filter; out of gas; power enrichment system not operating; choke partially closed; float level too low; fuel metering jets restricted; fuel pump, transmission, ignition, exhaust—get a new car, almost.

No. 9 (engine surges) caused by vacuum hose defects; PCV system clogged; loose carburetor, EGR or intake manifold bolts; leaking gaskets; low fuel pump pressure; contaminated fuel; fuel filter clogged; float level low; defective float and/or needle valve assembly; power piston binding; dirty fuel jets; ignition and exhaust system defects.

No. 10 (poor gas mileage) charged to the driver; vacuum hoses defective; engine and exhaust system misbehaving, including spark plugs; ignition, and other tuneup problems; fuel leaks; high fuel level in carburetor; carburetor malfunction in other systems; low tire pressure; transmission defects; but essentially a carburetor overhaul.

Carburetor cousins.

The Rochester M4MC (and its cousins, M4MCA and M4MEA) is a General Motors standby. It is found on Corvette and various other G.M. cars. Because it is a Rochester, it has certain "fingerprints" of componentry that anyone familiar with G.M. cars will recognize. But just because you have dealt with the old Rochester 2GC and earlier models, don't jump into the M4MC without looking carefully at it. There are many changes.

First, removal of the carburetor from the engine can be ticklish. Be careful with the fuel inlet coupling, which requires two wrenches—one to hold the carburetor side, the other to turn the pipe clamping nut. Never use only one wrench.

Next, all the accelerator linkage, the air tubes and connectors must be removed, including those that are intertwined with the air filter and its housing, atop the carburetor. Electrical connections should be removed carefully, and if you don't trust your memory, tab the lines, the leads, and the tubing. The accelerator linkage will usually be self-explanatory, but be careful with the fasteners—clips and whatever you encounter. It is easy to lose these little clips. Initially, get a rag and drape it around the outside bottom of the carburetor to catch any clips, springs, fasteners, nuts and bolts you might drop. Once dropped, these tiny parts are impossible to find, and impossible to replace, except as you make a special trip for them—a needless nuisance task.

Once you remove everything in and out of the carburetor—and that also includes the wire clips on

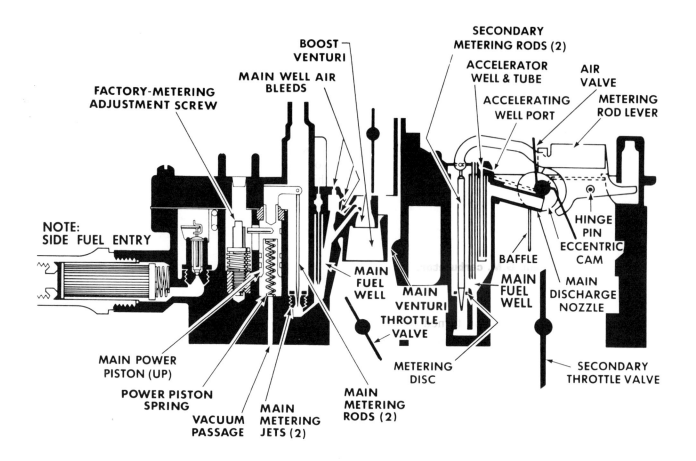

FACTORY-METERING
ADJUSTMENT SCREW

MAIN WELL AIR
BLEEDS

BOOST
VENTURI

SECONDARY
METERING RODS (2)

ACCELERATOR
WELL & TUBE

AIR
VALVE

ACCELERATING
WELL PORT

METERING
ROD LEVER

NOTE:
SIDE FUEL ENTRY

HINGE
PIN

ECCENTRIC
CAM

MAIN
FUEL
WELL

MAIN
VENTURI
THROTTLE
VALVE

BAFFLE

MAIN
FUEL
WELL

MAIN
DISCHARGE
NOZZLE

MAIN POWER
PISTON (UP)

POWER PISTON
SPRING

VACUUM
PASSAGE

MAIN
METERING
JETS (2)

MAIN
METERING
RODS (2)

METERING
DISC

SECONDARY
THROTTLE VALVE

Power system of M4MC carburetor.

the solenoid coils—you have only to remove the mounting bolts. One or two of them may offer little removal area, but you can always find some method of extraction. These include anything from the usual box wrench or socket extension with flexible joint, to the use of a hammer and screwdriver to knock the nut or bolt loose. If you use the last method, do it gently—tap the screwdriver lightly, exerting counterclockwise force on the nut or bolt to loosen it sufficiently so you can turn it off by hand. It may be necessary to put a little oil on the screw surfaces.

When you buy a carburetor repair kit, you will notice that among its many small parts there are washers and fasteners, gaskets and other things that you may not use, once you start assembling. Don't worry about it; it's not like the classic inept fixer who has a couple of parts left over. These kits are made to cover a range of models, not all identical.

When you get the carburetor off the car, it will have a chamber full of gas. Leave the gas in until you get the top off—the so-called air horn. You want to see how filthy the gas is. But don't pull on the accelerator pump or turn the carburetor over, unless you want a lap full of gas. There are 9 or 10 attaching screws between the air horn and the bowl. Notice

that they aren't very tight. Carburetors are delicate creatures and will not tolerate strong-arm abuse. Two of the screws are in sunken locations.

Once the screws are loosened, don't turn the carburetor over to get them out—remember the gas. But when the screws are fully loosened, you also have to remove the choke lever from the shaft, which you do by removing the screw that holds it. You must also remove the metering rods, the vacuum bracket assembly, and the vent valve cover, gasket and spring. Be careful not to lose the spring, and notice the way these parts fit.

With everything disconnected, lift up the top portion so that everything clears and doesn't get banged around. Separate the accelerating pump lever from the rod, and the carburetor is now in two halves. Inspect the gas and pour it out. If dirty, expect to replace the fuel filter.

Remove the gasket, the accelerating pump and plunger. Look at the pump skirt. If the car has been stumbling on acceleration, the skirt should have signs of wear—tears or shabbiness; no longer your Sunday-go-to-church skirt. Gasket removal requires that the metering rod and power piston assembly come out. The metering rod comes out first, then the

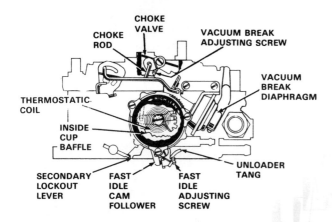

Choke system, G.M. carburetor.

so-called auxiliary piston can be turned toward a gasket slit that lets you get the gasket out. Of course, you can just tear the old gasket, since you'll be replacing it. But don't tear old gaskets until you can measure them against the new ones. Caution in these matters is desirable. Also, because there are so many small parts, compare them, as you take them out, with the exploded diagram that comes with the repair kit to make sure the diagram and your carburetor agree and the diagram is clear as to the order of parts replacement. In the illustrations accompanying this discussion we are trying to show all the parts and processes, but the kit diagram is also very helpful, or should be.

To remove the so-called power piston requires that you push down on the piston, then let it snap out. It can take several snaps. Take out the float and needle valve assembly, pulling out the pin that holds the float. Use a wide screwdriver on the float seat, otherwise you risk ruining the slot and making its extraction needlessly difficult. The pump discharge check-ball (a tiny metal ball) should come out for replacement. Its retainer is a screw and baffle that comes from the side of the pump well. Don't take the other jets out, unless you think they must be replaced and you have replacements for them. They get very little wear, if any. If your carburetor has a device called an adjustable part throttle (APT) and aneroid, it must be removed before you soak the unit for cleaning. It's near the fuel inlet side; it unscrews. It should be treated with great care, and the setting should not be changed.

Remove the choke cover and coil assembly, noting the setting on the outside of the cover—the degrees of lean or rich to which the choke is set. Return it that way.

Now take apart the throttle body from the rest of the bowl by loosening and removing the attaching screws. The idle adjustment needles with their

springs should be taken out for cleaning and examination. Remove the fuel inlet nut, and the contents of the inlet chamber, noting their order—nut, gasket, filter and spring.

Soak everything in a carburetor cleaner—Gunk is one such, but there are others. Soaking should be for several hours, at least, and preferably longer. The soaking is vital; it is almost the most important thing you can do to a carburetor. The next most important thing is to adjust the new needle valve and seat assembly.

Put the parts to be soaked (but soak no non-metal part) into a pan deep enough so that you can cover them with the solvent. Slosh them around from time to time. After soaking is concluded, take them out and rinse them in gas or kerosene. Soaking should make the parts gleam. Take a toothbrush to the throttle valve and clean it out completely; do the same to the choke valve on top. The accelerating part of the carburetor should move easily and smoothly; the choke valve should do the same. There must not be any binding of either of these valve systems. Also, their chambers must be completely free of carbon; so should the thin edges of the butterfly valves, otherwise they do not close properly.

You will undoubtedly have to remove the spring and metal container from the old accelerating pump skirt and install them on the new. If you are all thumbs this will be ticklish, possibly infuriating. But it shouldn't be.

When installing the new accelerating pump, be sure the skirt is started into its well properly tucked in everywhere.

The key to success in this endeavor is to get the

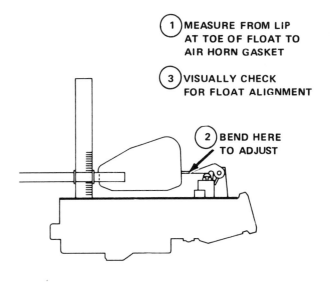

Float level adjustment on G.M. carburetor.

float and needle valve assembly properly installed. If you don't, nothing will work right. If you do, probably everything will work.

It really isn't that hard. Before you take the old one out, perhaps you should measure float distance —upside down distance from the rim and drop distance held in the correct posture. It should be about right—specifications are 15/32-inch (.460mm) with ruler from top of casting to top of float, the gauging point 3/16-inch back from end of float at the toe.

If the contents of the fuel chamber had much dirt, rust and other non-gasoline elements, it probably means you have fuel tank sediment sufficient to cause trouble. It could also mean much less—that the filter in the carburetor inlet was simply clogged. So look at both these possibilities as you take the carburetor apart. In any case, always replace the old filter. Be warned that repair kits may not have a new filter, so check and buy one separately if necessary.

In replacing the needle valve seat, first compare the old and new seats. They must be the same size, though they may differ in configuration. In other words, the relationship of float and valve to the seat should be the same in the new as in the old. When installing the new seat, screw it in tightly, but don't over-tighten. However, if you don't tighten it enough and it comes loose your car will behave crazily, developing all kinds of neurotic symptoms.

When you measure the distance of the float from the rim, it should be 15/32-inch without the gasket. If you measure with the gasket, add that width, which would be about 1/16-inch. It is important that this measurement be very precise. To adjust, bend the tab up or down at the needle.

If you get everything back correctly, including the choke and its thermostatic coil correctly set to the prescribed index mark (and the setting is 1 notch lean for carburetor numbers ending 202, 204, 210, 228, 585, 584, 216 and 217; or 2 notches lean with carburetors ending 203, 211, 502, and 504—the numbers are stamped on a thin metal strip), you will have few adjustments to make. That is, you will have few if the carburetor behaves properly. If it does not, you will have to reckon with adjustments. Chiefly the adjustments will be idle, solenoid, and air mix. But they could also involve the choke.

When putting the carburetor back on the engine, with the new gasket in place, clean out any sediment around the lugs and intake manifold opening. But don't let the stuff lie there; get it all out.

The order of reconnection is that once the carburetor is atop the studs and gasket, next connect the fuel line. That connection is best made with the carburetor loose, because the inlet line usually has little "give" to it and in order to get the locking nut started correctly you have to position the carburetor

itself in exactly the right way—a nudge here or there.

If you removed the idle mix needle valve and spring you will have to adjust it. A rough and ready adjustment can be made before you put the carburetor back, or it can be done on the car. Turn it all the way in until it bottoms—carefully so you don't damage the needle valve. Then back it out about 2½ turns. When the engine is running you can adjust it more carefully. However, it should be noted that G.M. prescribes a special kind of propane enrichment idle adjustment which can only be done at a shop which has the equipment and someone to use it. In fact, any other kind of adjustment is an actual law violation in California. And we have noted that the throwaway carburetor is next—it cannot be taken apart. So, once you have cleaned and repaired your Corvette M4MC carburetor, if you are overcome by a legal impulse to get it checked lawfully, take it in to a Corvette dealer. If the car runs perfectly when you get the carburetor back you may find the legal impulse extremely weak.

VW types

VW's Scirocco and other Volkswagens through 1976 used carburetors as well as fuel injection systems. In these cars the fuel pump is a mechanical pump mounted on the engine, operated by an eccentric cam. It poses no problems in replacement if tests determine the need for it. A filter screen and gasket can be removed for cleaning the screen or replacement of screen and gasket, but the pump itself cannot be repaired or serviced.

Recent VWs favor fuel injection.

In rebuilding the carburetor, follow step-by-step procedure given in the carburetor repair kit. In soaking the parts be sure that non-metal parts do not get put in the solvent. Compare the new gaskets and parts with the old. Some modifications in gaskets were made in 1975 models. Thus the carburetor flange gasket may have a hole that does not align with the hole in the carburetor. In that case, drill one (in the gasket, not the carburetor).

In rebuilding a carburetor, never remove more parts than necessary. Non-metallic parts, including all gaskets, must come off before soaking the carburetor. Non-metallic choke components, including the vacuum pull-down which controls choke plate opening, should not be soaked.

VW hasn't used many carburetors in the cars we're talking about for a number of years. The last ones they used were Zenith, with a mechanical fuel pump next to the distributor. This carburetor, which you find at the firewall, sits below a metal cap and

Idle mixture adjuster screw, VW 1975.

funnel that goes over to the filter. It's a long-wearing, patient carburetor, rarely requiring much attention. It has many virtues and few faults. It has four adjusting external screws that require extremely infrequent attention. About the only one of these four adjusters you might need to use is a large screw on the passenger side of the carburetor. It needs a stubby screwdriver because of close adjusting quarters. You turn it to the left to increase idle speed, to the right to slow it. You don't need to turn it very far. Note: if turning makes no difference in the idle speed that means you must look outside the carburetor for the problem, beginning with ignition (points, rotor—especially rotor, since these VW rotors are temperamental—spark plugs for carbon formation or incorrect gaps or simply worn out plugs). If ignition is exonerated you go back to the carburetor.

The air mix screw is the next adjuster. It is almost impossible to find. On the side of the carburetor, facing the left fender, it can be seen only if you use a periscope or push your face down near the bottom of the carburetor. It can only be turned with an extremely thin-bladed, small screwdriver, and it will require some careful adjusting. First of all, if the engine isn't running with sufficient evenness to make any adjustment possible, go back to the ignition system and check out the points. Remove the distributor cap, rotor and plastic shield. Push the points open so you can see the surfaces. If they or the rubbing cam are worn, no accurate adjustment is possible. You'll have to replace them. Sometimes they're not adjusted properly. If they're not opening at all, no spark is possible. The gap should be about .016 with the rubbing fiber block of the points resting squarely in the center of one of the cam lobes (as described under tuneup). If the gap differs much, you won't get proper adjustment—or performance. Also, you might find a set of points with the fiber

rubbing block so deteriorated that it can't do the job. Replace the points.

Now, let's go back to the carburetor and the air mix screw. If you have the points in shape, and everything else in working order—including the fuel pump, which you've checked out by pulling off the hose into the carburetor and watching the gas spurt out of it into a can as you turn on the ignition key for 15 seconds—turn this small adjusting screw all the way into the carburetor until it seats, just barely. Don't use any rough stuff, otherwise trouble. Then turn it out two or three complete turns, counting carefully, stopping at two. Now try the engine idle. It will start, unless you've tried to start it so many times that you've fouled the plugs. Alas, you simply have to remove each one of them, clean them off with sandpaper or a file, check their gaps (about .024) and put them back, tightening gently. Okay, the plugs are clean, you're still trying to get the idle adjustment in focus. If it isn't right yet, turn it a half turn and so on until it is right. The more you turn it out, the more likely you have a dirty, worn carburetor.

There is one more adjusting screw, affecting the throttle valve—the butterfly valve at the inside bottom of the carburetor, which you can barely see with the choke valve open. You shouldn't have to monkey with it. Finally, the fourth adjustment is on the accelerator linkage that holds the wire line. That one also is something you shouldn't monkey with. These last two adjustments will indeed be involved if you rebuild the carburetor.

If you rebuild a Zenith carburetor, following out the parts layout of the rebuilding kit you use, you will be forced to do a number of adjustments, both as you go and afterwards with the carburetor installed.

The key adjustment always is the float and needle valve. It's not difficult, merely important.

Disassembly of the Zenith carburetor follows usual procedure—the upper part, the choke components, the accelerator linkage and the pump attached to it, the throttle body at the bottom which has an electromagnetic cutoff valve attached. Remove that and everything else that doesn't get soaked in cleaner—all fiber or non-metallic parts do not get soaked!

You observe that the choke has two coolant hoses attached. When you unbolt them you will lose some coolant unless you use a pan underneath them. That is good policy, both to save the coolant and prevent a mess. (Water-cooled choke systems have gone out of style in recent years, to be replaced by electrical heaters. As it happens, the Zenith uses both.)

No other disassembly problems will be encountered, though you must take care with the accelerator cable to avoid kinking it. Don't disassemble more than necessary; follow the diagram of the repair kit you bought and don't buy a kit without a diagram. The simplest thing about removal and disassembly is taking out the long bolt at the top of the air chamber, but it just barely has room to come out without pushing in a bit on the body metal. That air chamber is attached by tube to the filter on the right fender. It's a good time to check out the state of the filter. If it's dirty, replace it by pulling up on the metal keepers that lock the filter chamber.

To avoid adjusting more than necessary, count the number of turns it takes to remove the air mix needle valve and after cleaning put it back that way. (You may have to alter it.) Other adjusters should not be changed, so long as you only clean them.

The float level adjustment (there are two of them; a primary and secondary float) can't be avoided. With the upper part of the carburetor removed, turn it upside down. Measure from the uppermost part of the float to the surface of the inverted carburetor. That's roughly the center of the float to the metal flange surface below. That dimension, with the needle valve fully seated, is 1.102-inch (28 mm). (The primary float is nearest the name Zenith on the body). The secondary float similar dimension differs slightly—it's 1.181-inch (30 mm). There is a "play" factor in these dimensions; plus or minus .020-inch. That's not an amount for a klutzy adjustment, so get it right on the nose. Bend the tang of the float hinge that rests on the needle valve. These measurements are without the gasket.

Many other adjustments are possible but not probable, so long as you restrict your disassembly procedures to those parts in your kit. Thus you don't touch the throttle and choke valves, other than to make sure they are cleaned completely and work freely. Any choke adjustment should be restricted to getting the index mark back to where it was (the mark on the outside of the choke housing which aligns with the mark opposite it on the choke cover, as you found it—but if the catalytic converter has been removed the index mark on the cover will be roughly 3/6-inch clockwise from the corresponding mark on the choke housing).

Citation

General Motors' Citation engines will be the dominant U.S. engines of the decade. At the moment they are found in sporty models of X-body cars. They may one day shift to Corvette or to other lines of sporty cars. These engines have carburetors rather than fuel injection. How long that will last is anybody's guess, but while it does we might as well get used to it.

There are, of course two Citation engines—the L4 and the V6. They use the 2SE carburetor on both engines, and while the carburetors are basically alike they have some differences—they are not interchangeable between the two engines. Another carburetor, somewhat similar, is the Model E2SE, on the 2.5 Litre L4 and 2.8 Litre V6 engines. It responds to electronic sensors for its various permutations and it is practically an electronic fuel injection system inside a carburetor—not exactly a wolf in sheep's clothing since it is hard to know what is wolf and what is sheep in this equation, but it does represent a carburetor design aimed at bridging the gap between the two beasts. Its adjustments are not for amateurs, though it is possible to replace worn needle valve assemblies and to clean out the dirt and grime, provided you do not tamper with the pre-set adjustments of its vital organs.

The 2SE carburetor, by contrast, and despite its general similarity to the other one, can be taken apart and rebuilt, with great care. It's a two-barrel carburetor with an electric choke and riveted choke cover, a sealed idle mixture needle that requires an excavation not unlike entering a sarcophagus to open it, and various other tamper-resistant features which point to the totally sealed carburetor just down the pike.

Nevertheless, the 2SE is not yet that creature.

Before digging into the 2SE, in response to the usual carburetor complaints, do some external, on-car tinkering. For starters, test the choke plate. Remove the air cleaner, hold the throttle half open and open and close the choke plate several times. Look at all linkage to check for smooth, easy operation—no hangups anywhere. Any binding or sticking can be corrected to some extent with a good choke cleaner—G.M. recommends United Delco Choke Cleaner X-20-A (or equivalent). But if that doesn't work you have to either replace the binding parts or take the carburetor off and soak it.

Look at all vacuum hoses for cracks and other signs of wear and see that they are connected properly. Examine all the levers that move when the choke plate is opened and closed by the control diaphragm. They must all move easily, without binding anywhere. But if they don't, you can't grease them. Either they must be replaced or cleaned or both.

If the choke fails to open, first check the electric supply. Using either a test 12-volt lamp or voltmeter, check voltage at the choke heater connection, while the engine is running. Pull off the clip and put the lamp or meter between the clip and the post. If voltage is below 12 or nothing, examine and clean all connections and look at wires for breaks. If voltage is between 12-15, replace the choke unit. Then look at the oil pressure switch connection. Turn the igni-

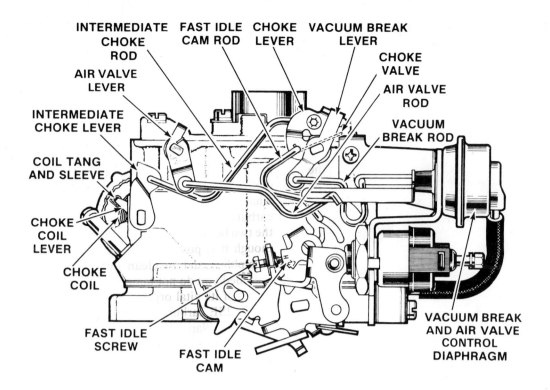

Choke system on the G.M. L4 engine.

tion key on, but don't start the engine. The temperature pressure warning light will be off if the oil pressure switch is faulty. If you can't clean off the oil switch connection and make it work, replace it.

The basic symptoms, as we've noted, that cause carburetors to be overhauled are stumbling on acceleration, flooding, hard starting, etc., when you have eliminated ignition and emission controls.

To disassemble the 2SE carburetor, take off the air cleaner and its gasket, disconnect all the tubes, linkage and electrical connectors, putting tabs on them if you don't trust your memory, removing the hold down bolts, and the carburetor will now lift off. Notice the condition of the filter when you remove the fuel inlet nut. If it is dirty or plugged in such a way as to restrict the flow of fuel, change it and try the car before removing the carburetor. A fuel filter that isn't passing fuel can cause a lot of bad performance.

The order of installation is fuel inlet nut, gasket, filter with hole in the filter toward the nut, and spring.

Also, check the idle solenoid. The solenoid plunger extends out when it is on. Turn on the ignition and push open the throttle (all the way), with the engine off. Disconnect the wire at the solenoid, and the plunger should drop away from the throttle lever. Now re-connect the solenoid wire. The plunger should push out, contacting the lever. If no movement is there, check for voltage. If the voltage is

12-15 the solenoid is defective; if voltage is either very low or zero, electricity isn't getting to the unit and the problem is in the supply somewhere along the line. This requires electrical troubleshooting—not an easy task. Trace the electrical connector back (but first clean it off with sandpaper or a file) to the nearest outlet, and check the connector there. Despite the fact that these connectors appear foolproof, they are not. Vibration and corrosion erode them, though it isn't likely in a new car. There you expect components rather than wiring to be at fault.

Disassembly of the 2SE begins with removal of the upper section (the air horn). Don't take off the air valve rod or the vacuum break rod. The vacuum break assembly (it opens the choke plate) and solenoid cannot be soaked in cleaner. The rods may sometimes need replacement but it is neither routine nor likely. You can see what needs to come off in order to separate the major components of the carburetor. Only those parts that connect the three major sections are to be removed—the pump lever, for example, comes off when you open its attaching screw. Save all the small attaching clips. They are easy to lose and the kit may not have suitable replacements.

To get the float assembly and needle valve out—the key replacement items in any malfunctioning carburetor—requires removal of the pump plunger from its well, the pump return spring from the well,

Pump lever screw removal.

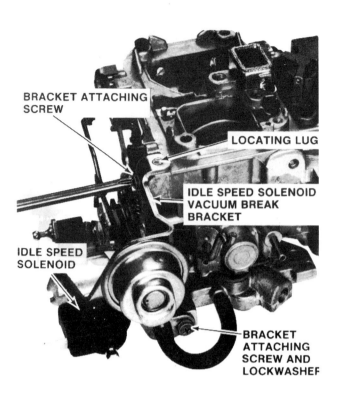

Vacuum break removal.

and the plastic block over the float valve. Float assembly and needle come out by pulling up on the pin. The needle seat and gasket should be unscrewed with a wide blade screwdriver. (If the blade isn't wide enough you could ruin the seat.) The power piston and metering rod assembly come out by pushing in on the piston stem and letting it snap out.

You may have to snap it a couple of times, but resist using pliers on it. The metering rod must be removed carefully so as not to damage the tip of it. To get the metering rod out, compress the spring on top and align the groove on the rod with the slot in the holder. To get the main metering jet out, use a broad screwdriver that fits across the slot fully. There's a plastic

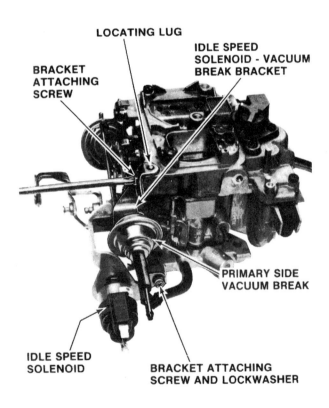

Vacuum break removal V-6.

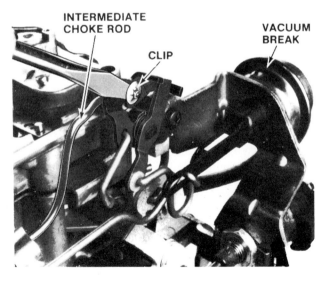

Intermediate rod and clip removal.

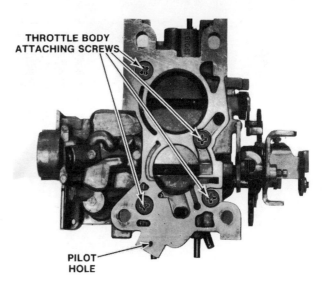

Air horn removal.

Throttle body screws in relation to throttle body.

retainer that holds the pump discharge spring and check ball (it's a little ball bearing), and you need some kind of small slide hammer or similar tool. The point is that you need something to hook on to it that will in effect tap it out. Do not use a screwdriver to pry it out; you could ruin the bowl casting surface and have to buy an entire new float bowl.

The choke cover and choke should not be soaked. Take the choke assembly off by removing the choking housing attaching screws. Then remove the throttle body attaching screws, and you have the carburetor ready for soaking. What you don't soak are: solenoid, electric choke, all rubber and plastic parts including diaphragms, also the pump plunger and plastic filler block. However, the plastic bushings on the various rods (vacuum break, rod and air valve rod on L4 Citations) can be dunked in cleaner solvent.

Whenever you remove a float, shake it and listen for fluid (gas) inside. If that happens, you need a new one. Floats don't routinely come with rebuilding kits, nor do they routinely become defective.

Flooding is caused by the float needle and seat, which you will be replacing. When installing the new seat for the needle, put it back as tightly as the old one. That means not too tight, but securely. If it comes loose your labors will have to be repeated. The car will misbehave horribly. Hesitation will be cured with a new accelerator pump, but examine the skirt of the old one just to make sure that the defect was there. You can't always see wear on these things—they may look normal—but cracks do appear, causing leaks.

Hard starting and dismal cold weather performance are caused by the choke valve failure to close—usually caused by dirt and carbon formation. Make sure, when you finish, that the choke valve runs as smoothly as silk. But look also at the fuel filter.

Poor gas mileage and other complaints about performance arise from dirty fuel and air passages inside the carburetor, and from a sticking choke valve, as well as failure by the power piston, metering rod and other sticking, binding parts.

Rough idle, when it is not caused by ignition failures, is caused by gasket failure, or the idle screw adjusters (which are needle valves supposedly set for all time). But all the various diaphragm pumps must be checked for leaks. Blow on them, if you can't see any leaking holes.

Putting everything back in working order is a challenge—a juggling act of sorts. You can start with the fuel inlet filter, spring, gasket and nut. Or start with the throttle body. You didn't take anything off that part of it—or shouldn't. It was soaked. Make sure it's clean and the throttle valves are free of all dirt and anything that could prevent their smooth operation. Blow through the jets—by mouth if you don't have compressed air. Put the float bowl components back, next. Replace the fuel inlet parts, if you didn't do it already. Put the choke housing back in place, also the choke shaft and lever assembly, the thermostatic coil lever and note the coil alignment. It is right when the coil pick-up tang is at the top position.

Put the pump discharge steel check ball (that little ball bearing) and spring in their passage next to the float chamber. Push the new plastic retainer into the end of the spring and install it in the float bowl, tapping it in place.

PUMP DISCHARGE
SPRING AND BALL
RETAINER

Pump discharge spring and ball retainer.

Install the main metering jet into the bottom of the float chamber and tighten it. Put the needle valve seat assembly into place with its gasket. Put the needle on the float arm by sliding the float lever under the needle pull clip and hook the clip over the edge of the float on the float arm facing the pontoon of the float. Push the pin into the float arm with the

end of the pin loop facing the pump well. Install the float assembly—it's a bit tricky getting all these little parts together. Float level adjustment must be exactly right. Measure from the top of the float bowl surface (without the gasket) to the top of the float at its toe with the gauging point 3/16-inch back from the end of the float. The measurement is 3/16-inch (5.15 mm). Incidentally, it is well to measure the old needle valve-float adjustment before taking it out, as a clue to former behavior contrasted with the new.

Replace the power piston spring in the piston bore and install the piston and metering rod assembly into the float bowl and main metering jet. Press the plastic power piston retainer down firmly to make sure that it is seated in the recess of the bowl, the top flush with the surface. You can tap it in if it isn't.

Get the air horn gasket on the float bowl—carefully. Install the pump return spring in the well and the pump plunger assembly back in the well.

Now put the air horn back. Install the fast idle cam rod in the lower hole of the choke lever, getting the tab on the rod to line up with the small slot in the lever.

Turn the fast idle cam to its full UP position; tilt the air horn so as to engage the fast idle cam rod in the slot of the fast idle cam. Then, holding down the pump plunger assembly, lower the air horn into the float bowl, guiding the pump plunger stem through its hole in the air horn casting. Don't force; the two

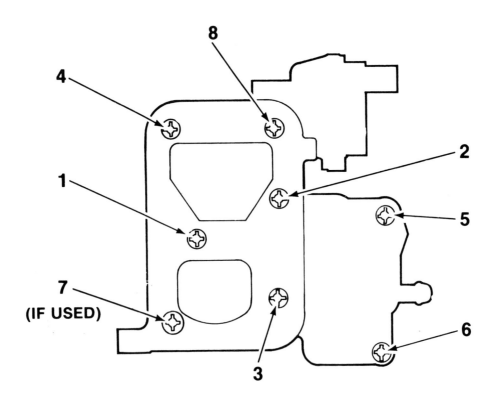

Tighten air horn screws in this sequence.

110

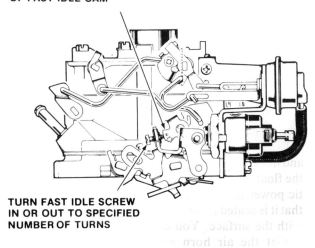

PLACE FAST IDLE
SCREW ON HIGHEST STEP
OF FAST IDLE CAM

TURN FAST IDLE SCREW
IN OR OUT TO SPECIFIED
NUMBER OF TURNS

Fast idle adjustment.

parts must mesh gently and easily. If they don't, pull back the air horn and check all the possible mistakes of placement.

V6 carburetors differ slightly in some fastening details, most of which are self-evident.

The rebuilding kit will contain a diagram that can be followed as far as individual component systems are concerned. Always keep in mind that you deal with mostly fragile parts, so never use force on them. There are a few exceptions; sometimes a needle float seat will be tightened ruinously and only force will get it out (using a wide blade screwdriver that fits across the two slits).

Once the air horn is back and properly tightened, with all the rods and levers attached, the choke is the final installation. Make sure that the thermostatic coil lever inside the choke housing is properly installed in the pickup-tang—if you took off the choke cover. (It isn't necessary to take the choke apart if it's doing its job.)

Note that the ground contact for the electric choke is by a metal plate at the rear of the choke assembly. Don't put the choke cover gasket between the electric choke and the choke housing, otherwise the choke won't work. It needs the ground.

Anyone who has worked on earlier Rochester carburetors will recognize this one as the latest in a long line. Rochester carburetors have been a mainstay of the U.S. auto industry for decades. The 2SE has some adjustments in common with earlier models, but it is getting close to the closed unit. If, when you get the carburetor back on the engine it doesn't idle or otherwise behave properly, the following adjustments can be made.

The fast idle adjustment requires that you place

the fast idle screw on the highest step of the fast idle cam and after it contacts turn three complete turns. This is a bench adjustment before you put the carburetor back, but the on-car adjustment is the same, subject to whatever slight changes engine performance dictates.

Idle adjustment is about what it always has been, with a few exceptions. Turn on ignition key to energize the solenoid; open the throttle slightly to allow the solenoid plunger to become fully extended; start engine and turn the solenoid screw to desired idle speed; turn the idle speed adjusting screw to desired speed after disconnecting the solenoid.

Omni and Horizon

Chrysler's Omni/Horizon cars (sporty and other models) use the Holley 5220 carburetor. Holley, like Rochester, is an industry standard. It presents no special problems of disassembly or assembly. Like other Holleys, this one uses two pump discharge balls, so that when you take the discharge nozzle screw out and turn the carburetor upside down, with the palm of your hand over the discharge nozzle, don't be astounded by the appearance of the second ball. It is simply a weight and must be put back on top of the regular discharge check ball. The accelerator pump system differs from Rochester and other makes in that it uses a pump diaphragm assembly activated by the pump lever and accelerator linkage. The pump must always be examined during tear

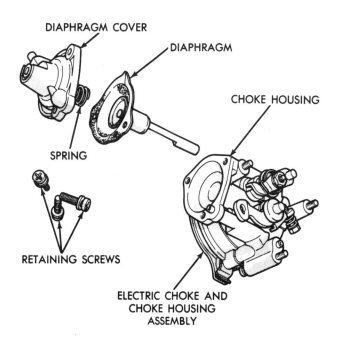

Choke diaphragm assembly.

111

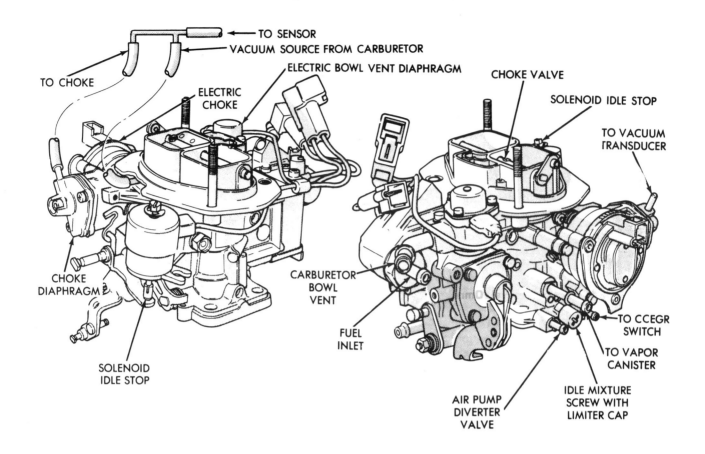

To SENSOR
VACUUM SOURCE FROM CARBURETOR
ELECTRIC BOWL VENT DIAPHRAGM
CHOKE VALVE
SOLENOID IDLE STOP
TO CHOKE
ELECTRIC CHOKE
TO VACUUM TRANSDUCER
CHOKE DIAPHRAGM
CARBURETOR BOWL VENT
SOLENOID IDLE STOP
FUEL INLET
TO CCEGR SWITCH
TO VAPOR CANISTER
AIR PUMP DIVERTER VALVE
IDLE MIXTURE SCREW WITH LIMITER CAP

Omni and Horizon carburetor views.

down, though most kits will replace it routinely. The choke is electric, and can be removed as a unit during cleaning. For ordinary adjustment and superficial, on-car cleaning, it isn't necessary to touch the choke unless it's misbehaving. The choke setting is not adjustable.

Carburetor disassembly begins with removal of the air cleaner, the fuel tank pressure vacuum filler cap (to relieve pressure on the fuel inlet), the fuel inlet tube (put a can or glass under it, in case); all the wiring harness, the throttle linkage and hoses, and the mounting nuts. Don't lose the small fasteners.

Unbolt the fuel inlet fitting, the choke operating rod and choke rod seal, the three mounting screws and harness mounting screw of the bowl vent solenoid diaphragm; the solenoid idle stop with its two retaining screws; the 5 air horn mounting screws and now pull up the air horn assembly, carefully.

Take off the float lever pin and pull out the float and needle. Unscrew the 3 power valve diaphragm mounting screws and remove it. The needle seat assembly comes out with a small socket wrench. With a screwdriver, take out the retaining clip and separate the diaphragm assembly from the air horn. Remove the power valve and the two main metering jets—secondary and primary—the high speed bleed,

both primary and secondary, and keep all these jets in separate little bins, marked so that you put them back in the right places. They don't have to be

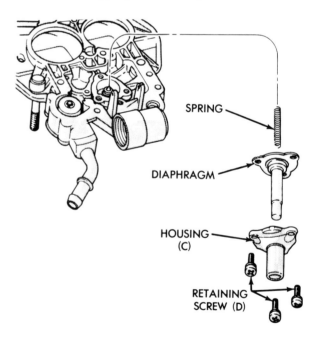

SPRING
DIAPHRAGM
HOUSING (C)
RETAINING SCREW (D)

Power valve diaphragm assembly.

112

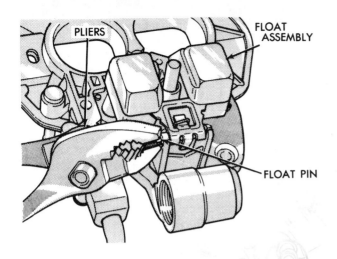

Float pin removal, Omni.

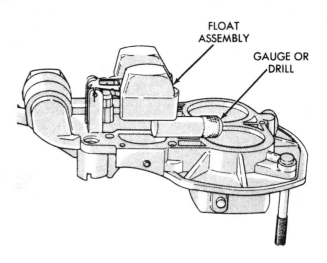

Float assembly.

soaked, but their chambers do. So wrap them in paper and mark each paper. Take off the accelerator pump discharge nozzle and the accelerator pump cover. Look at the pump diaphragm for holes or tears. Remove the throttle A/C cut-out switch. Take off the choke diaphragm assembly and housing as a unit and leave it alone unless it was not performing properly.

Soak all the metal parts.

One test you should make is the effectiveness of the discharge check balls (two of them). Put one ball (a used one) in the passage and fill the fuel bowl with clean fuel, holding the check ball down with a small thin tool of some sort. Operate the accelerator pump plunger by hand to pump fuel. If there is a leak at the ball and seat, no resistance will be felt at the pump plunger. If there is a leak at the ball, tap it lightly with whatever tool fits—some kind of a drift, replace the ball you tapped with the two new ones and try again. That should cure it.

Replace the parts you removed in reverse order with new parts in the kit, taking the usual care with the proper needle valve and float assembly adjustment. The float adjustment (there are two floats), should be done with the air horn upside down, and the gauge or whatever you use (a drill bit .480-inch—12.2 mm) between the air horn surface and float minus the gasket. Bend the adjustment tang for the right gap. Then check float drop. Turn the air horn upright, and let the float assembly fall. Measure at the lowest point of the float to the required gap, which is 1-7/8-inch drop (47.6mm). To adjust, hold the float assembly with one hand and bend the adjustment tang with the other using a screwdriver.

You'll have to set the fast idle and idle speed adjusters, (fast idle is to overcome cold engine friction, stalls after cold starts and because of carburetor

icing). To set, run the engine to normal operating temperature, with transmission in neutral. Remove air cleaner top, disconnect and plug the vacuum hoses to the EGR valve and the distributor (turn off air conditioning). Open the throttle slightly and place the slowest speed step of the fast idle cam (the top one) under the adjusting screw. Start the engine (choke valve now fully open) and adjust to 1,700 rpm with carburetor models R8838A, R8839A, R9110A, and R9111A; adjust to 1,400 rpm with models R8726A, R8837A, R9108A, and R9109A.

Chrysler recommends that you run the electric fan throughout the adjusting process, which would slow the speed slightly. But it's a tricky maneuver, so reduce the rpm adjustment somewhat under the figures above.

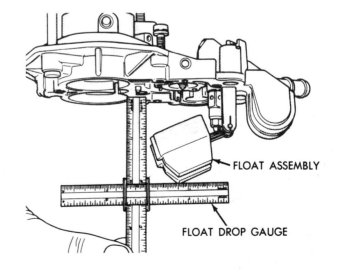

Float drop measurement.

113

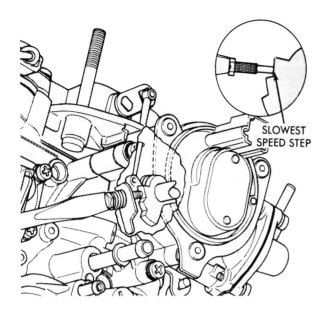

Fast idle adjustment, Holley 5220.

The regular curb idle adjustment is prescribed using the new propane tank method of adjustment. Since you won't have such a device, you'll have to use the idle mixture screw at the bottom of the carburetor (it's hard to see) and the idle adjusting screw on the solenoid idle stop. The air conditioning idle solenoid (on cars so equipped) is a separate solenoid that you adjust with an allen wrench to an idle speed of 750 rpm—a typical idle speed. The adjustment without air conditioning is a regular screw adjuster on the solenoid idle stop. Make this adjustment on the solenoid plunger with a screwdriver, the transmission in neutral, the solenoid wire disconnected. The adjustment should be 700 rpm.

FUEL INJECTION

Fuel injection systems represent a more complex way of doing carburetion—mixing fuel and air and getting it to the cylinders. Many more components are involved; many more processes at work. Fuel injection offers more control over more engine speeds than the carburetor.

Fuel and air demands of an engine vary with temperature and speed. An engine should have a slightly rich mixture for idle; a rich mixture for starting and cold driving and for maximum power. At partial load—"normal" speeds—the engine needs a lean mixture. The air sensor responds to these requirements more sensitively than the carburetor, and the fuel injectors can deliver the air-fuel mix with greater

precision than the intake manifold under the carburetor. However, the differences are very slight, and the much greater costs of fuel injection systems rule out replacement of the carburetor entirely, nor is there any sign that this is happening. It may, when computers take over the fuel systems of cars entirely. But that's another story.

Meanwhile the intrusion of government regulations reaches new heights, centering on the carburetor, of all things. Soon it will be illegal to do any of the things we're talking about to a new carburetor. That instrument will be hermetically sealed, in order to render it inviolate to any would-be fixer. The purpose, stated and implied, is to keep its functions pure—free of the change of air-fuel ratios some tinkerer might see fit to bestow. It is interesting that purity is thus legislated upon the innocent carburetor. We look forward to a stunning success in the legislation of purity for the carburetor, confident that such success will smooth the path for the legislation of purity in other errant fields.

Fuel injection is a system for measuring gas/air more accurately in terms of need than the carburetor can before sending the mixture into the cylinders to be fired. The system requires a fuel pump (some of them have two, one in the gas tank), a fuel filter, and the injectors—one per cylinder. Injectors are valves at the end of the fuel injection system that thrust the fuel mix into the combustion chamber. A complex system precedes them. It is far more complicated than the carburetor; it's a different animal. It may include, in addition to the main outlines above, many additional devices; a fuel accumulator, fuel distributor, warm-up regulator, airflow sensor plate, cold start valve, injection valve, auxiliary air valve, throttle plate with deceleration valve, all of which (and more) are found on a typical Bosch Continuous Fuel Injection System, which is standard on Saab 99 cars and others.

Consider the Scirocco, the VW sporty model. VW uses several different fuel injection types, including the famous diesel Rabbit injection system. Scirocco has a continuous injection system. Both systems are designed for high mileage, low or no maintenance service. But the best systems are like the best intentions—the road to somewhere is paved with them. Every mechanical system can break down.

Diesel systems

Fuel injectors dispense diesel fuel. (Keep it off your hands.) The injectors can become worn and corroded. You can clean or replace them as needed. Symptoms of such need are knocking in a cylinder, engine overheating, loss of power, smoky black

114

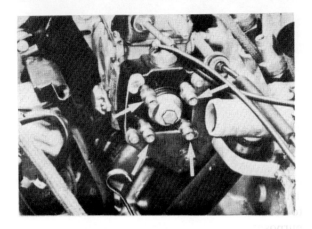

Bosch diesel fuel injector delivery valves, which may need tightening on occasion.

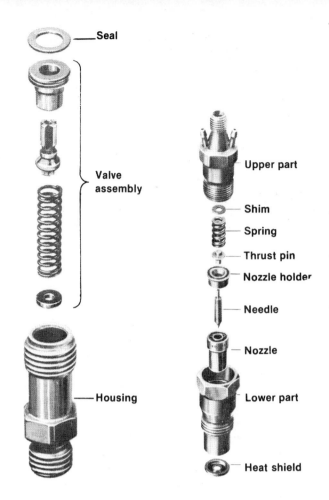

- Seal
- Valve assembly
- Housing
- Upper part
- Shim
- Spring
- Thrust pin
- Nozzle holder
- Needle
- Nozzle
- Lower part
- Heat shield

Fuel delivery valve housings may need replacing or cleaning.

exhaust, and increased fuel consumption.

It isn't likely that all the injectors will require cleaning and/or replacing. You can pinpoint the guilty injector by loosening the pipe union on each of the injectors in turn, with the engine running at fast idle. If engine speed is unchanged when the pipe union is loosened it means that injector needs work.

To remove an injector requires removing the pipe fittings and pipes. You must disconnect the fuel return hoses and the injectors can be removed next.

In handling fuel injector parts it is of the utmost importance that no dirt get on or into them. When cleaning the parts you can use gasoline to clean carbon deposits, but diesel fuel should be used to rinse them immediately. Wherever possible, clean with diesel fuel. Examine the parts carefully for wear and corrosion.

The injector has a lower and upper part, with a nozzle, needle valve, spring and supporting parts. A heat shield is at the bottom. The two parts must be unbolted for examination, cleaning and replacement.

Replace the heat shield every time, but before replacing anything else, clean it carefully and examine it for wear. The needle valve is the most obvious candidate for replacement. If you replace the needle you must replace the nozzle and holder. You can buy a kit for these parts and others, as the need arises.

When replacing the parts, install new heat shields, and tighten the injectors as they were—51 ft lbs, (70 Nm) which is tight. Then tighten the injector pipes to 18 ft. lb (25 Nm). Replace the fuel return hoses, and start the engine. Accelerate it a few times to clear out air bubbles.

When removing and replacing the fuel injectors, great care must be taken with the injector pipes, otherwise you can easily foul the fuel delivery valve fittings. If that happens and they leak, you have to start over and remove the fuel injector pipes, and tighten the fuel delivery valves to 33 ft lb (45 Nm). If

that doesn't stop the leak, the fuel delivery valve housing and seal must be replaced. The components of the fuel delivery valve housing contain the valve

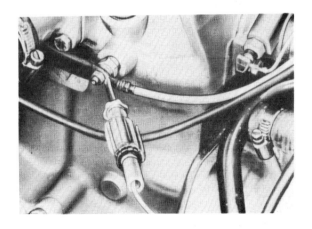

If glow plugs fail the test prescribed in the text they are probably defective; but other components such as the glow plug relay, ignition switch, or fuse box relay plate may be faulty.

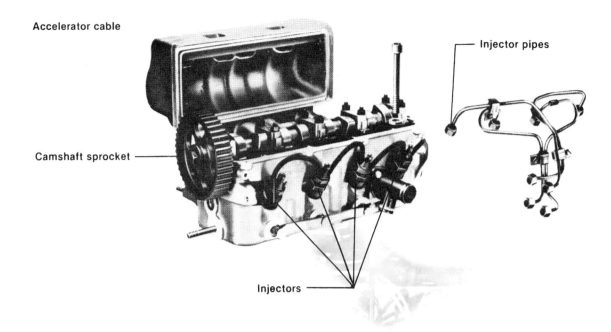

Diesel injection pipes and injectors.

assembly, spring, seal, and the housing. Replace the seal at least, and if the valve is worn or corroded replace that, though it should only be necessary to replace the seal.

You can check glow plugs or, if one of them doesn't seem to be working, simply replace it. The test is to connect any test light between the No. 4 cylinder glow plug and a ground. Turn the ignition key to the heat position. The light should go on. If it does not, the plug is bad.

The major components of the diesel fuel injection system consist of the pump and various supporting devices. The pump is the heart of the system and can only be serviced by people who have had training in it. No part of it is subject to amateur work without the specialized equipment. But so much equipment is necessary that one cannot recommend acquiring it.

Gasoline injection systems

Gasoline fuel injection trouble shooting requires some knowledge of the major systems. These are by Bosch, mostly.

The VW system, which is most familiar, is the CIS. It is also found on Audi Fox and 100 LS; the Mercedes Benz 450; the Porsche 911 and Turbo Carrea; the Saab 99, and Volvo 240 and 260.

Datsun 280Z and ZX use a Bosch Air Flow Controlled (AFC) system.

The CIS system is mechanical, not unlike the car-buretor in that a series of events take place that are mostly caused by mechanical relationships. The Datsun system (AFC) is electronic. It depends on signals sent to the electronic control unit from air pressure sensors in the distributor and manifold. The contact breaker points in the distributor tell the electronic control unit when to start fuel injection and what the speed of the engine is; the sensor in the manifold controls duration of the fuel injection cycle. The control unit is in effect a pre-programmed computer that processes the signals it receives from the sensors.

Electronic fuel injection repair takes electronic equipment and cannot be recommended to amateurs, unless you like to acquire equipment that can be used only occasionally. Not so the mechanical system, despite the complexities of it.

Though fuel injection has many more components and complications than a carburetor, the Bosch Continuous Injection System is designed to be serviced by a reasonably intelligent person, and that is the individual we are talking to, so it presents no unusual problems.

We assume that before you test a CIS system you have eliminated electrical and ignition problems. You suspect ignition problems first. And if the car has mileage in excess of 20,000, you also begin to think about such mechanical problems as valves and valve train wear symptoms. You also check exhaust and mechanical malfunctions, and that is a large order.

Ignition and electrical problems center on spark plugs, cables, distributors, batteries, fuses and wiring harnesses. It is impossible to dismiss these com-

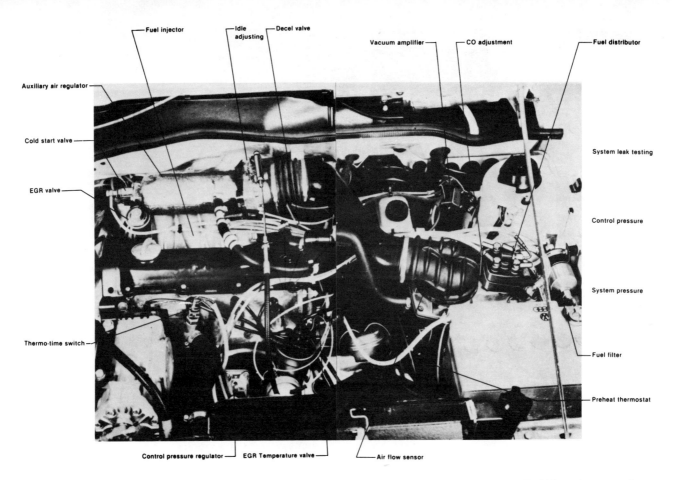

Fuel injector · Idle adjusting · Decel valve · Vacuum amplifier · CO adjustment · Fuel distributor

Auxiliary air regulator

Cold start valve

EGR valve

System leak testing

Control pressure

System pressure

Thermo-time switch

Fuel filter

Preheat thermostat

Control pressure regulator · EGR Temperature valve · Air flow sensor

The component parts of a Bosch Continuous Injection System (CIS) as used on Scirocco, Rabbit and many other cars.

ponents in a quick scrutiny. Ignition troubleshooting should follow the patterns suggested in engine tuneup. Exhaust system components are more easily checked.

Hard starting, failure to start, and performance failures, should not be blamed on fuel injection (or carburetor systems) unless you have eliminated everything else. The reason is simply that the fuel system, for all its complexity, is less likely to be the culprit. Electrical and ignition problems arise first, next come such purely mechanical problems as slipping fan belts which don't turn the alternator properly, and finally the fuel system. But the most common fuel system problems with the CIS are air leaks—into the engine. If the cover gasket over the top (and the pan gasket below) admit air, or the oil filler cap is worn and admits air, or the ventilation hoses leak, the engine won't run properly because the CIS fuel metering system will be disturbed. Correct operation of the system demands that air enter through the mixture control unit, and that it be a precisely measured flow.

A visual check of the CIS system sometimes leads to a quick fix of its problems. Loose wires, tubes and pipes sometimes can be seen—indeed, sometimes are disconnected because of engine vibration and

wear. If you see loose wires be sure you connect them to the right posts. The problem is more likely to be loose tubes and pipes, which result in leaks. Cables and wires, especially as part of a harness, may corrode but are less likely to come apart. Corrosion is the enemy and rarely can be spotted visually, since the corrosion is inside the insulated terminals and joints.

Because fuel pressure is so vital to correct operation of the CIS (and any other) fuel system, you begin by checking at the gas tank and forward of it to the engine. To check the fuel tank connections properly, it is best to raise the rear end. You can examine the joints at the tank, the fuel pump and the fuel pressure accumulator. Both pump and accumulator are under the car, near the fuel tank, bolted to the body. If any joints leak there will be telltale signs—discoloration tracks around the joints. There could be gas fumes and leaks, with the engine running. It is best to wipe the joints off with paper or a rag since leaks are more apparent on a clean, dry surface.

Fuel line connections—especially plastic—won't stand much tightening, if you find a leak. However, tighten them securely and that could stop the leak. If leaks persist after tightening there is only one cure—replacement. What you replace usually is a

Connecting the pressure gauge from the fuel distributor control pressure regulator, lever set to position A.

System pressure is checked with gauge in B position.

gasket, less often the coupling unit or the line itself. The lines must be visually checked for cracks and wear.

If no evidence of leaks at the joints or in the tubing lines shows up, you must next test the fuel pump.

Because you cannot test the pump independently of other components, using the simple test of the pan and the disconnected line, you must use the proper fuel pressure gauge with three-way lever, designed for Bosch CIS systems. However, with this gauge, an ohmmeter and test lamp you can test any phase of the system, so it is hard to quarrel with an investment in such a gauge.

The pressure gauge (VW 1318 or 378 by number) should be connected from the fuel distributor to the control pressure regulator. To do that, disconnect the line from the top center of the fuel distributor—alongside the battery and between the fuel filter (bracket-mounted cylinder) and the air flow sensor. Install the outlet hose of the three-way valve of the gauge to the fuel distributor in place of the line you remove. Connect the other line of the gauge to the disconnected hose going to the control pressure regulator (a device on the side of the engine). Note that the operating lever on the gauge's three-way valve has several positions; position A, which points away from the gauge, and position B, which points in parallel to the gauge or at right angles to it (see illustrations).

The first test should be with a cold engine—that means one that hasn't been run for at least several hours. CIS systems test like this:

Remove the electrical plug connectors from the control pressure regulator; and the auxiliary air regulator. The three-way gauge valve should be in a position that puts the valve above the gauge (for bleeding purposes). With the ignition on, move the operating lever of the gauge back and forth between

position A and B at 10-second intervals, four or five times (the fuel pump is operating), to bleed the lines. Now start the engine. Move the valve to A. If it's about 68 degrees F, the gauge should register a cold control pressure reading of above 18 psi (pounds per square inch) but not much over 24 (or 1.35 and 1.7 bar reading).

Don't run the engine for more than a minute.

With the engine stopped, the gauge yet in place, reconnect the electrical connectors you removed. Control pressure reading should rise after 2 minutes to 3.4-3.8 bar (48-54 psi). Readings outside these ranges mean the control pressure regulator is defective.

For a warm control pressure reading: gauge lever is in A position. Leave electrical connection attached at the control pressure regulator and alternator. Run engine until warm (60 C/140 F). As the engine warms fully the reading should stablilize at 48-54 psi (3.4-3.8 bar). If the reading is not within these tolerances the control pressure regulator is defective.

To test fuel delivery rate and general system pressure:

Connect (that is don't disconnect) electrical connectors on the control pressure regulator and auxiliary air regulator. Install gauge as before, with lever in position B. Run engine at idle until pressure reaches 4.5-5.2 bar (64-74 psi). If results vary, clean the fuel distributor pressure relief valve. (See below.) With the gauge installed and the engine running at idle, bleed the pressure gauge as before—hold the gauge down and move the lever several times back and forth (A to B, open to closed) positions. Now put lever in A position. Warm up engine to 140 F. Pressure should read 3.4-3.8 bar (48-54 psi).

Turn off the engine and wait 10 minutes. Reading should drop below 1.8. If not, wait another 10 minutes. Minimum pressure at 20 minutes must be 1.6 bar (18 psi). If the pressure is below 1.6 bar (18 psi), put the lever in position B and repeat the entire procedure. Run the engine at idle until the gauge reads 4.5-5.2 bar (64-74 psi). If the pressure does not then drop below 1.8 bar in 10 minutes or 1.6 bar in 20 minutes, the control pressure regulator must be replaced. If pressure drops in position B as it did in position A, the lines probably leak, or there may be a leak in the fuel distributor, in the fuel injectors, the cold start valve, the fuel pump or the fuel pump check valve.

Fuel pump delivery rate is tested by removing the fuel return hose and disconnecting the high tension cable from the ignition coil (center post). Hold the end of the opened line hose in a one-quart glass or other container. Run the starter for 15 seconds and if the pump is working and the filter is not clogged you should collect about 12 ounces of fuel. But if the pump doesn't run check the electrical connections. If the amount of fuel isn't correct, try replacing the fuel filter.

To replace the filter, disconnect the negative cable from the battery. Remove the fuel filter mounting nuts (one is on the bracket holding the filter, the other is concealed by the tubing line). The filter can now be removed from the mount. Loosen the fuel filler cap; loosen slightly the fuel lines on the filter to relieve fuel pressure. Keep a can handy to catch spilling fuel. Remove the filter from the lines next; replace with new filter. Replace the four sealing rings on the through bolts and tighten the fuel lines to the new filter about 14 ft lb—securely but not excessively.

Fuel line testing can be done if you are willing to disconnect the line from the rear of the car at the tank and test it through the fuel accumulator simply by blowing through it. That tests for obstructions but

Checking the sensor plate.

not leaks. The fuel tank strainer, which can get so clogged that fuel pump pressure is affected severely, is below the fuel gauge sending unit. Working on the gas tank is dangerous and not recommended. The chances are, however, that the fuel pump itself needs replacing when it fails to pump gas at all, but when it pumps insufficiently it may well be the strainer, a line obstruction, a leak and lastly the pump itself.

Electrical fuel pump tests begin with the relay. First locate the fuse for the fuel pump, which is on top of the relay. It has a cover which you remove to get at the relay. The fuse that controls the fuel pump and relay is separate and is just above the number 6 and 7 fuses on the panel (there are 15 fuses in that line on the panel; the fuel pump fuse is all alone). Check the fuse carefully. Take it out and clean the terminals, if it appears to be good. Once you are satisfied that the fuse works, and the fuel pump does not, and you have eliminated the other culprits above, the relay and pump remain as sole possibilities. To test you need to eliminate the relay from the circuit. Remove the relay from the fuse relay box. Disconnect the alternator hot wire. (That's to save the alternator diodes from any mistake.) Use a jumper cable across the L13 and L14 terminals—vacated when you removed the relay switch from the fuse panel. If the pump now starts to work with the ignition switch on, replace the relay. If it does not, replace the pump. You can buy new fuel pumps for not much more than $25 or $30 that equal original equipment and perhaps surpass it. You don't have to buy the pump from the dealer parts counter, unless you feel some obligation about it.

The relay switch, if defective, may not be so easily found (but it isn't likely to need it—the fuel pump will be the culprit virtually every time).

If you replace the fuel pump be prepared with a can to catch fuel when you disconnect the tubing. It

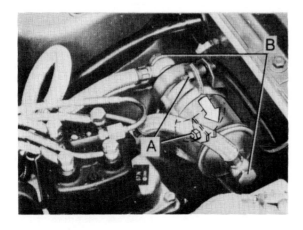

Replacing fuel filter follows the sequence of removing bolts and lines.

Testing movement of sensor plate.

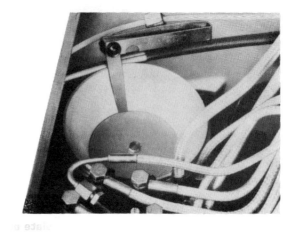

Checking sensor plate injection quantity with feeler gauge.

goes without saying that you never smoke around gas lines or do anything that could make a spark.

The fuel pump is underneath the car near the fuel tank (as is the fuel accumulator). In removing the pump for replacement, the sequence is to disconnect both fuel lines, remove bolts that hold the pump's sound-absorbing box, then both box and pump come out. The pump's check valve is next, followed by the pump. Whenever disconnecting fuel lines keep a can around to catch dribbling gas.

Central to CIS fuel injection performance is the sensor plate and its action in conjunction with the fuel distributor. The sensor plate and lever/control plunger, in effect and in conjunction with the air sensor and the fuel distributor, control the air/fuel mixture that is sent to the fuel injectors. Air, from the air cleaner, passes between the sensor plate and its surrounding passageways, then forward to the fuel distributor. It is mixed with gas by a series of events in the pressure regulating valve.

The first test requires that you expose the sensor plate by disconnecting the duct from the air flow sensor—the rubber duct connecting to the plastic duct that goes in turn to the throttle valve or idle adjusting unit (see layout). Next, turn on the ignition key briefly—long enough for the fuel pump to turn on and introduce pressure into the system (a few seconds). This forces the metering unit control plunger against the sensor plate's lever. For the first test you need a magnet of some sort (or a small electrical pliers). With the magnet, lift the sensor plate, noting whether there are drags at any point. If you use a pliers, use it gently. The movement of the plate should be uniformly free through its travel. Now, with a feeler gauge, .004-inch (10 mm) test around the rim of the plate. If it isn't .004 loosen the centering bolt slightly and move the feeler gauge around again so that centering takes place, then tighten the bolt.

Note that the bolt takes a lot of tightening (46 ft lbs). Next move the sensor plate quickly from its raised position to rest. If the sensor plate lever is hard to move up but moves downward freely, the control plunger needs to be cleaned. Remove the fuel distributor and pull the control plunger out. Clean it in solvent (note that the longest land of the plunger moves away from the fuel distributor to the air flow sensor and plate). If cleaning the plunger doesn't cure sticking, the fuel distributor must be replaced. If when the sensor plate is moved quickly from raised to rest and there is noticeable resistance, the air flow sensor must be replaced. Warning: be careful with the plunger; it's delicate and easily ruined.

Sensor plate height must be checked. To do that requires that you loosen the control pressure line at the pressure regulator, to remove line pressure. When you do that, catch the fuel that will be pushed out. The sensor plate edge nearest the fuel distributor must align in this way: upper edge must be even with the bottom of the air cone taper or no more

Checking the sensor plate.

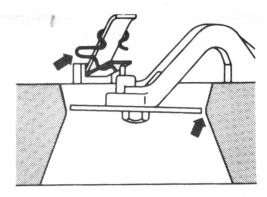

Height adjustment on the air flow sensor plate of the CIS.

Accelerator cable adjustment. Arrow shows throttle lever and cable.

than .020-inch (.5 mm) below the bottom of the taper. To adjust, lift the sensor plate by taking out the retaining screws. Bend the wire clip so as to adjust the spring stop to bring the sensor plate into correct alignment with the venturi.

These are all delicate adjustments; thus when loosening and tightening the sensor plate bolt be very careful with it so as not to scratch the venturi of the air flow sensor.

To adjust system pressure when it falls outside the correct specifications noted above, you remove or add adjusting shims in the pressure relief valve of the fuel distributor. The addition or subtraction of a .020-inch shim (.50 mm) will add or subtract about 4 psi (.30 bar). But all this presupposes that you have checked out the fuel pressure throughout the system, as described above. If the pressure isn't in the system the shims won't help.

To adjust the fuel distributor when you've done major replacements—a new fuel distributor or air flow sensor repair or replacement— pull out all the fuel injectors from the cylinder head. Turn on the ignition key to activate the fuel pump. Hold injectors

To check a new fuel distributor, pull out each injector.

in a container and lift the sensor plate several times to bleed the lines. Turn off the key. Using a special adjusting tool (wrench P 377, an inexpensive tool you'll need if you plan to get this far in fuel injection), turn the CO adjustment screw counter clockwise one or two turns. Turn on the fuel pump again, and turn the CO adjustment screw clockwise until the injectors begin to spray. Then turn the screw counterclockwise one half turn. Turn off the fuel pump and replace the injectors. Start the engine and let it warm, and adjust idle speed, if necessary.

There are other adjustments and components to the CIS system, but we have covered the major problem areas. A minor adjustment involves the accelerator cable, which can get out of adjustment. If with manual transmission the accelerator pedal fails to respond properly, push it to its stop position and hold it there (prop it or have someone hold it). Loosen the cable locknuts; adjust cable so that throttle valve reaches stop. Tighten locknuts. When the accelerator is released the throttle valve should be closed. For automatic transmission you turn the adjuster on the accelerator cable support bracket until no play remains in the cable.

To test the fuel injectors, pull them out of their cylinder head bushings and put them in measuring glasses. Run the fuel pump (turn on ignition key) and raise the sensor plate until one glass measures 50 cc, noting whether the spray from the injectors comes out in an even cone-shape when the plate is lifted. Close the sensor plate; no fuel droplets should be noticed on an injector in 15 seconds. And the fuel quantity in all the glasses should be within 7 ccs of each other. If there are greater differences, exchange injectors on the lines where the greatest differences occur. Repeat the volume test. If the same injector shows the low volume, examine it carefully and assume that it is defective. Assume also, if the same

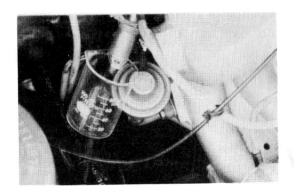

Checking the CIS cold start valve.

fuel line shows low volume, that the fuel distributor is defective and must be replaced.

The cold start valve can be checked, if the car won't start in cold weather and everything else seems to be working. The valve (see illustration for location) should be removed from the intake manifold and held in a container with the fuel line connected to it. Connect a jumper wire from one terminal of the cold start valve to the ignition coil terminal #15. Ground, with a second jumper wire, the second cold start valve terminal. Turn on the ignition. The pump is on. Check valve nozzle for steady, cone-shaped spray. Turn off ignition. The pump will continue to run (it is wired to terminal #15). Wipe the nozzle. If drops form within one minute the valve is defective.

You can check the thermo-time switch. It must be done with a cold engine. It requires a simple test light. Remove the electrical lead from the cold start valve and connect a test light between the two prongs of the harness. Remove the connector from the coil terminal #15 (it is so marked) and insulate it. (That will keep the engine from starting.) Remove the electrical connector from the control pressure regu-

Thermo-time switch location and check.

lator and auxiliary air regulator. Turn on the starter for 10 seconds; the test light must go on. If not, replace it.

Datsun

For an example of an other type system, the Datsun 200FX is an electronic fuel injection system, with integrated circuits, (ICs), resistors, thermistors, all of which control the amount of fuel made available to the engine at each speed and operating condition. Fuel from the tank goes into the pump, then to a mechanical fuel damper. The fuel is filtered, then goes into the line and is injected into the intake manifold cylinder. Surplus fuel goes into a pressure regulator which returns it to the tank. The pressure regulator controls injection pressure so that the pressure difference between the fuel pressure and the intake manifold vacuum is always 250 kPa (2.55 kg/cm^2, or 36.3 psi). Air from the air cleaner is metered at the air flow meter; it flows through the throttle chamber and into the intake manifold, then into each intake manifold branch where it is channeled into each cylinder. Air flow is controlled by the throttle valve in the throttle chamber. During idle, the throttle valve is almost closed and air goes through a by-pass line.

The electrical system works through various sensors. There are altitude (in California), air temperature and water temperature, sensors, as well as other controls with electrical components. The fuel injectors are connected electrically in parallel in the control unit. Injectors receive the injection signal from the control unit simultaneously, so injection is independent but coincidental with engine operation. Fuel is not injected directly into the cylinder, but goes into an outside portion of the intake valve. The mixture is sucked into the cylinder when the intake valve begins the suction stroke. The air-fuel mix is blocked from the intake valve in other strokes (compression, combustion, exhaust).

Amount of fuel injection and character—that is, the type of fuel mix needed under each operating condition—are determined by sensors which report their findings to the control unit. That brain in turn decides what goes to the injectors. The control unit's function is to generate a pulse whose duration coincides with the injector's open valve time period. The optimum quantity of correctly mixed fuel is what the control unit must produce with its pulse. The unit itself consists of three integrated circuits on a printed circuit board. Its reliability should be high—these auto control units are supposed to last the life of the car. Some do, some don't.

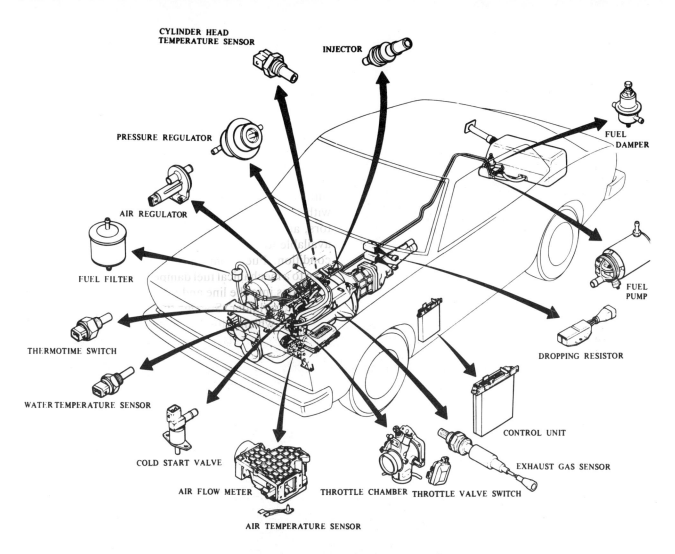

CYLINDER HEAD
TEMPERATURE SENSOR

INJECTOR

PRESSURE REGULATOR

FUEL
DAMPER

AIR REGULATOR

FUEL FILTER

FUEL
PUMP

THERMOTIME SWITCH

DROPPING RESISTOR

WATER TEMPERATURE SENSOR

COLD START VALVE

CONTROL UNIT

AIR FLOW METER

THROTTLE CHAMBER   THROTTLE VALVE SWITCH

EXHAUST GAS SENSOR

AIR TEMPERATURE SENSOR

The engine placement and components of the EFI system.

To go troubleshooting in this Datsun (by Bosch) electronic system requires certain preliminary agreements and procedures, as with the CSI system. The EFI harness connector is a 35-pin connector to the control unit and the various engine units. The connection must be secure, since a poor connection can cause voltage surge in the coil and condenser and damage to the IC circuit. The EFI harness should be about 4 inches (10 cm) from other harnesses, so as to isolate it from reception of external noises, and the possibility of a defective IC circuit operation. All EFI parts and wiring should be kept dry. Battery ground cable should be removed when working on—i.e., removing and replacing—parts. The air flow meter should be treated especially carefully. Do not press accelerator pedal when starting and don't rev the engine after starting. Never run the fuel pump when there is no fuel in the lines; don't put anti-freeze in the fuel.

The symptoms that send you troubleshooting into this complex, delicate system (which, however, is remarkably trouble-free), consist of the usual:

Causes of starting failure are: air leakage at PCV valve; VC valve; dipstick seal; oil filler cap; blow-by hoses; air flow meter hoses and clamps; manifold and other gaskets; fuel pump does not work; improper ignition signal input; EFI relay or control unit or injector have failed; water temperature sensor; air flow meter potentiometer; or start signal circuit are mal functioning. Battery failure.

Causes of engine starting then stalling are most of the above, plus air regulator.

Causes of too-fast engine idle which cannot be adjusted, or unstable engine idle, are intake and exhaust valve clearance wrong, or malfunctioning air regulator.

Causes of engine mis-firing are poor or corroded EFI harness connectors, fuel line failure somewhere in the components, control unit out of order, improper fuel pressure, wrong EFI circuit.

Causes of lack of power are: throttle valve, air flow meter, fuel line blockage, fuel pressure failure due to ignition coil trigger input circuit, control unit power input circuit, injector circuit, air flow meter

123

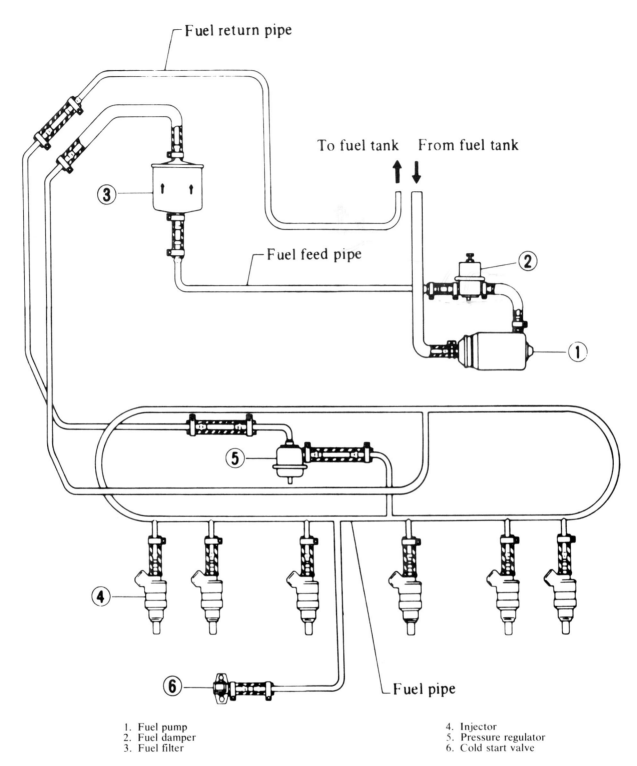

Fuel return pipe

To fuel tank   From fuel tank

③

Fuel feed pipe

②

①

⑤

④

⑥

Fuel pipe

1. Fuel pump
2. Fuel damper
3. Fuel filter

4. Injector
5. Pressure regulator
6. Cold start valve

Fuel hoses, injectors, and other parts of EFI.

potentiometer, throttle valve switch, idle contact and full throttle contact, vacuum switch, air temperature sensor, water temperature sensor, altitude sensor, air regulator and fuel pump circuit failures.

Causes of hesitation are most of the above, plus incorrect idle CO% adjustment.

Causes of poor gas mileage are ignition timing wrong, air cleaner filter incorrect or clogged, and/or

problems in sensors, switches, air, fuel pump, and injector circuits.

Causes of engine surge are any of the system components.

Causes of backfiring are: air leakage; also wrong fuel pressure and CO% idle adjustment; also any of the component systems.

Causes of afterfire or after-burning are: the sen-

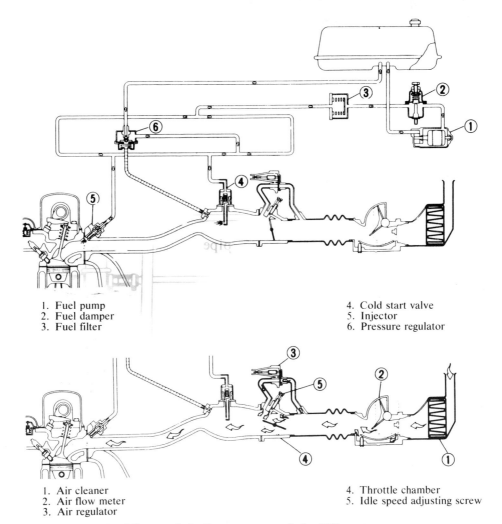

1. Fuel pump
2. Fuel damper
3. Fuel filter

4. Cold start valve
5. Injector
6. Pressure regulator

1. Air cleaner
2. Air flow meter
3. Air regulator

4. Throttle chamber
5. Idle speed adjusting screw

Fuel flow and air flow systems of the EFI system.

sors, the throttle valve switch, idle contact and full throttle contact, the injection circuit, or possibly any component malfunction.

Continuity testing

Checking, adjusting, repairing and replacing so complex a system can be done in two ways—continuity testing using an ohmmeter—and in the test of individual components using a voltmeter, test light, ohmmeter, or other simple devices such as a thermometer, or continuity tester. Much of testing consists of establishing continuity or its absence between the components involved. Problems often arise simply because vibration plays havoc with electrical connections, while the atmosphere corrodes them. So, cleaning and restoring original connecting surfaces can cure a lot of such problems. However, there are many wearing components in the system, and while they are tough and durable they can all destruct.

Ignition problem troubleshooting should begin by eliminating the question of electrical supply. Disconnect the cable from one spark plug and hold it away from the plug to see whether there is spark—with the ignition on. If spark is present, go next to air flow meter hoses and clamps, PCV valve, dipstick seal, oil filler cap, and all gaskets, including manifold gaskets, looking for air leaks. Air leaks are hard to track down, but the least alteration in the air-fuel mix caused by a leak can upset engine performance drastically. Visual inspection of connections and gaskets can tell you a great deal about air leaks, but you are pretty much on your own. You can try such measures as taping suspected connections to see whether it makes a difference. However, tape is no solution, and if it reveals a leaking connection the tape must be replaced with a new gasket, connector, or whatever is at fault. But tape does work as an initial testing procedure.

Once air leaks are eliminated, and you have established the existence of electrical current at the spark plugs, proceed to a check of all harness connectors. But first, turn off the ignition switch. Also, remove

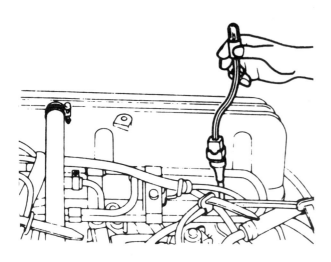

Test light for the control unit of the EFI and its use.

the negative battery terminal. If you do not take these precautions when removing harness connectors—especially the 35-pin connector—you will ruin the control unit.

You can test a control unit (on the left dash side—driver side). The EFI harness' 35-pin connector goes to the control unit and also to the various components in the engine compartment: air flow meter, throttle valve switch, cold start valve, air regulator, thermotime switch, water temperature sensor, dropping resistor and injector, among others. The battery supplies electric power to the injector and control unit through a special fuse—a fusible link. Whenever removing the 35-pin connector from the control unit for examination, use care not to distort any of the pins, and when replacing the connector use twice as much care. It would be a disaster of some magnitude to ruin this connector. But if it must be cleaned—if any of the pins are corroded—it can be done exactly as porcupines are reported to make love, with the utmost caution and minimum of abrasiveness. Use a small file or knife or sandpaper.

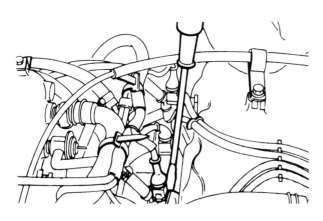

Sound test on EFI connectors of Datsun engine.

But if you use the latter blow out the grains.

A true test of the control unit requires a small test lamp which you connect to the harness side connector of the injector. You then turn on the starter. If the lamp flashes that means the control unit is generating its pulse voltage, and is normal; but to confirm the finding, disconnect the harness of the cooling water temperature sensor. If the lamp flashes more brightly, when you turn on the ignition and starter, that is confirmation that the control unit is normal.

If the control unit fails the test, it is very easily removed and replaced. Remove the bolt that holds the cover over the control unit on the left side dash panel, pry off the cover. Disconnect the coupler, remove the two bolts (there is variation from year to year on retainers and fasteners, but there is little trouble in any case). It is best, in any dealings with the pin connector, to remove the battery negative cable before removing the connector or installing the new one. It's to protect the control unit from any mistakes. (Yours, not its.)

To test the fuel pump, disconnect the starting motor lead wire at Terminal ''S'' and turn the ignition switch to starting position, listening to the fuel pump operating sound. If it makes one, you have to do a fuel pressure test. That requires a fuel pressure gauge, which you aren't likely to possess. But if the pump is operating electrically the chances are that any failure of pressure is not in the pump but elsewhere, for example in the lines. Look for bent tubing, or you can disconnect the lines (which are under pressure so they have to be drained) and check for obstructions by blowing through them. This is not as easy as it sounds, but it can be done.

To test fuel injectors if the engine is running, use the tip of a screwdriver to take a sounding on each injector. A low sound usually means that the injector in question is faulty. You can get the same effect with an engine that won't run by getting someone to turn the starting motor on. But first, disconnect the electric lead of the cold start valve, thus preventing damage to the catalytic converter. If you hear no sound from any of the injectors in this test, that is probably a sign that something is amiss in the harness or the control unit. But if sounds can be heard from numbers 1, 2 and 3, or 4, 5 and 6, but not from both groups, the control unit is defective.

To test other main components of this system involves greater complications of equipment and procedure then it is wise to undertake at this stage of the game. The main components are those we've discussed and if they require replacement you can do it easily enough if you've followed the discussions so far. Electronic fuel injection, however, is the most complex system on your car and in order to proceed to the testing of the remaining components—the sensors and switches, primarily—one must have the

- Securely connect EFI harness connector. A poor connection can cause an extremely high (surge) voltage to develop in coil and condenser, thus resulting in damage to IC circuit.
- Keep EFI harness at least 10 cm (3.9 in) away from adjacent harnesses, to prevent an EFI system malfunction due to reception of external noise, degraded operation of IC circuit, etc.
- Keep EFI parts and harnesses dry.
- Before removing parts, turn off ignition switch and then disconnect battery ground cable.

- Do not apply battery power directly to injectors.

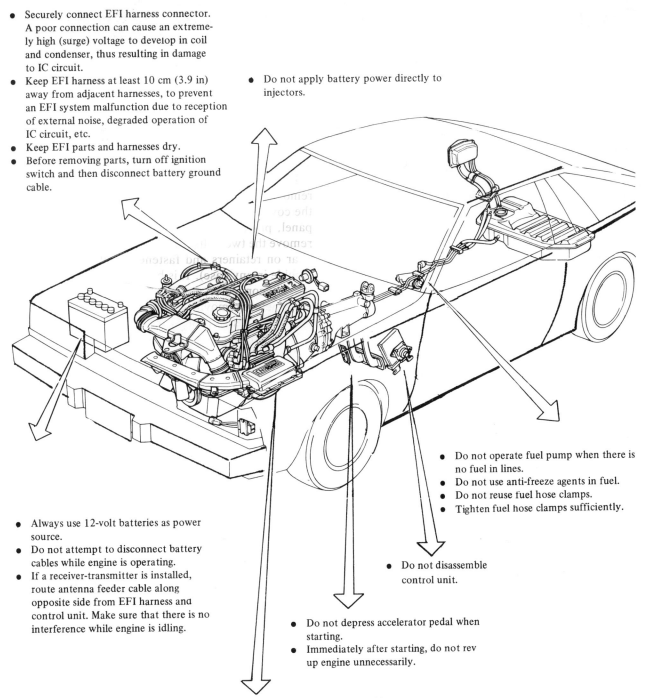

- Do not operate fuel pump when there is no fuel in lines.
- Do not use anti-freeze agents in fuel.
- Do not reuse fuel hose clamps.
- Tighten fuel hose clamps sufficiently.

- Always use 12-volt batteries as power source.
- Do not attempt to disconnect battery cables while engine is operating.
- If a receiver-transmitter is installed, route antenna feeder cable along opposite side from EFI harness and control unit. Make sure that there is no interference while engine is idling.

- Do not disassemble control unit.

- Do not depress accelerator pedal when starting.
- Immediately after starting, do not rev up engine unnecessarily.

- Handle air flow meter carefully to avoid damage.
- There should not occur even a slight leak in air intake system.

Troubleshooting an EFI system.

willingness to trace out the EFI circuit diagram nearby. It then requires that you follow the inspection procedure table; unfortunately it is very tedious, complicated testing. Fortunately, it rarely has to be done.

We have examined in detail the mechanical fuel injection system CIS ("continuous injection system") and the Datsun Electronic Fuel Injection or EFI system. All other types are variants of these systems.

Chapter Six

Engine Details

VALVE LASH ADJUSTMENT

On Scirocco and other VW engines, valve lash adjustment requires two special tools (US 4476 and VW 546), which aren't worth buying unless you plan to keep the car for awhile, since valve lash adjustment isn't terribly expensive at the garage. You can improvise tools to force the valve spring down and fish out the disc with a screwdriver and magnet, but that's doing it the tricky way. One of the tools is a special pliers that removes the valve adjusting disc, while the other tool is a rod that pushes down on the cam followers and allows you to remove the disc for replacement.

It is best to adjust valve lash with the engine warm, the cylinder head moderately warm.

You must remove the cylinder head cover and gasket, held by eight attaching bolts. You can reuse the gasket if you don't ruin it and if there are no signs of leaks around it.

Turn the camshaft by using a wrench on the crankshaft bolt as you did in engine tuneup until the cam lobes of the cylinder you are testing both point upward. With a feeler gauge, check between the cam lobe and its follower—actually the adjusting disc on top of the follower. The first measurement should be the first cam lobe at the No. 1 cylinder, at the side nearest the belts and pulleys. This is the intake valve and should be .008 to .012-inches (0.20 to 0.30 mm).

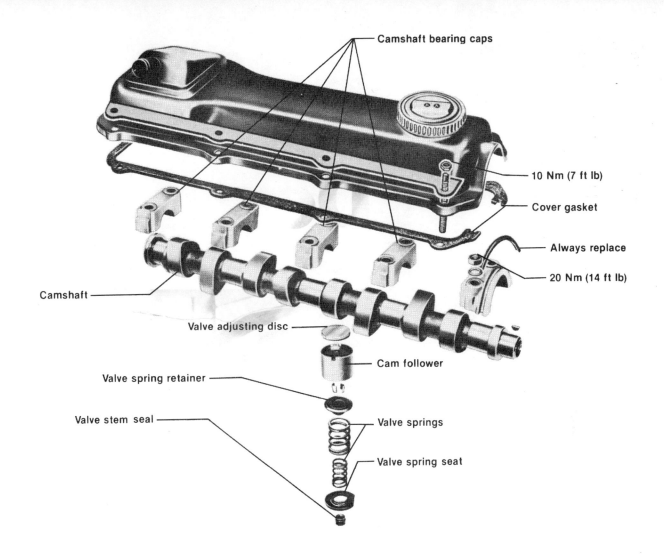

Valve rocker details showing camshaft and valve adjusting disc.

Camshaft bearing caps

10 Nm (7 ft lb)

Cover gasket

Always replace

20 Nm (14 ft lb)

Camshaft

Valve adjusting disc

Cam follower

Valve spring retainer

Valve springs

Valve stem seal

Valve spring seat

The exhaust valve next in line should be .016 to .020-inches (0.40 to 0.50 mm). If the measurement is larger than these numbers, you must remove the disc and replace it with a thicker one. If the measurement is smaller, use a thinner replacement disc.

For example, if you come up with an intake measurement of .004-inches, (0.10 mm) you will have to replace the existing disc with one that is at least .004-inches thinner, to arrive at the required

Valve adjusting disc tools on VW engine.

Using a feeler gauge to check valve clearance.

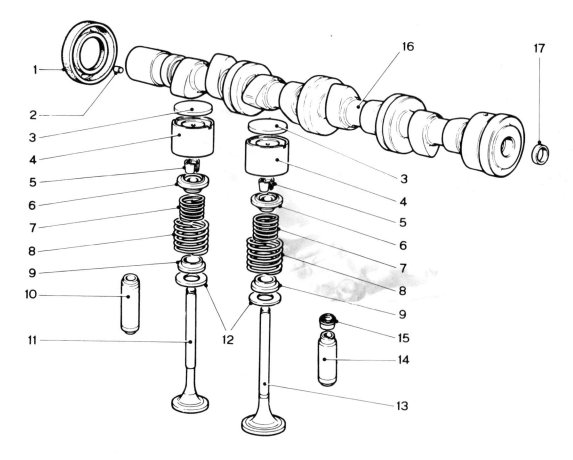

1. Seal
2. Dowel
3. Plates of adjusting valve clearance
4. Tappets
5. Locks
6. Upper cups
7. Inner spring
8. Outer springs
9. Lower cups
10. Exhaust valve guide
11. Exhaust valve
12. Flat washer
13. Intake valve
14. Intake valve guide
15. Oil seal
16. Camshaft
17. Welch plug

Valve mechanism on Fiat X 1/9.

minimum of .008-inches. The discs come in various thicknesses; the most common replacements are apt to be between 3.00 to 4.25 mm (.118 to .167-inches). To get the right thickness of the new disc, remove the old one and add its thickness to what is required (or subtract it).

An example of an exhaust measurement in which a thicker disc would be required: you measure .024-inches (0.60 mm) but you need .020-inches (0.50 mm). So you need a new disc that is .004 inches (0.10 mm) thicker. Any VW parts counter will have these discs.

To measure each valve in turn, you must have the cam lobes of each cylinder pointing up. Incidentally, you can measure a cold engine. The cold tolerances are these: Intake is .006 to .010-inches (0.15 to 0.25 mm); exhaust is .014 to .018-inches (0.35 to 0.45 mm), and disc measurements are etched on one side.

When installing, the disc markings should face down against the cam follower.

Fiat X 1/9 valve lash also has discs or "tappet plates" as it calls them which require replacement as the adjusting method. You get at them by removing the air cleaner, disconnecting the throttle rod and the hoses that are in the way, and then taking off the cover after removing the six nuts that hold it. Then turn the crankshaft until the lobe on the camshaft is pointing up at a right angle to the valve. Measure the clearance with a feeler gauge. Intake is .012-inch (0.30 mm); exhaust is .016-inch (0.40 mm). These are for cold engine. To remove the existing tappet plate and to replace it with the required size takes a special tool, as with VW and most other cars. The tool depresses the spring while it enables you to get out the adjusting plate.

Fiat 131 and Spider valve lash is intake .017 to

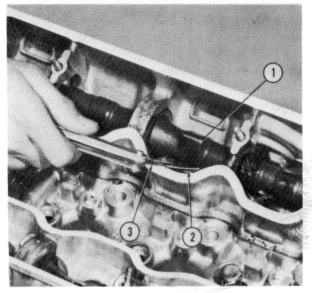

1. Camshaft lobe
2. Tappet
3. Feeler gauge

1. Tool
2. Camshaft lobe
3. Notch on tappet
4. Tappet

Fiat 131 valve lash adjustment procedures—measuring and prying the tappet down with special tool.

.019-inch (0.43 to 0.48 mm); exhaust is .019 to .021-inch (0.48 to 0.53 mm). These specs are for mid-and late-70s Fiats. Intake and exhaust valves are driven by their separate camshafts. To adjust requires a special holding tool that will enable you to pry out the tappet plate as you depress the valve spring. You can also turn the crankshaft down so as to push the tappet in, and then install a holding tool that will hold the tappet in while you turn the camshaft back up and release the tappet plate. But you need one tool or the other.

Fiat Strada valve lash is (cold engine) intake .011-inch (0.28 mm); exhaust is .015-inch (0.36 mm). Strada allows a .003-inch margin up from these specs.

Valve lash adjustment is similar to other Fiats.

If you're ever in doubt about the location of intake or exhaust valves look for the exhaust manifold ports, which attach to the exhaust valve chamber of the engine.

Citation and other G.M. cars use hydraulic lifters which require no adjustment. Chrysler Omni/Horizon engines are basically VW Rabbit engines and they follow the specifications and procedures given above.

Datsun 280ZX valve lash should be checked with engine at operating temperature. Remove the rocker arm cover and check valves 1, 3, 7, 8, 9, and 11 with the No. 1 cam lobe set to point straight upward. Intake clearance is .010-inch (0.25 mm); exhaust is .012-inch (0.30 mm). Adjustment is by rocker pivot and lock nut. Loosen the lock nut and turn the valve rocker pivot until correct lash is achieved. Tighten

the pivot lock nut to 36-43 ft lb (5.0 to 6.9 kg-m). Check clearance again. Now turn the crankshaft so that the high point of the No. 1 cam lobe points straight downward. Adjust valves 2, 4, 5, 6, 10, and 12.

Toyota Celica valves should be set with warmed engine. Remove the valve cover, and set No. 1 cylinder to TDC. Turn the crankshaft with a wrench until the timing marks are aligned, with the groove (timing mark) on the pulley at the 0 mark. Rocker arms on the No. 1 cylinder should be loose; rockers on the No. 4 should be tight. If they are not, turn the crankshaft one complete revolution with marks aligned as above.

Adjust the clearance of half the valves, as illustrated. Intake lash is .008-inch (.2 mm); exhaust lash is .012-inch (.3 mm). Loosen the lock nut with an open end wrench and turn the adjusting screw with a

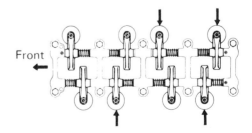

Toyota Celica valve lash adjustment begins by setting No. 1 cylinder to TDC. The first adjustment is to those valves indicated by arrows.

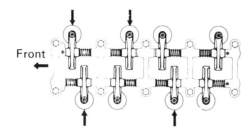

Front

Toyota Celica valve lash adjustment—second step.

Toyota valve lash adjustments using open end wrench and screwdriver.

screwdriver. The feeler gauge should pull through with a slight drag.

Now turn the crankshaft one revolution and adjust the other valves. (The timing marks should be aligned as above.)

Celica lash adjustment is about as easy as they come, and involves no special tools. Clearly the range is between Celica and Rabbit type engines—in terms of difficulty and special tools.

TIMING BELTS

Timing chains and belts wear out and sometimes break altogether. A broken timing belt is one of the catastrophe events that disable the car. Nothing will make the car run when the timing belt or chain break.

Are there warning signs? Not unless you are willing to make investigations periodically. A loose distributor pole is the sign of a timing chain that is tiring or about to break. Inability to set engine dwell correctly is another such sign. Take the distributor cap off and grasp the rotor. Turn it right and left. There should be only a minimum of movement. If movement is pronounced you should investigate further.

With cars such as VW Scirocco and its relatives—the Rabbit, and the Audi engines—it is possible to examine the belt with a minimum of component removal work. The timing belt cover comes off without major problems. Such is the case also with the Chrysler Omni/Horizon engines, which are close relatives of the VW engine family.

Such is not the case with many other engines. To get at the timing chain of the typical V-8 or V-6 engine requires removing the radiator, water pump and, in some case, the harmonic balance wheel on the crankshaft. That may require removing the engine oil pan, which is itself a major piece of excavation.

VW and Audi engine timing belts can be replaced with a minimum of disassembly. You can test them informally in many cases without removing the cover. You can reach the belt and get some sense of the amount of slackness in it by pulling on it at the opening near the valve rocker cover at the front of the engine. It should not be loose. If it is, you need to remove the timing belt cover. You have to remove the carburetor air cleaner and ducts, probably also the V-belt down below, the water pump pulley, and any electrical cables that get in the way—only you push them out of the way and tie them up, if necessary, but don't disconnect them. To get the old belt off, loosen the tension adjuster and turn it counterclockwise. Work the belt off the sprockets.

To replace the belt, turn the camshaft sprocket (the one on top) until the center mark is in line with mounting flange of the cylinder head cover. Then turn the crankshaft pulley and the intermediate shaft sprocket until marks on each wheel line up with each other—the v-notch on the pulley and the centerpunch mark on the sprocket. Start the new belt at the bottom and work up with care, so that there is no

VW timing belt adjustment point.

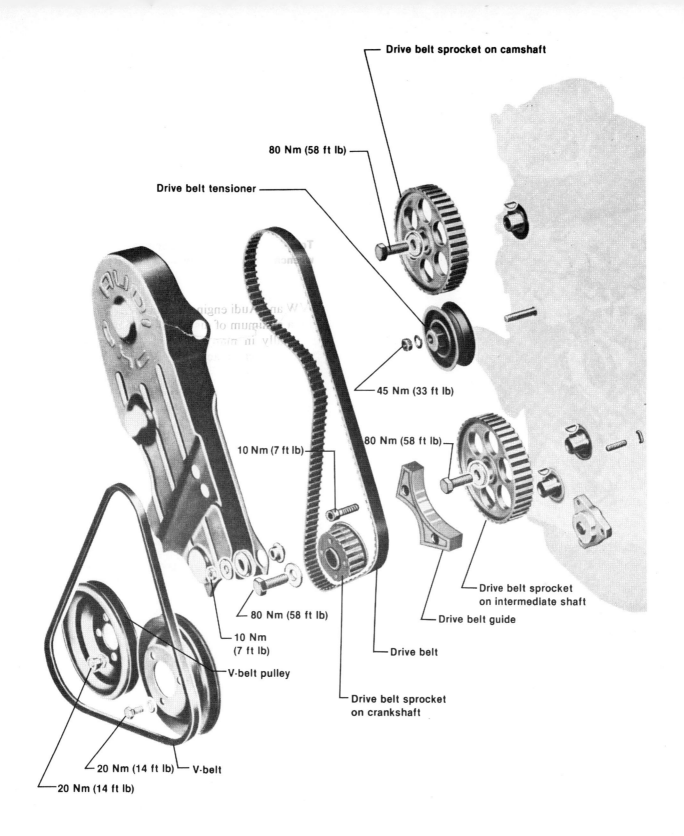

Drive belt sprocket on camshaft

80 Nm (58 ft lb)

Drive belt tensioner

45 Nm (33 ft lb)

10 Nm (7 ft lb)

80 Nm (58 ft lb)

Drive belt sprocket
on intermediate shaft

Drive belt guide

80 Nm (58 ft lb)

10 Nm
(7 ft lb)

V-belt pulley

Drive belt

Drive belt sprocket
on crankshaft

20 Nm (14 ft lb)   V-belt

20 Nm (14 ft lb)

VW timing belt, pulleys, and other components of the system.

slack between crankshaft pulley and intermediate sprocket, or between intermediate shaft and camshaft sprockets. Any slack should occur at the tension adjusting wheel, where you remove it by turning

the wheel. The locknut on the tension adjuster should be very tight (33 ft lb).

You can test the timing belt for tension either by twisting it, as noted above, or by pushing it in. It

Alignment of the drive belt sprocket on the crankshaft with the intermediate shaft mark, on VW and Audi engines.

Adjusting tension on the timing belt of VW engines.

shouldn't push more than about a half-inch. Specifically, it should be between 3/8 to 9/16-inch (10 to 15 mm).

The Chrysler version of this engine is more or less identical in respect to the timing belt change. Chrysler notes that if you hear a whirring noise from the timing belt when the engine is running, you have made the belt too tight. "It will have less than normal life" notes Chrysler with fine understatement.

Fiat X 1/9 timing belt replacement, though similar to VW engines, has its own ways of getting there.

You have to set the engine on top dead center, firing on No. 4 cylinder (meaning, that cylinder has to be up). See that the pulley timing mark on the crankshaft is aligned with the support finger visible

Testing tension on the drive (timing) belt of VW engines.

through a hole in the pulley cover. Put the car in 4th gear; apply the hand brake.

Remove timing cover bolts, the right engine guard from below the engine, the lower bolt holding the cover, and remove the cover. Remove the alternator belt; remove the water pump drive pulley from the crankshaft.

Remove bolts through the rear of the air pump and support brackets. Loosen the top bolt of the air pump and remove the belt.

Next, remove the camshaft cover and see that cam lobes of the No. 4 cylinder point up. Mark and remove the distributor. Loosen the idler pulley lock nut. Push in on the support and tighten the lock nut. Remove the old belt, starting at the idler pulley.

To install the new belt, start at the crankshaft pulley and twist it carefully to get it around the crankshaft pulley. Avoid kinking it. Also, keep slack out of it. Slip the new belt over the camshaft pulley—you may have to turn the camshaft pulley slightly to align its slots with cogs in the belt. Next coax the belt over the idler pulley. If you can't get that step to work, start over and see where you lost a cog or two. The trick is in having no slack. Don't pry the belt!

Release the idler pulley lock nut, then tighten it after tension is on the belt. Release the hand brake and push the car forward while in gear one-half turn of the belt. Release the idler pulley lock nut and see whether all slack is removed. Now again tighten the lock nut. Continue to push the car forward until the No. 4 cylinder is again on firing stroke, with the cam lobes up. Do not push the car backward in gear or allow the engine to rock backward while you're pushing the car. Slack will develop in the belt, causing the belt to jump timing.

Put the belt cover back. Get the crankshaft timing mark on top dead center with the camshaft mark exactly on the pointer. Tighten tension pulley to 32.5

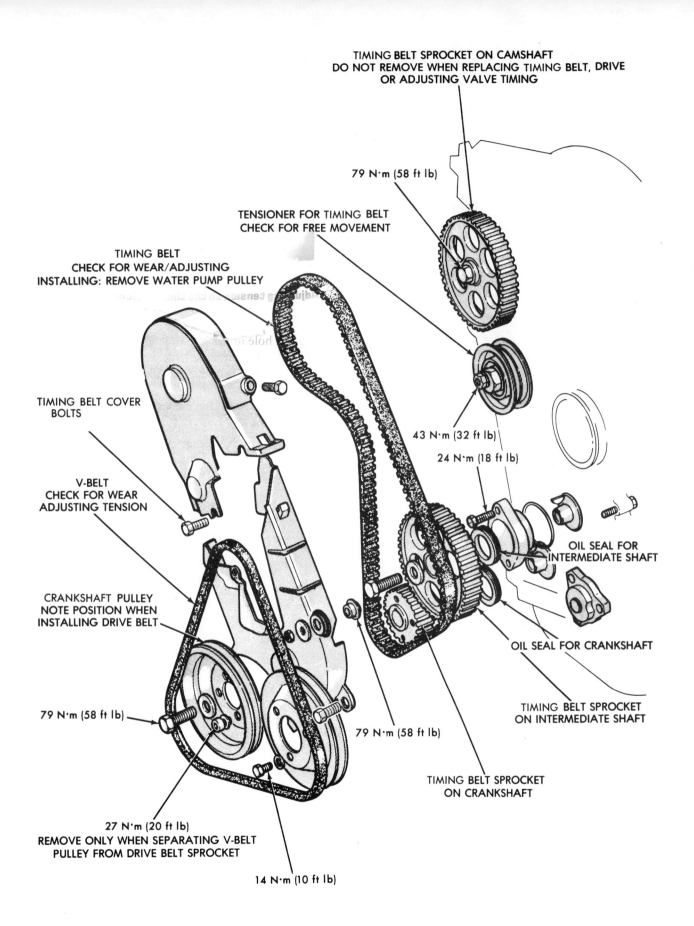

TIMING BELT SPROCKET ON CAMSHAFT
DO NOT REMOVE WHEN REPLACING TIMING BELT, DRIVE
OR ADJUSTING VALVE TIMING

79 N·m (58 ft lb)

TENSIONER FOR TIMING BELT
CHECK FOR FREE MOVEMENT

TIMING BELT
CHECK FOR WEAR/ADJUSTING
INSTALLING: REMOVE WATER PUMP PULLEY

TIMING BELT COVER
BOLTS

V-BELT
CHECK FOR WEAR
ADJUSTING TENSION

CRANKSHAFT PULLEY
NOTE POSITION WHEN
INSTALLING DRIVE BELT

79 N·m (58 ft lb)

43 N·m (32 ft lb)

24 N·m (18 ft lb)

OIL SEAL FOR
INTERMEDIATE SHAFT

OIL SEAL FOR CRANKSHAFT

TIMING BELT SPROCKET
ON INTERMEDIATE SHAFT

79 N·m (58 ft lb)

TIMING BELT SPROCKET
ON CRANKSHAFT

27 N·m (20 ft lb)
REMOVE ONLY WHEN SEPARATING V-BELT
PULLEY FROM DRIVE BELT SPROCKET

14 N·m (10 ft lb)

Chrysler timing gears, belt and other components of Omni/Horizon.

Fiat X 1/9 timing belt replacement requires eight procedure points as illustrated—1. timing cover, 2. drive pulley, 3. drive belt, 4. alternator, 5. bolt, 6. adjusting bracket, 7. brackets, and 8. air pump.

Fiat X 1/9 timing belt replacement involves 1. camshaft pulley, 2. belt, 3. lock nut, and 4. idler pulley.

Fiat X 1/9—further details of timing belt change involve 1. lock nut, 2. idler pulley, 3. timing belt.

ft lbs. Install pulley on crankshaft, drive belt on air pump, water pump and alternator belts, and adjust belt tension. Put back the timing gear cover, and everything else you took off. Put the distributor back—it should point to the No. 4 cylinder.

To replace timing chains on other types of engines is not recommended, since it often involves major engine disassembly, including cylinder heads, balance wheels and many other components. Such engines as Toyota Celica, Corvette, or even the G.M. X-body engines fall into the difficult category. Major engine work is involved. The Fiat represents the outer limit of complexity for the amateur mechanic.

Replacing gaskets on oil pans is possible, but in most cases it involves more surgery than you might expect. For one thing, it often involves raising the engine, and that requires unbolting the engine mounts. You can do it provided that you have the right supports for the raised engine—jack stands for

both sides. Usually you don't have to raise the engine very far, but it's still a big job. The automatic transmission pan is much simpler since in many cases it is regularly indicated maintenance. Drain the oil and remove the filler tube and the attaching bolts. It comes right off. Sometimes it's messy to drain the oil.

WATER PUMPS

Water pumps are supposed to last the life of the car, but like fuel pumps they don't always read the script that says so.

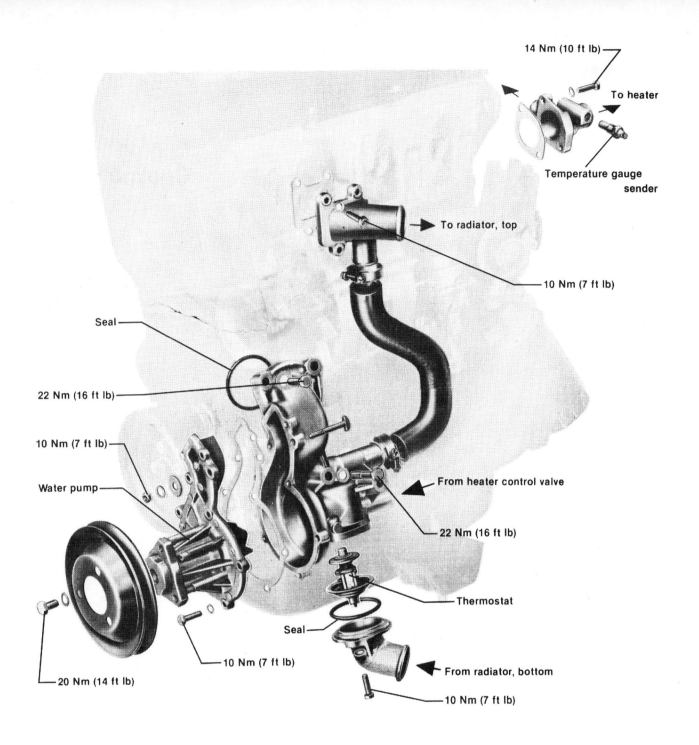

14 Nm (10 ft lb)

To heater

Temperature gauge
sender

To radiator, top

10 Nm (7 ft lb)

Seal

22 Nm (16 ft lb)

10 Nm (7 ft lb)

Water pump

From heater control valve

22 Nm (16 ft lb)

Thermostat

Seal

10 Nm (7 ft lb)

From radiator, bottom

20 Nm (14 ft lb)

10 Nm (7 ft lb)

VW cooling system in isolation showing water pump and other components. The system is very similar to Omni/Horizon, though details differ.

Water pumps are usually not difficult to replace, but you do have to drain the cooling system. When do they need replacement? When they leak. Water pumps are simple souls, having only rudimentary skills. They push water along through the engine. When they fail it is usually from simple wear—the bushing and bearing wear out and cause a leak. That ruins the pump. Sometimes the impeller in the pump

gets loose and doesn't move coolant along. Engine overheating is the result. That's rare; engine overheating is usually caused by other malfunctions

As an example of a standard water pump replacement, the procedures involved in the Chrysler Omni/Horizon cars, are given as follows. Drain the cooling system by placing a pan under the radiator and opening the valve down at the bottom. Remove

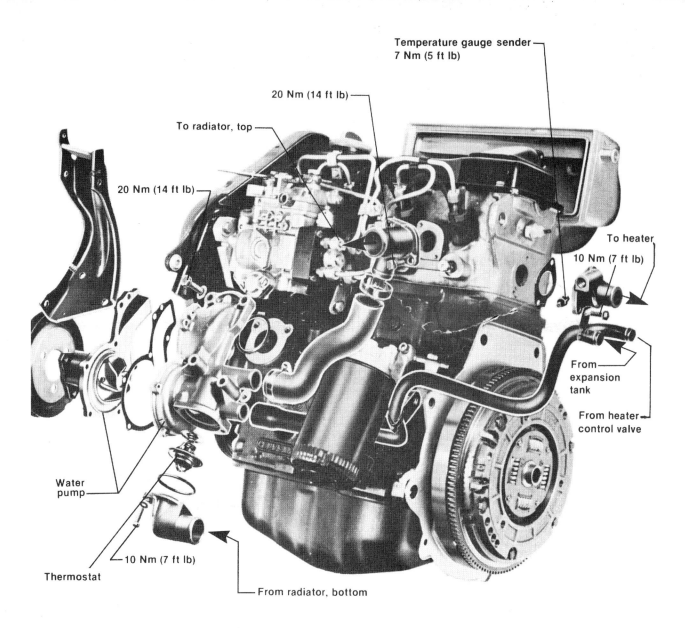

**Temperature gauge sender
7 Nm (5 ft lb)**

20 Nm (14 ft lb)

To radiator, top

20 Nm (14 ft lb)

To heater

10 Nm (7 ft lb)

From
expansion
tank

From heater
control valve

Water
pump

10 Nm (7 ft lb)

Thermostat

From radiator, bottom

VW cooling system (and Omni/Horizon—though details are different) in relation to the engine.

the upper radiator hose. If the car has air conditioning it will be necessary to remove the compressor from its engine brackets and put it to one side, without discharging the system. Remove the alternator altogether. Remove the water pump pulley. If the car has a diverter valve, disconnect the diverter valve hose at the diverter valve, remove the rear air pump bracket and the front air pump bracket. Now remove the alternator bracket that is attached to the water pump. Remove the water pump by disconnecting the lower radiator hose, the bypass hose, and unbolting the timing belt cover bolt and two top water pump bolts.

The Omni/Horizon water pump involves perhaps an extreme of unrelated component removal. Many cars require the removal of the water pump itself, only. However, these are the extremes.

To install the Omni/Horizon pump, apply a gasket sealer (Chrysler recommends RTV, a "room temperature vulcanizer") to the housing gasket groove. Allow the sealer to set before running the engine. Finger-tighten the bolts, then tighten them in an opposing sequence, securely but not excessively. When you took the bolts off you must have noticed that they were not terribly tight. Use just a slight, tightening turn. You deal with soft metal.

Datsun water pumps, of aluminum casting, have a thermostat-controlled fan coupling in front. If the pump develops a squeak, try using a water pump seal lubricant on it, before condemning it. Rust and corrosion eventually ruin water pumps, even those of aluminum. You look for excessive end play (push up and down on the coupling, push in on it, and listen for bearing noise), as well as leaks. If you can push the

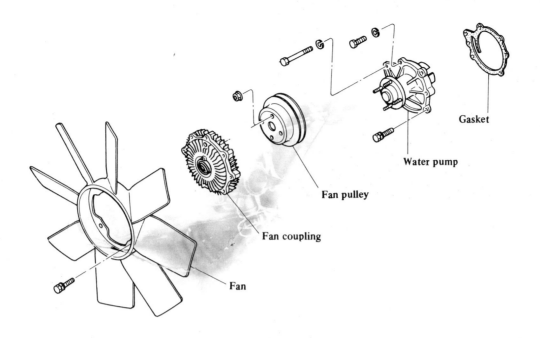

Datsun water pump and related components.

impeller around, the bushing is defective. Impeller failure—the inability to force water along—is rare, but it can happen. That would cause quick engine overheating.

There is no repair for a defective Datsun pump—you replace it. Replacement of Datsun pumps is easy in that you don't have to take off too many unrelated components to get at it. You do, of course, have to drain the cooling system in the usual way.

Open the drain valve at the bottom of the radiator and drain the coolant into a pan. Remove the radiator

shroud, then loosen the fan belt. Loosen the alternator bolts and move it toward the engine. Now remove the fan, fan coupling and fan pulley (as an assembly). Unbolt the water pump, noting the slight tightness involved. Clean off gasket surfaces before putting the new pump on. Examine the fan coupling for oil leaks or any other defect—a bent bi-metal thermostat, for example.

Use gasket cement sparingly, on both metal and gasket surfaces. Hose connections should be cemented; don't over-tighten them.

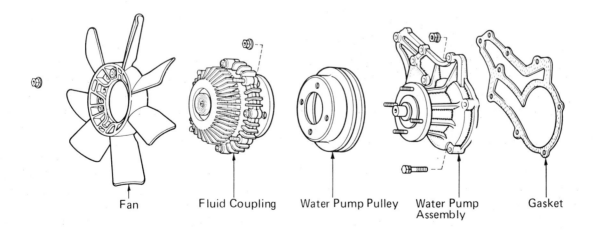

Toyota Celica water pump, fan, fluid coupling and other details.

The Datsun pump, behind the radiator, and the VW or Omni pumps, alongside the transversely mounted front drive engine, are the two basic types of pump you encounter nowadays. Obviously, the buried transversely mounted pump involves more disassembly, but that's progress. It never came serenely.

Cooling system maintenance and repair also involves other components.

RADIATORS

Radiators, if coddled with yearly flushing and anti-rust chemicals, can last quite a few years—say five or six. Mostly they develop leaks and holes in three or four, because of the soft metals in them and the corrosive nature of the coolant.

Cooling systems are pressurized, (Subaru is an exception), and somewhat fragile on that and other accounts. You know never to open a hot radiator cap—it can blow scalding coolant all over. You also know that radiator caps aren't easy to open (you push down on them, forcefully with one hand, turning counterclockwise with the other).

The only service you can perform on a radiator is to replace the hoses when they need it, and to take the radiator off and get it "rodded out" and repaired when it needs that. It needs that when it leaks. Leaks show up as steam under pressure, or as green, coolant discolorations. They always show up as coolant loss. Some loss is normal because of condensation. But you shouldn't have to add much anti-freeze or water between changes. You should change the anti-freeze each year or two. You can avoid that by adding anti-rust chemicals each year so long as anti-freeze levels test out acceptably. The glycol

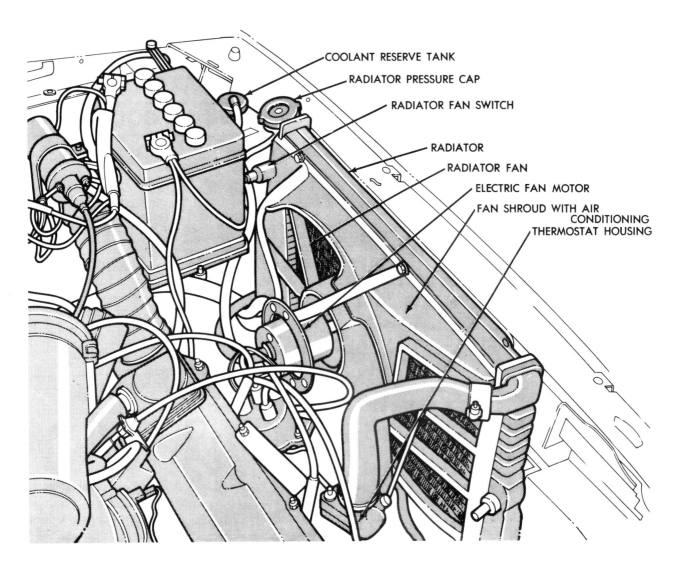

COOLANT RESERVE TANK
RADIATOR PRESSURE CAP
RADIATOR FAN SWITCH
RADIATOR
RADIATOR FAN
ELECTRIC FAN MOTOR
FAN SHROUD WITH AIR
CONDITIONING
THERMOSTAT HOUSING

The cooling system showing the radiator and supporting components of the Omni/Horizon—a typical front-drive system.

140

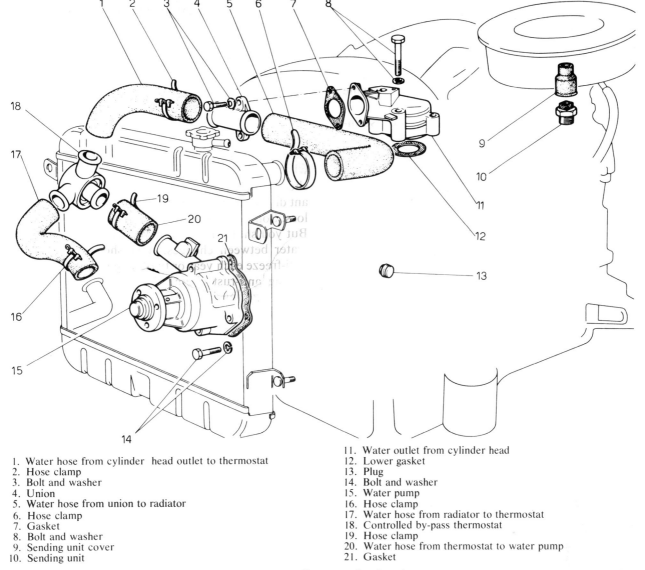

1. Water hose from cylinder head outlet to thermostat
2. Hose clamp
3. Bolt and washer
4. Union
5. Water hose from union to radiator
6. Hose clamp
7. Gasket
8. Bolt and washer
9. Sending unit cover
10. Sending unit
11. Water outlet from cylinder head
12. Lower gasket
13. Plug
14. Bolt and washer
15. Water pump
16. Hose clamp
17. Water hose from radiator to thermostat
18. Controlled by-pass thermostat
19. Hose clamp
20. Water hose from thermostat to water pump
21. Gasket

Fiat 131 water pump, radiator, and related components.

base of the anti-freeze never loses its capacity for protecting against freeze, but the anti-freeze does lose its rust protection abilities. Restore those and you are safe.

When the radiator appears to be losing coolant, examine the rest of the cooling system first before taking the radiator off. Look first at the water pump —at the bottom of it and at its hose connections.

Then examine all the hoses and their connections, especially at the heater. The drain cock or valve at the bottom of the radiator can leak. The upper hose and its terminus at the thermostat can leak. The thermostat in its engine housing can leak at its gasket.

If the thermostat gasket leaks, you don't have to drain the entire engine to replace it, only the coolant amount that is level or below the location of the thermostat. When replacing a thermostat gasket, try the bolts for resistance. If they don't want to come

off easily, as they should, use penetrating oil on them, and tap them with a hammer and drift, or whatever will do the job. Don't use excessive force. When you take off the thermostat housing, notice that the thermostat fits in one way. If you get it back in the wrong direction, it won't work. Thermostats themselves may need replacement, every two or three years. They freeze in open position, and you get little heat, even though there seems to be nothing else wrong.

Thermostats may be found in unlikely places. In Scirocco and other VW cars the thermostat is mounted in the water pump. It can be serviced separately there. The thermostat is mounted on one side of the housing of the pump and actually has nothing to do with the pump. It's just there. To get at it, you have to remove the belt from the alternator. You have to drain the entire radiator and engine when removing the VW (and the Omni/Horizon) thermo-

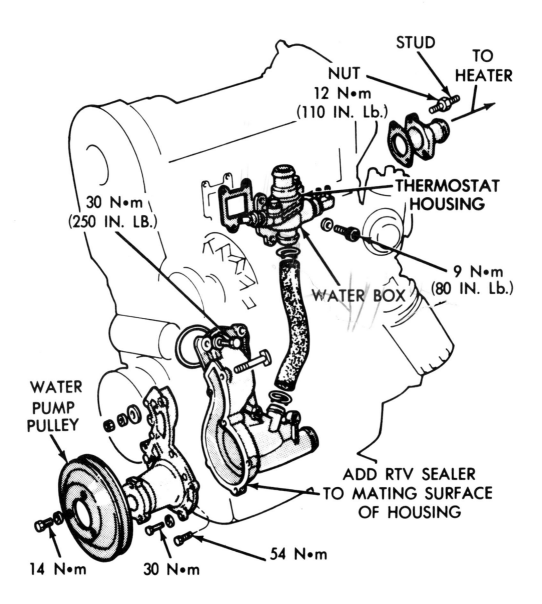

STUD

TO
HEATER

NUT
12 N•m
(110 IN. Lb.)

THERMOSTAT
HOUSING

30 N•m
(250 IN. LB.)

9 N•m
(80 IN. Lb.)

WATER BOX

WATER
PUMP
PULLEY

ADD RTV SEALER
TO MATING SURFACE
OF HOUSING

14 N•m   30 N•m   54 N•m

Thermostat and other details of Omni/Horizon cooling system.

stat and/or water pump. You may also find that you have to remove the pulley on the water pump shaft in order to gain easier access to the thermostat housing side of the pump. It comes off with three loosened bolts.

Nowadays you may find water hoses going to such odd places as carburetor chokes or exhaust or intake manifolds. So you have to look at the connection for leaks. If you find no leaks at these and the more familiar hose outlets—at the heater, especially—you must admit that the radiator has to come off for repairs (or replacement). To get the radiator off, drain it and remove the shroud. On cars with electric fans, radiator removal also entails fan removal, usually. Disconnect the fan electric harness, first. Then disconnect the fan. The oil cooler lines for automatic transmission will also have to be removed, from the bottom.

It is important that you take the radiator to a place you can trust not to abuse it in the test. If they use more than 15 pounds of pressure on the radiator it will be ruined. How you find out about the character of the radiator repairman is beyond the scope of this book.

EXHAUST SYSTEMS

Mufflers

Exhaust systems are not likely candidates for immortality. Made of thin steel when new, they deteriorate quickly under the constant devastation of expelled engine gases. Mufflers can be expected to

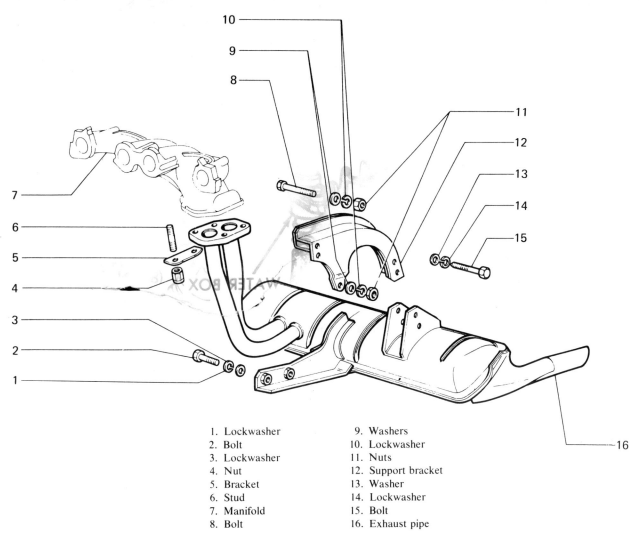

1. Lockwasher
2. Bolt
3. Lockwasher
4. Nut
5. Bracket
6. Stud
7. Manifold
8. Bolt
9. Washers
10. Lockwasher
11. Nuts
12. Support bracket
13. Washer
14. Lockwasher
15. Bolt
16. Exhaust pipe

Fiat's X 1/9 exhaust pipe and related parts.

need replacement at any point after two years, and along with them will go tailpipes and connecting pipes of various types. Crossover pipes from the engine, or exhaust pipes, also from the engine, have somewhat longer life expectancies, but all will require replacement at a time in the car's life when it seems to be in the pink. Is it worth the bother to replace mufflers and other components when Midas and others beckon? It isn't easy to do muffler and other exhaust work. You save about half if you do it yourself, more if you know how to buy components. But it is hard work, or can be.

The catalytic converter is also part of exhaust system work. Designed for the life of the car, it remains a political football and a mechanical mystery. How long does it last? It varies. What happens when it doesn't last? Usually nothing—emission levels may rise, but who knows that? Only a gas gauge and only if it is applied. Local laws may require exhaust testing, but mostly they don't. So the catalytic converter is one of those imponderables.

We don't know what to do with it, though plenty of them have been taken off, their insides discarded and the shell put back, to resume their role in appearance, if nothing more.

In U.S. cars the catalytic converter is often accompanied by other components. The Omni/ Horizon, for example, has the converter and a special California mini-converter that is an added oxidation catalyst. There are also the usual pipes, muffler, and the various couplings, including a special ball joint coupling in Omni/Horizon. There are plenty of other unusual exhaust devices.

Mufflers and pipes need replacement when holes burn through their exteriors and cause hissing, booming and other strange noises. Noisy exhaust warnings should always be heeded because they signify the escape of deadly gases. With windows closed, they can escape into the passenger compartment.

Whenever you hear such noises, track them down. The way you do that is to turn on the engine when it is

143

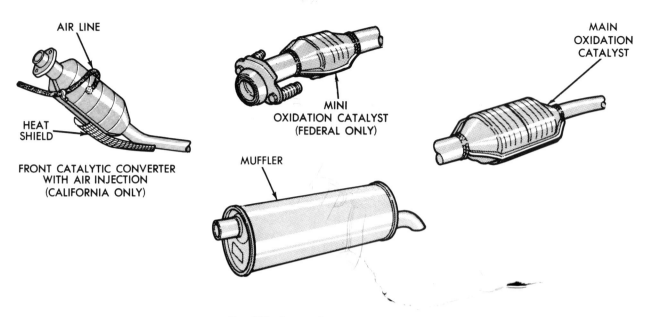

AIR LINE

HEAT SHIELD

FRONT CATALYTIC CONVERTER
WITH AIR INJECTION
(CALIFORNIA ONLY)

MINI
OXIDATION CATALYST
(FEDERAL ONLY)

MAIN
OXIDATION
CATALYST

MUFFLER

Omni/Horizon exhaust components.

cold, and listen for the escaping gases—their noise. Put your hand over the area and pinpoint it. That will identify the defective component. (The hand test is the reason a cold engine is specified; hot pipes will burn your hand disastrously.) You then assess what you need. If the defective component is the muffler, examine the pipes in and out of it carefully. If they are pitted, or with holes, or they appear to be close to death's door, don't economize; replace them. Every component attached to something you have to replace must be in extraordinarily good condition to escape also being replaced. That is because their cost isn't great, but the labor involved in replacing them separately, later on, is enormous.

Sometimes joints in exhaust pipes leak only because they aren't tight enough. Admittedly that's a remote chance. Still, don't overlook the possibility that tightening the joints will save a replacement job.

Mufflers and tailpipes are easy to replace. You jack up the car on the muffler side with the usual jacks, jack stands or your favorite support. Spray penetrating oil on all the clamp bolts. Spray the inlet and/or outlet muffler pipe joint itself if the pipes leading in and out of it are to be saved. Allow the oil to soak in for an hour or so, then tap on the sprayed areas with a hammer. The point of the hammer is to try to loosen the joints. Remove the clamps, but before you remove the hanger straps and clamps put a support under the muffler. That will make things easier.

Usually the muffler and tailpipe will be replaced and in many cases they come as a unit. But the forward joint can be difficult, and if that pipe is to be saved you need to use some diplomacy with it. First, remove the clamp, and don't worry if the clamps

break off—you'll be replacing them. Next, pound on the joint, if it refuses to loosen, but not so much that you knock it out of shape. If the joint doesn't loosen you'll have to use stronger methods. First try to hammer a screwdriver or something with a sharp edge into the recalcitrant joint. Don't use a thick punch. Drive it into the joint all around it, then try to work the joint loose. If that doesn't work, use an electric drill with a sanding stone on the end ot it, or use a hacksaw and cut into the muffler side, but don't

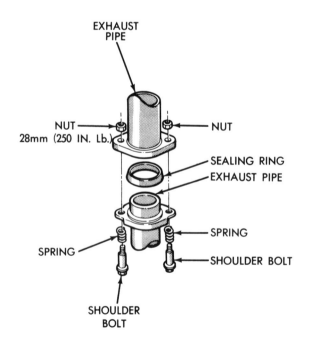

EXHAUST
PIPE

NUT
28mm (250 IN. Lb.)

NUT

SEALING RING
EXHAUST PIPE

SPRING

SPRING

SHOULDER BOLT

SHOULDER
BOLT

Special ball joint connector in Omni/Horizon exhaust pipe.

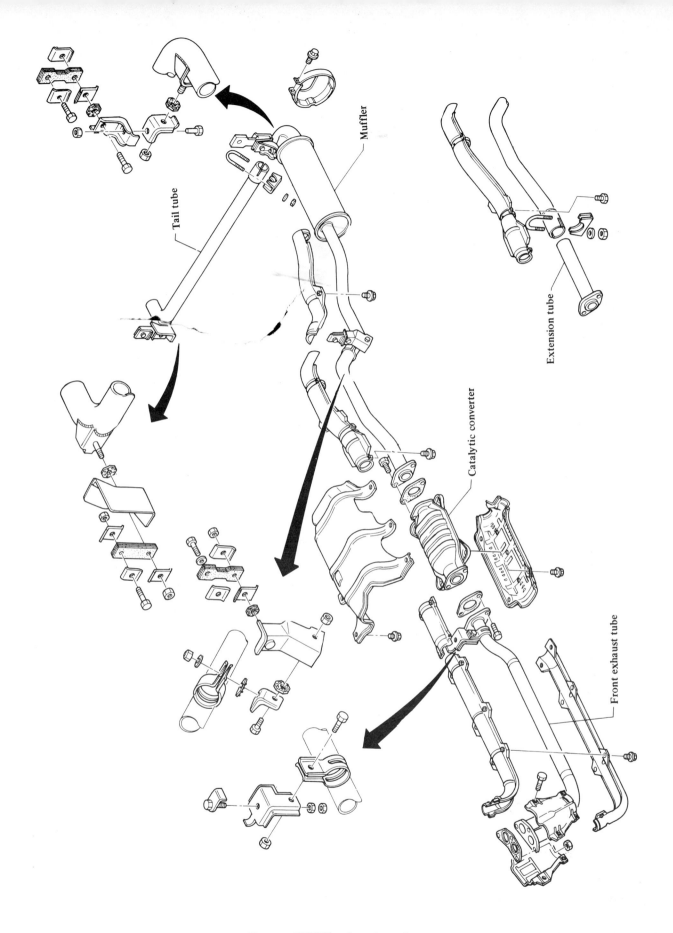

Tail tube

Muffler

Extension tube

Catalytic converter

Front exhaust tube

Datsun 280ZX exhaust system.

145

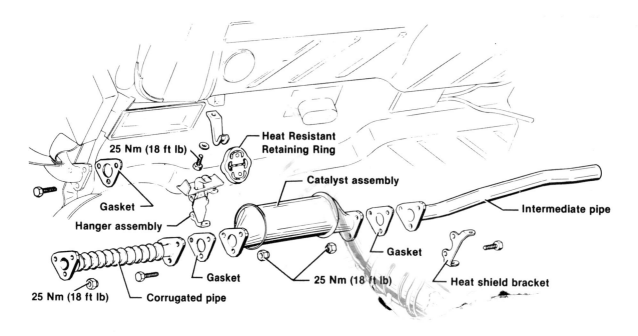

VW exhaust components including catalytic converter.

cut into the pipe connection you want to save. These joints are rust-welded, hence the problem. But they all come out, sooner or later, with prodding.

The only difficult exhaust replacements are up front, coming out of the engine. Exhaust pipes from the exhaust manifold usually cause trouble because they bolt into clamps or joints that resist easy opening, or can break off and require difficult extraction.

Any exhaust pipe at the engine that leaks and requires replacement must be doused in penetrating oil for several hours, then pounded in an effort to loosen the bolts, clamps, and joints.

Working space will be extremely cramped at the engine; getting the old pipes out, the new ones in, can be extremely difficult. So, you may wish to consider letting the professionals replace such defective

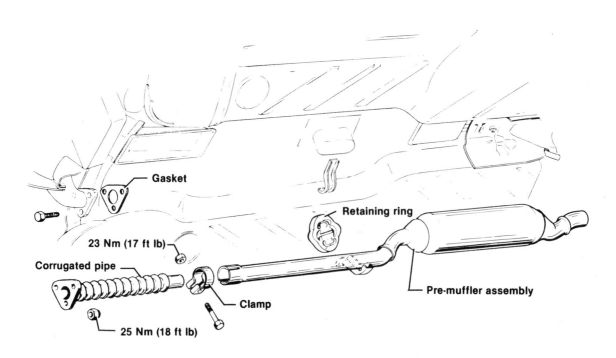

VW exhaust system without catalytic converter.

146

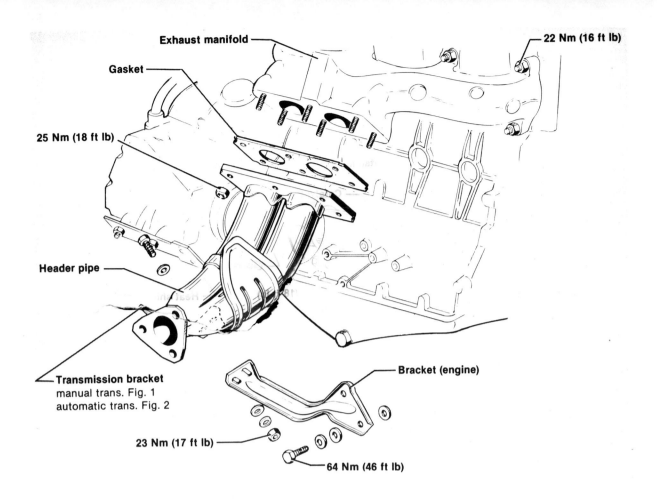

Exhaust manifold

Gasket

22 Nm (16 ft lb)

25 Nm (18 ft lb)

Header pipe

Transmission bracket
manual trans. Fig. 1
automatic trans. Fig. 2

Bracket (engine)

23 Nm (17 ft lb)

64 Nm (46 ft lb)

Front assembly components on VW engine exhaust system.

pipes. But you can do all the others, and if you are willing, you can also do the pipes from the exhaust manifold to the catalytic converter.

If the exhaust system is several years old and the muffler goes bad, it is likely that you will have to replace the entire system (excepting the catalytic converter) sooner or later. If that is the case, you will save much labor by doing everything at once. Savings, in such a case, will be at least half the cost at a garage. They don't over-charge; there's a lot of labor involved.

When you replace the entire system you don't have to worry about saving any components, except the catalytic converter, and it is always tougher than anything around it. So, you have only to remove and save the joints at the engine and the converter, and the hanging clamps at the muffler, if they're still good. The only problem with replacing an entire exhaust system is the lifting of the car. The way you solve the problem is to lift it at the front, first, to get the exhaust pipes off the engine. Once these are released, the same lift will enable you to open the pipe at the catalytic converter. Then jack up and support the car at the side and/or rear, sturdily.

Loosen everything else.

When installing the new parts, start at the front and move back. You will discover that the catalytic converter can make problems. So begin with it and work the new parts forward to the engine couplings.

Exhaust couplings cause trouble because the high temperatures ruin the bolts, even though these bolts are designed to withstand such extremes. That is why soaking them in penetrating oil is important. If, heaven forbid, you should break one of the bolts off at the exhaust pipe flange in the engine, you will have to drill it out. It is not a job to be envied. You start with a small drill into the center of the bolt, and move up to a larger one. Sometimes you can extract the broken bolt or stud simply by using penetrating oil on it, tapping it on the end, then grasping the exposed end (once the clamp and pipe are removed) and turning it out with a vise pliers. If you can't get it to loosen that way, you'll have to use the drill on it. Once you drill out the center, a bolt extracting tool will get the remains out. Sometimes it will be loose enough to turn out with a screwdriver, if you pound a notch into it. Generally this kind of problem won't arise.

Cylinder Head Side

Clean Hose

Intake Manifold Side

The PCV valve can be checked by removing it, blowing on the large diameter side and noting that air passes through easily; then blowing on smaller diameter, and noting that air passes through with difficulty. It must pass both tests, otherwise replace it.

EMISSION CONTROLS

Engine work may include emission control devices. While many of the controls that arose in the 70s have been eliminated by the catalytic converter, many others remain. To test most of these devices requires a vacuum gauge and sometimes a vacuum pump. These are not terribly expensive tools, but without them you can't get very far in testing, though as you'll see you can test some things without them.

One of the earliest devices is the PCV valve, which you find on virtually all cars. You may have to

hunt for it. It's a small, cylindrical valve somewhere on or near the rocker panel, in a hose going to the carburetor, usually. It should be pulled out and checked every 12,000 miles, as we've noted already. You shake it; it rattles if it's good. If not, replace it.

The charcoal canister filter, located usually at the front of the engine, needs a new filter every 12,000 miles or according to individual specifications for the car involved. It too is an easily changed item, though not nearly as easy as the PCV valve. Some

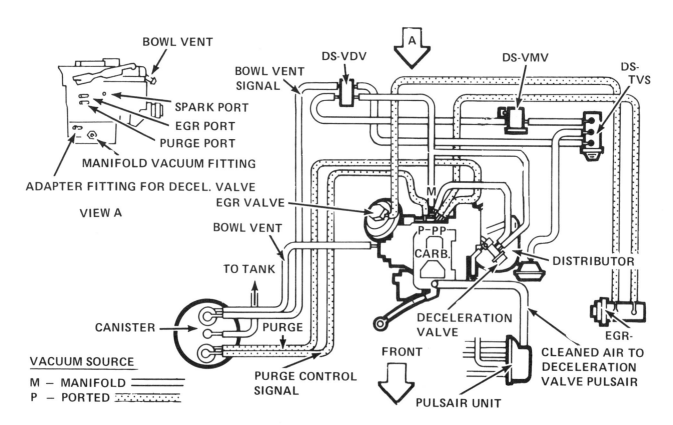

Citation 2.5 Litre L4 engine canister and other emission control related components.

1. Nut   5. Mounting
2. Bracket   6. Shield
3. Drive belt   7. Air pump
4. Bolt

Fiat Air pump and components.

belts even less so. They are checked for pump pressure and noises. The noise takes no gauge, but pressure takes a special pressure gauge. It doesn't mean you should rush out and buy one. If the pump isn't noisy and you're worried about its pressure, take off the outlet hose and feel it. A strong blast of air should remove some of the pressure from your anxiety.

Toyota Celica (and other Toyotas) have the usual emission systems, refined and complicated to meet Japanese anxieties and the EPA. The EGR system uses a vacuum modulator with a filter that requires periodic inspection and cleaning—or replacement if it is damaged or cannot be cleaned. You can check the EGR valve by taking the hose off the valve and attaching it to the gauge. The engine should idle properly. At 2,000 rpm the gauge should read zero, with coolant temperature below 86 degrees F (30 C). Any departures from these numbers indicates problems in the system. Remove the EGR valve and look for a sticking valve and heavy carbon deposits. Unless the valve moves freely, replace the device. If it appears to be moving properly, clean it out and put it back.

The vacuum modulator of the EGR system is on top of the engine at the rear, atop the EGR valve. It

cars have AIR pumps which are driven by belt off the crankshaft. These pumps are not immortal, their

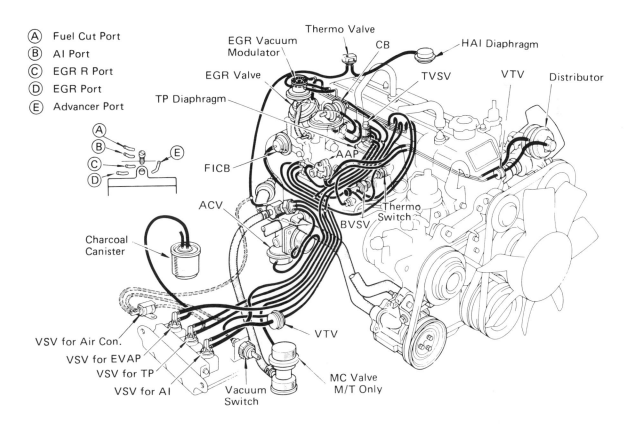

(A) Fuel Cut Port
(B) AI Port
(C) EGR R Port
(D) EGR Port
(E) Advancer Port

Toyota Celica's emission control system spans a complex relationship of components involving every engine system.

149

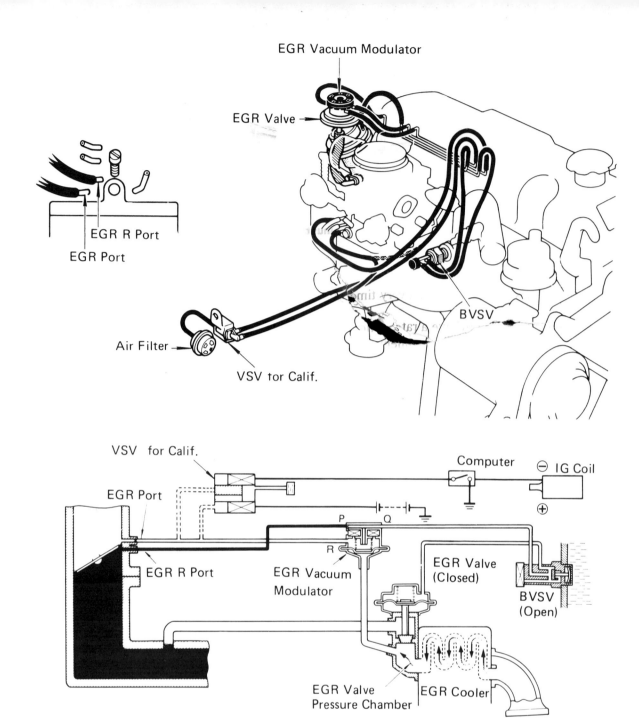

EGR Vacuum Modulator

EGR Valve

EGR R Port

EGR Port

Air Filter

VSV for Calif.

BVSV

VSV for Calif.

EGR Port

Computer

IG Coil

P Q

R

EGR R Port

EGR Vacuum Modulator

EGR Valve (Closed)

BVSV (Open)

EGR Valve Pressure Chamber

EGR Cooler

Toyota Celica's EGR system showing the vacuum modulator above the EGR valve.

should be taken apart periodically to check its filter for dirt. The filter can be cleaned out.

The vacuum modulator can also be checked by disconnecting the hoses from its ports, plugging the two closest to each other with a finger and blowing air into the other one. Air should pass through to the air filter side. Then, start the engine and let it idle rapidly. Do the same test and feel for strong resistance to air flow.

A bi-metal vacuum switching valve (BVSV), on the side of the engine, with two pipes and an air filter, can be checked with engine temperature below 86 degrees F (30 C). Blow into the pipe nearest the engine and air should come out of the filter. Warm up the engine, repeat the test and the air should come out of the other pipe.

Air injection systems on Toyota Celica and other Toyotas begin with the air pump. Visual checks of

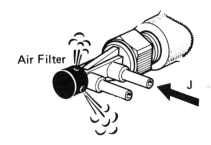

Air Filter

To check the bi-metal vacuum switching valve you must blow into the valve when the engine is cold and then warmed.

the belt and hoses should be made every time you tune the engine.

The pump is supposed to have a rated flow that requires a tester for accurate assessment of its capacity. If you suspect that the pump is not producing enough air pressure, you can disconnect the outlet hose and feel the pressure. If it seems to be pushing a lot of air, it probably doesn't need work or replacement. But the air injection system has an air by-pass valve, a check valve, the vacuum switching valve, a vacuum transmitting valve, a mixture valve (on manual transmissions), and other paraphernalia. So, in troubleshooting any air injection system, once past the air pump and its belt and hoses and the superficial examination (above), you are faced with a battery of valves. Most of these valves operate by air or electrical pressure or both. For example, to test the vacuum switching valve (VSV), connect its

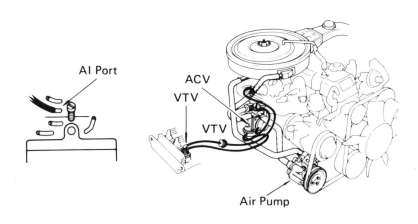

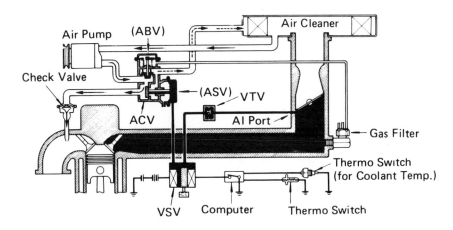

Diagrammatic view of the Celica air injection system showing components and connections.

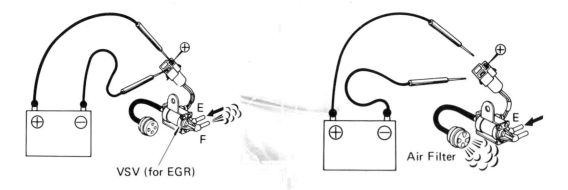

Testing the vacuum switching valve (VSV) is done by blowing through its pipes with the valve connected to the battery.

electrical terminals to the battery. Then blow into pipe E (as shown) and feel pipe F, where air should emerge. Disconnect the battery; now blow into pipe E and the air should come out of the air filter. If it doesn't work that way, you have to replace the valve. But you also need an ohmmeter to make sure that there is no continuity between the positive terminal of the valve and the valve body. If there is, the valve is shorted. Finally, you have to check for an open circuit, by putting an ohmmeter between the two terminals of the valve. It's a lot of testing for one valve, especially as the system has so many others. But it's the only way to go if the pump seems to be functioning but the system is causing trouble, either because it isn't passing emission tests or is causing poor engine performance, both at idle and acceleration. Pumps cost far more than valves.

(It goes without saying that you always check ignition, first.) It also goes without saying that California cars have more control equipment on them. For example, California cars have an outer vent control valve, not present on other cars, that must be open when ignition is off, closed when on, with hoses disconnected. It's an electrical valve, which means it relates to fuses, to connections, and to the ignition switch itself.

Virtually all cars, Toyota included, have a charcoal canister for cleaning up the evaporations of gas from the carburetor and fuel tank. The canister has a filter that is supposed to be inspected and cleaned about every 12,000 miles, but nobody does this and cars go on. They pollute more, but not much more. This is not said to intimidate you or to give you guilt feelings about canister filters. It is a fact that emission control equipment gets more complicated at every turn of the EPA screw, which requires the perfect non-polluting car, though Mother Nature herself holds her sides in laughter at such a scenario as she goes about blithely spewing up every conceivable gas.

A device called the throttle positioner (TP) may interest you. What it does is to open the throttle valve slightly more at idle—as if adjudicating a case—than when decelerating, thus causing the air-fuel mix to burn more completely. Simple enough in theory, but not in fact.

The throttle positioner, like any referee, is prone to error. If, when the engine is at idle, the throttle positioner is not released, it can upset correct idle. To check the throttle positioner, put its hose on to the vacuum connector on the intake manifold. Now you need a tachometer to reflect engine speed—it

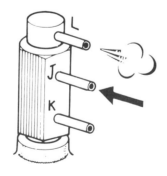 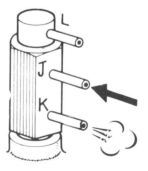

The thermostatic vacuum switching valve (TVSV) on Toyota Celica is checked by blowing into pipe J with coolant temperature below 50 degrees C (122 F) and feeling that air comes out of pipe L; then, with engine warmed, blowing into pipe J and feeling air come out of pipe K. Either failure disqualifies the valve.

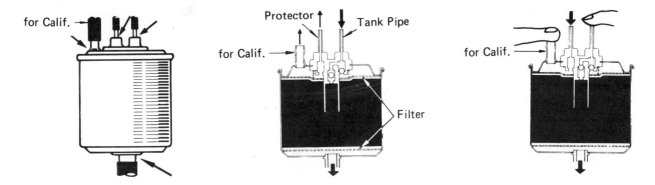

for Calif.

Protector ↑ ↓ Tank Pipe

for Calif.

Filter

for Calif.

Canister inspection means visual inspection for dirt, cracks and damage. Shown is the California Celica model. If the filter is clogged it can be cleaned by blowing air into the purge pipe while holding the two smaller pipes closed, as shown.

must be 1,050 rpm. If the engine isn't running at the correct speed—1,050 rpm—get the throttle positioner adjusting screw adjusted so it is, by turning it in or out as required.

The mixture control system (MC) allows fresh air into the intake manifold when you suddenly take your foot off the accelerator. It too is a device that won't change performance very much, if at all, but it does reduce emissions when it does its duty. It works on increased vacuum that occurs on sudden deceleration, and routs fresh air into intake manifold. You can check it by disconnecting the air inlet tube and putting your hand over the bottom of the valve with the engine running. No vacuum should be felt. When

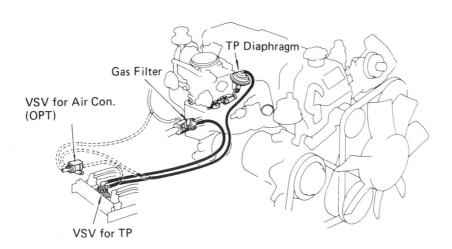

TP Diaphragm

Gas Filter

VSV for Air Con. (OPT)

VSV for TP

Deceleration

Deceleration

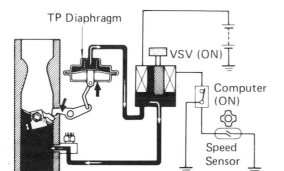

TP Diaphragm

VSV (ON)

Computer (ON)

Speed Sensor

Carburetor

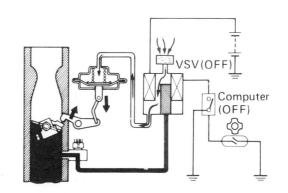

VSV (OFF)

Computer (OFF)

The throttle positioner valve or diaphragm can be checked by pulling on the throttle and releasing it. The TP should release when engine speed decelerates and returns to idle.

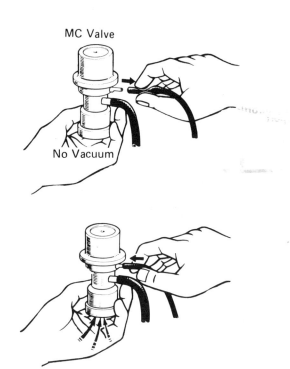

MC Valve

No Vacuum

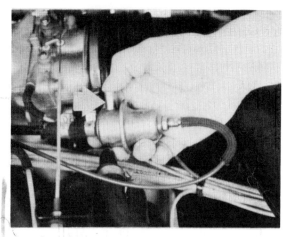

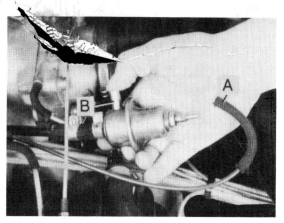

To test the mixture control valve (MC), disconnect the air inlet tube and put your hand over the bottom of the valve, with engine running. Reconnect the hose; vacuum should be felt.

you put the hose back, vacuum should be felt on the palm of your hand; also, the engine should be in a rough idle or quit altogether.

Toyota Celica's emission control system is elaborate, but not essentially different from other car systems.

VW emission controls

A typical VW system shows the exhaust gas recirculation system, charcoal filter valve, catalytic converter, and supporting gadgetry, including such components as the deceleration valve, which limits emissions during deceleration, as part of the EGR system. The system can cause trouble—starting troubles, rough idling, stalling, and general poor performance in cold weather.

To test the EGR system, look at all the hoses for leaks and cracks.

Start a system test with the deceleration valve, by removing the hose from valve to intake air duct, and plugging the hose. Run the engine at 3,000 rpm (about). Snap the throttle closed; check with a finger for suction at the hose connection. It should occur. If you don't feel suction at the connection (on top of the valve), remove the vacuum hose (at ''A'' in illustration) at the end of the valve and plug the hose. Run the engine rapidly, at about 3,000 rpm. There should

The VW deceleration valve is checked by removing line A and noting suction or lack of it at B. Adjustment is by turning vacuum line connection 1½ to 2 turns clockwise, after loosening locknut (bottom arrow).

now be no suction at the top connection (where there was supposed to be suction before). If there is suction, the valve must be replaced.

The deceleration valve can be adjusted to reduce engine delay in returning to the correct idle. The engine must be warm. Loosen lock nut on the vac-

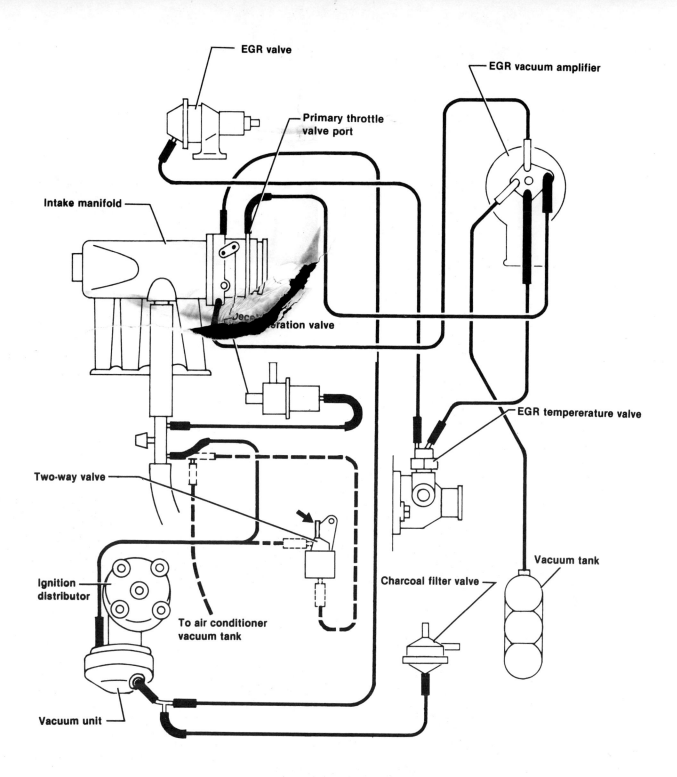

EGR valve

EGR vacuum amplifier

Primary throttle valve port

Intake manifold

Deceleration valve

EGR temperature valve

Two-way valve

Ignition distributor

To air conditioner vacuum tank

Charcoal filter valve

Vacuum tank

Vacuum unit

VW emission control system showing relationships between the basic involved components.

uum line connection and turn the vacuum line connection 1½ to 2 turns clockwise. Then tighten the lock nut.

To check the EGR valve, remove the vacuum hose from the distributor vacuum retard, and connect it to the EGR valve. If idle speed drops or the engine stalls, the EGR valve is good. If idle speed does not change, the valve or line is dirty, blocked or defective and must be replaced. First clean out the valve passages by removing the valve from the engine and cleaning out the passages near the bottom of the valve. Note that modifications on some 1975 and 1976 VW engines disconnected and capped the EGR valve.

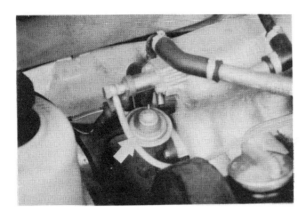

VW exhaust gas recirculation valve checking should be done regularly.

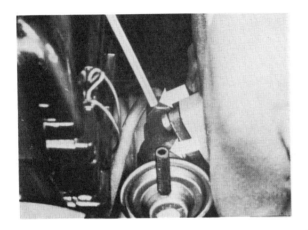

Checking the EGR temperature valve.

Later engines have an even more complex EGR system. It includes the temperature valve, the vacuum amplifier, as well as the EGR valve, charcoal filter, and the two-way valve on air conditioned cars.

Checking the VW vacuum amplifier.

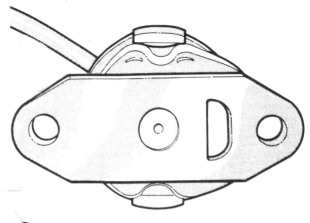

A ___ view of the Omni/Horizon EGR valve.

To check an EGR temperature valve with warm engine, attach a vacuum gauge (engine is running) between the EGR temperature control valve and the EGR valve. The gauge should read between 50-90 mm (2-4 inches) Hg. If not, replace it.

To check the EGR vacuum amplifier (engine running), connect the gauge between the vacuum amplifier and the primary throttle valve port (see illustration). The gauge should read 5-8 mm (.2-.3-inches) Hg. The throttle valve port could be clogged; clean it out. Then connect the gauge between the vacuum amplifier and the temperature valve. Reading should be 50-90 mm (2-4 inches) Hg. If not, replace the amplifier.

On the Chrysler Omni/Horizon version of the VW

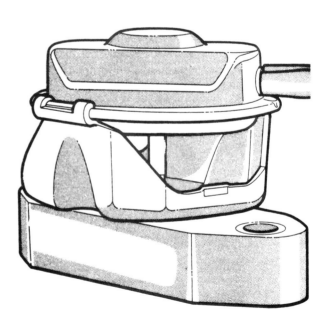

EGR valve on Omni/Horizon.

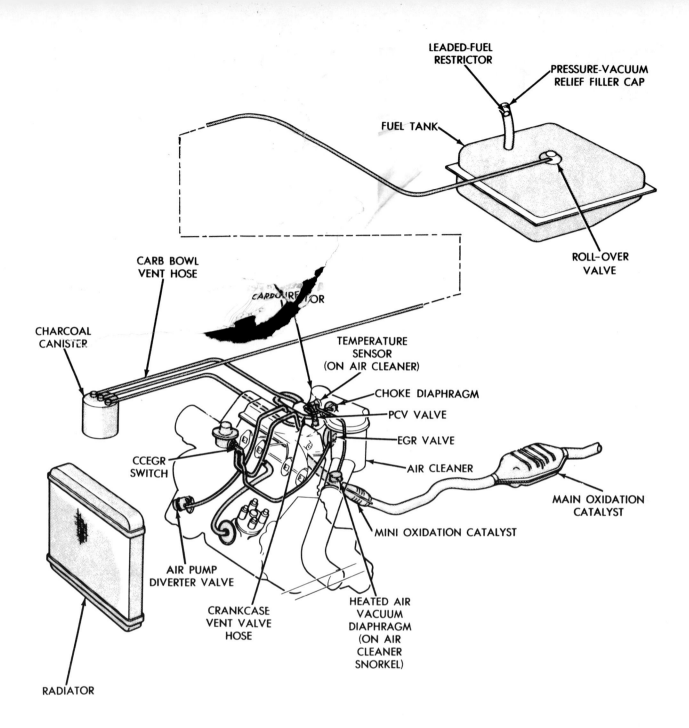

Omni/Horizon emission control system.

engine the emission controls are somewhat similar. The EGR valve, in the carburetor throttle body, can be checked by looking for movement of the EGR valve stem when you move the engine abruptly from idle to about 2,000 rpm (but not over 3,000). The groove on the EGR valve stem should be seen moving. Otherwise, replace the valve. The thermostat housing has a gas recirculation valve. You can't test it without a lot of rigamarole and equipment, so look elsewhere if the car is misbehaving without any apparent reason. Clean the EGR valve at the seat and

poppet area. Use a heat control valve solvent or some other strong cleaner that allows the hard deposits to soften, but be warned that the cure can be worse than the trouble—solvent can ruin the valve diaphragm. Also, to get at the deposits requires some tactic that will open the valve without ruining it. The best solution, if the engine won't idle properly or it dies out on return to idle, or idle is rough and slow, with the EGR valve closed at idle, is simply to replace the valve. It's inexpensive and easy to replace, as you can see by looking at it.

Datsun

Emission control on the Datsun 280ZX involves three systems; (1) is a closed type crankcase system; (2) is an exhaust system and (3) is an evaporative emission system. Also, California models differ from U.S. models and both of them differ from Canadian models.

The crankcase system takes blow-by gas from the engine crankcase to the intake manifold and throttle chamber. It goes through the PCV valve to the manifold, and with the engine running you can check the valve by removing the ventilation hose from it. If the valve works you should hear a hissing noise, and feel a strong vacuum when you put a finger over the valve inlet.

The exhaust system has an EGR valve as well as other components. The air induction valve is one of them, as is the E.A.I. tube. The air induction valve is a 2-reed valve inside the air induction case, between the air cleaner, the E.A.I. pipe, and the exhaust manifold. All these components are subject to wear and tear, as anything is involving the exhaust manifold.

The EGR system has the usual control valve. It also has a thermal vacuum valve, a B.P.T. valve, and other components. You may be appalled at these emission systems, knowing that they do nothing to make the car go forward—indeed, prevent it—but that's life in the modern world. It is impossible to be optimistic about such developments; one notes them, hopes they will go away, suffers them in silence and goes on to the next problem. Problems, after all, are both optimistic and pessimistic. Emission control is pessimistic.

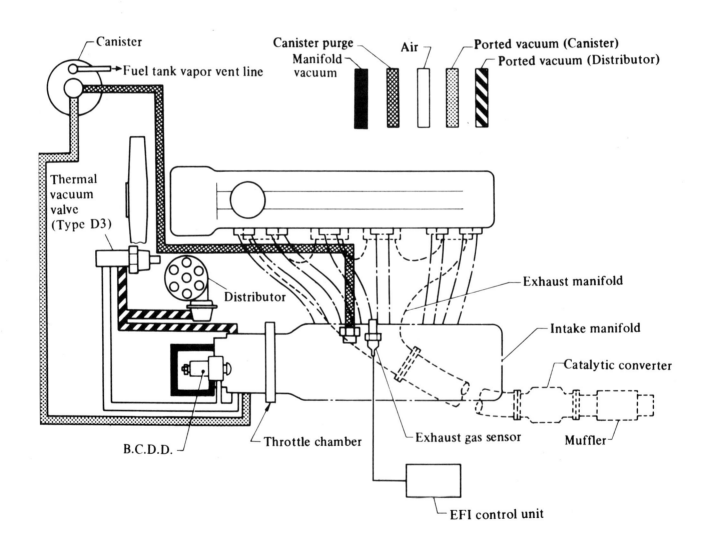

Datsun 280ZX California emission control system.

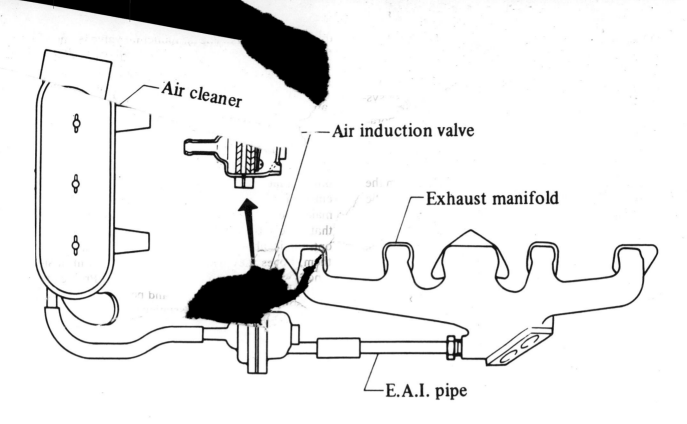

Datsun air induction system.

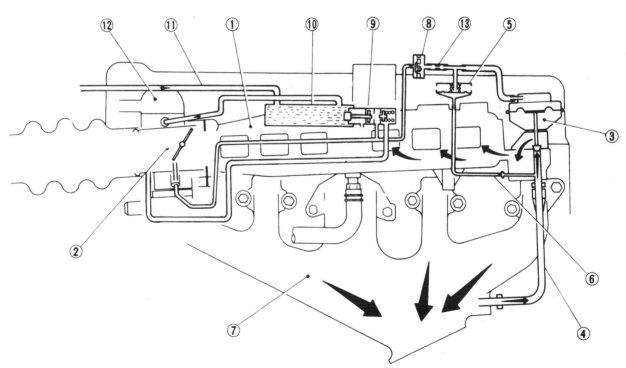

1 Intake manifold
2 Throttle chamber
3 E.G.R. control valve
4 E.G.R. tube
5 B.P.T. valve (Except Canada)
6 B.P.T. tube (Except Canada)

7 Exhaust manifold
8 Vacuum delay valve (Except Canada)
9 Thermal vacuum valve
10 Heater housing
11 Water return tube
12 Thermostat housing
13 Vacuum orifice (Except Canada)

The EGR system on Datsun 280ZX.

Chapter Seven

Suspension Systems

Suspension systems of sports cars differ from larger models only in their size. Their operations and parts are similar, though parts are not often interchangeable.

Increasingly the MacPherson strut is the solution to the front suspension problem of front drive cars. The way things are going, it appears that no other suspension system will be found in the next few years.

That is both good and bad news for home mechanics, since it is a remarkably troublefree way of tying together a lot of movements that required more systems the way it used to be done. But merely to do the simplest job in strut suspension systems—replacing shock absorbers—is no longer simple. To change shock absorbers in MacPherson struts requires much disassembly and one special tool, the spring squeezer, a compressor that pushes the coil

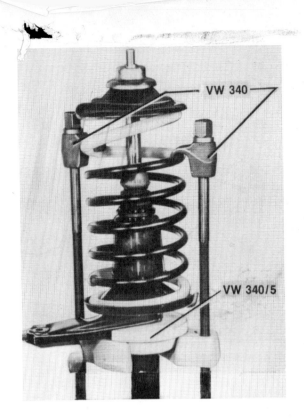

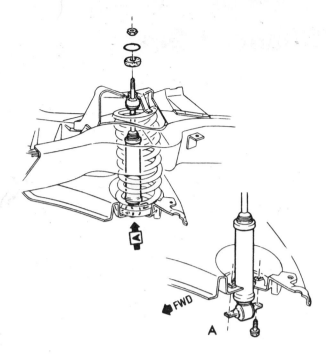

A spring compressor holding an Audi MacPherson strut spring.

Corvette shock absorber placement details.

spring's ends into manageable size so you can get the shock absorber off and on. Not all front drive cars have struts, and struts have not entirely eliminated the control arm designs that they replace. Vestigial, gill-like remnants of control arms are still out there. They are small, lower control arms that continue to play a key role, and even have ball joints, whose elimination is a consummation devoutly to be wished but never to be achieved in this age, apparently.

The rear suspension system may also use struts in conjunction with a metal frame member across the bottom of the car that links two "trailing arms" as they are called. These arms are what hold and support the wheel assemblies and axles as well as anchoring everything to the car frame. They are simple, sturdy systems.

In addition to the MacPherson (and other) strut systems, there is also the old familiar upper and lower control arm system, with upper and lower ball joints, with sway bars and bushings, and other paraphernalia.

Steering systems are either ball recirculating, in which case you deal with elaborate linkage, or they are the simpler rack and pinion. In front drive cars you also deal with the constant velocity joints at the wheels and at the transaxle. These joints are a kind of universal joint, with built-in permanent lubrication. They are a big job to take apart.

Corvette

Corvette suspension consists of standard General Motors components, beginning with the ball recirculating steering, pitman arm, steering linkage with idler arm, tie rods, ball joints, control arms, coil springs with shock absorbers inside, stabilizer bar, and brake and wheel components. It's far more complex than the strut system, and it has wear points every step of the way. It doesn't mean you get wear at those points; indeed, if you lubricate each wear point regularly you can drive such a system for 100,000 miles or more without replacing a single element in the system. Don't count on it.

Metal fatigue can make it necessary to replace any component at any mileage.

Shock absorber replacement is one of the most common tasks, but you must ask the question, is it worth doing? Many places use shock absorber replacement as a lure and charge so little that you can hardly save any money doing it yourself. However, resolute do-it-yourselfers will not be swayed.

Shock absorber replacement is easy once you get the old one off—at least in the type of suspension system we're discussing.

Corvette shock absorbers need replacement when they leak a lot (tiny leaks don't count), or when they

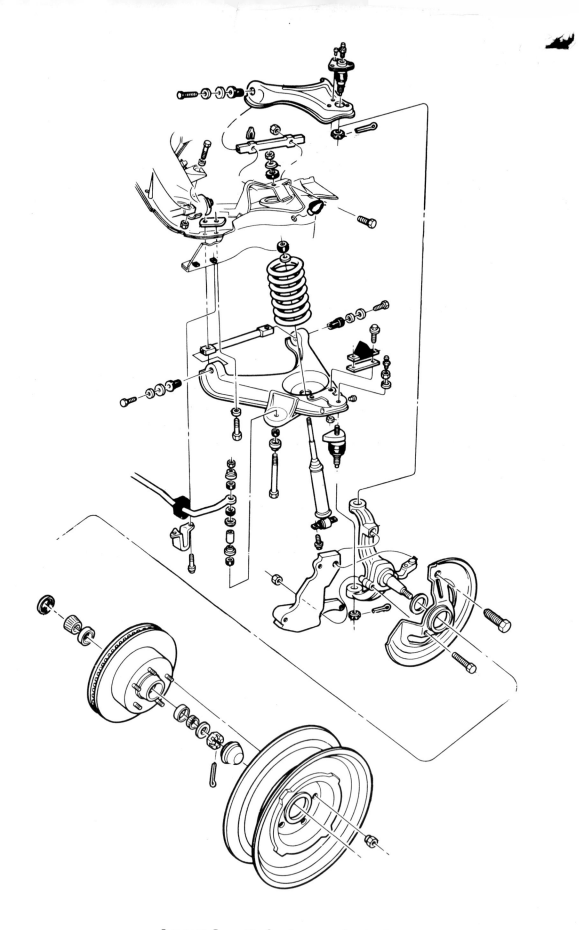

A recent Corvette front suspension system.

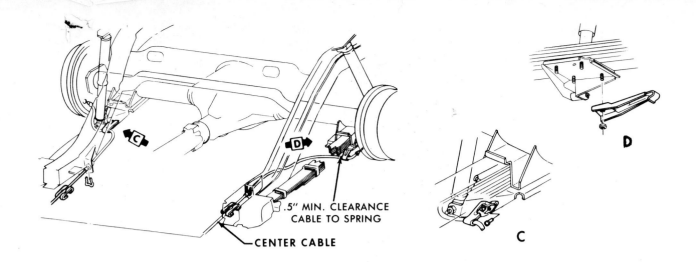

.5" MIN. CLEARANCE
CABLE TO SPRING

CENTER CABLE

G.M. rear assembly showing various components.

fail a test by pushing. Push hard on the bumper until you get the maximum possible movement. Then release the bumper suddenly. The movement should stop instantly. If one side of the car stops, for example, and the other doesn't you have one worn shock. You can also test for noise from wear and loose joints this way.

To replace shocks, jack up the car and support it for under-car work. You don't have to take off the wheel, but it helps—gives you more room, which you will appreciate. Use a lot of penetrating oil on the mounting bolts, both at the top (it's a nut) in the engine compartment and at the bottom. You can simplify removal of the top nut by oiling it and then using a cutting screw to remove the rust and corrosion. Otherwise, some of these nuts can cause a lot of removal distress. So too the bottom bolts and their retainers.

Usually the bottom bolt doesn't cause trouble—if you oil it. Once the old shock is off, follow installation directions with the new. Get the rubber grommet and steel washers in the right place at the top (the rubber grommet goes between them).

Rear shocks on front engine/rear drive cars are about like the front insofar as replacement goes. The upper bolt may cause trouble, thanks to some perverse placement of it, but usually rear shocks are easier to do than their front brethren.

Shock absorbers rarely last much more than 30,000 miles. All other suspension components can last much more or less. Coil springs rarely need replacement, but they lose their tension in time. Usually they don't break, though it can happen. They are tricky to replace. Ball joints, if not lubricated, will wear out in 50,000 to 60,000 miles. If lubricated, they rarely wear out. Pitman arms and idler arms, which move and support steering linkage,

also will last more or less forever if lubricated. Some idler arms, however, make no provision for lubrication. So they wear out. They aren't too hard to fix.

Bushings in control arms and sway bars wear out because they are made of rubber and steel and the rubber eventually gives way, leading to the steel of the bushing bouncing against the steel of the frame. That is what causes front end "clunk" hence the "clunker." It also causes misalignment of wheels and front end instability.

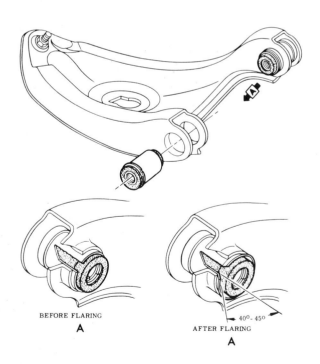

BEFORE FLARING
A

40° - 45°

AFTER FLARING
A

Bushing details on a Corvette lower front control arm. Installation is by press fit. Fitting must also be flared with a special tool.

163

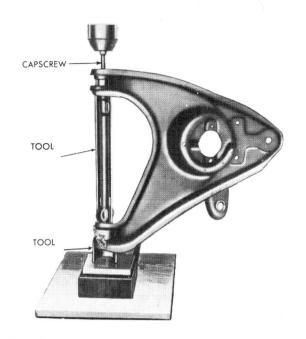

CAPSCREW

TOOL

TOOL

Pressing out an upper control arm cross shaft and bushing, Corvette.

Tie rod ends, which control steering and alignment, also are subject to wear, but you can grease them regularly—they have fittings or jets that take grease.

To do front end work in which all these parts must be pressed out of each other by considerable force, in some cases, requires mostly a large steel fork with tapered fingers that fit between the leeway that is provided. When you hit the other end of this tool, it forces the joints apart—once you unbolt or unscrew the fastener. Some of the fasteners have cotter pins in their ends. If you are going to fix any front end press-fit component you have to buy such a tool. It doesn't cost much—not over $15—and less in some catalogs. It will enable you to replace all front end components, however. The pitman arm, which attaches the steering gearbox to the steering linkage, requires a puller in some cases, rather than the blunt tool above. But try the simpler tool first. If you have to replace a pitman arm it must be marked exactly in relation to the splined shaft that turns it, otherwise you'll get the steering all out of kilter.

When do you replace these components? When there is instability that shocks and alignment don't cure. Some play is allowed in all front end components. Ball joints generally have a warning device that tells when replacement is needed. Idler arms don't; but some play is allowed. Use a rod or jack handle to pry on suspension components. Any that have distinct wobble rather than a tiny amount of play need replacement. Tie rod ends, however, should have no play. Play should not interfere with smooth operation of all front end components. When you push them around with a testing rod, there should be a clear, instant response through all connecting links. Any links that fail to respond smoothly probably need replacing.

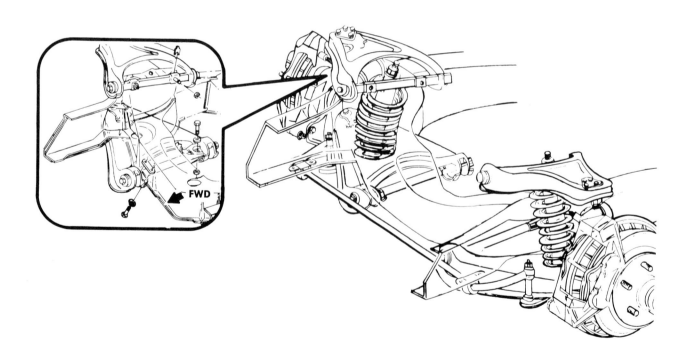

FWD

Older Corvette front suspension system.

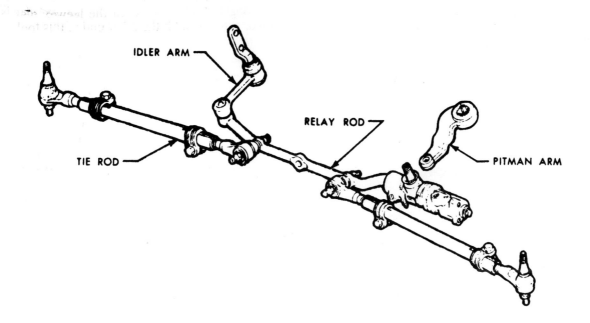

Corvette steering linkage.

But before replacing any component, all must be tested.

Bushings that are worn out, whether in stabilizer bars along the front of the system (or in the back), in the control arms, or wherever they occur, can usually be seen. The rubber portion of the bushing sometimes will be frayed obviously, and the steel socket of the bushing will be up against metal rather than riding against rubber.

Any loose tie rod end must be replaced.

Coil spring replacement

To replace a coil spring in this type of suspension, when the spring is between upper and lower control arms, requires that you remove the front wheel and the shock absorber. Then place a hydraulic jack below the lower control arm, unbolt the lower ball

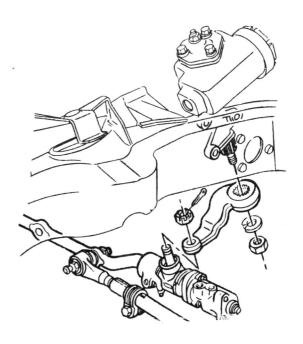

Idler arm play should be very slight, as indicated in this Corvette illustration.

Tie rod end positioning on recent Corvettes.

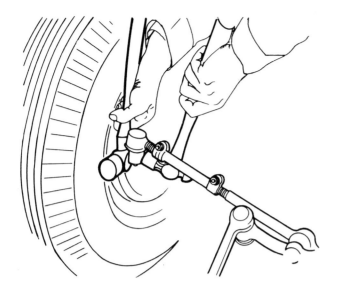

Using two hammers to free ball joint studs.

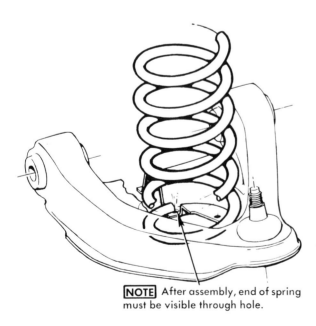

> **NOTE** End of spring must be .38 ± 12 from spring stop.

A

Corvette coil spring positioning, recent models.

joint and knock it open with the tool described above or you can do it with two hammers, one smaller hammer hitting the side of the ball joint housing, while you hold a large hammer against the joint. You can also use the force of the spring to push down on the ball joint as the spring pressure is released with the jack. If you use a hydraulic jack, make sure you control it carefully. If you are not sure, use a scissors jack, turning it slowly. When replacing the spring, it must be positioned so that the end is within .50-inch

from the spring stop, which you will have no trouble identifying.

You may also have to use the hydraulic jack to push the spring up and in place. The top of the jack can fit through the shock absorber opening and push the spring into place, if it doesn't go there without a push. Coil spring replacement is ticklish business. It doesn't happen often. When it does, the professional manuals recommend that you wind a chain around the coil, as you lower the control arm to release the coil's tension. I have never found it necessary, but the spring is indeed powerful and if you have a chain it won't hurt to use it.

> **NOTE** After assembly, end of spring must be visible through hole.

Positioning of coil spring in front suspension of early 70s G.M. system.

Upper and lower ball joints, recent Corvette models.

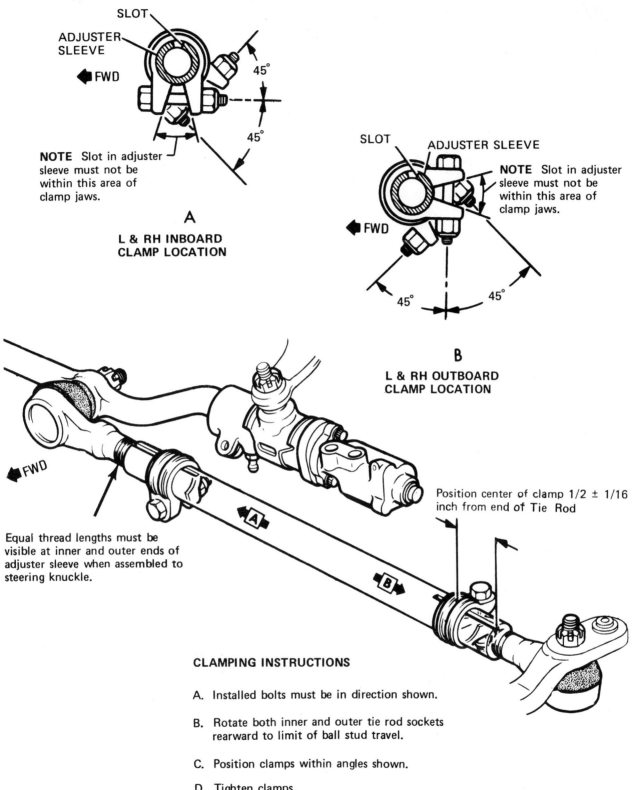

SLOT

ADJUSTER SLEEVE

◀ FWD

45°

45°

NOTE Slot in adjuster sleeve must not be within this area of clamp jaws.

A

L & RH INBOARD CLAMP LOCATION

SLOT   ADJUSTER SLEEVE

NOTE Slot in adjuster sleeve must not be within this area of clamp jaws.

◀ FWD

45°   45°

B

L & RH OUTBOARD CLAMP LOCATION

◀ FWD

Equal thread lengths must be visible at inner and outer ends of adjuster sleeve when assembled to steering knuckle.

Position center of clamp 1/2 ± 1/16 inch from end of Tie Rod

CLAMPING INSTRUCTIONS

A. Installed bolts must be in direction shown.

B. Rotate both inner and outer tie rod sockets rearward to limit of ball stud travel.

C. Position clamps within angles shown.

D. Tighten clamps.

E. With this same rearward rotation, all bolt centerlines must be between angles shown.

Corvette tie rod end adjustment details.

167

Bushing replacement

Bushings on Corvette and similar suspension systems, with upper and lower control arms, require that the worn bushing be removed, the new one pressed in. Getting the old one out requires a lot of disassembly. If it's the upper control arm you also have to remove whatever is in the way of removal, and the upper ball joint at least. It's no big deal to remove ball joints, if you have the patience and time. The upper control arm bushing may be buried under a mound of equipment, like an air conditioner or some other hefty component. Also, you will have to get the new bushing pressed in at a shop; it's highly specialized pressing which no amateur can undertake. Still, jobs like these are terribly expensive done completely at the garage, and the total cost to you, doing it yourself, will be the price of the new bushing and the pressing in and out. It shouldn't cost more than a few dollars; professionally it would cost and be worth a rather large sum.

The point of doing suspension work is that basically you can do a lot of expensive tasks for the cost of parts, which aren't much when bought at the big chains, in the catalogs, or at your neighborhood parts store. You rarely even disturb wheel alignment, unless you have to change tie rod ends. If you're willing to buy fairly inexpensive equipment, you can even do that, though professionals charge so little for alignment that it may not be worth your doing.

If you do have to change tie rod ends, measure the old ones exactly as you take them out, and adjust the new ones to those measurements. That could save the need for alignment.

If alignment has been altered in an attempt to compensate for worn bushings, the new bushings will make alignment essential. New shock absorbers and other steering linkage will not usually require alignment.

Strut suspensions

The trouble with taking apart a front strut suspension in many front drive cars is twofold; you must compress the spring, which takes a special tool, and you must buy wheel alignment or do it yourself. These are not insuperable problems. The spring compressor can be bought rather inexpensively, as noted elsewhere, and wheel alignment is inexpensive, done professionally. Also, if you mark the camber adjustment bolt, when you take it out of those cars that require it, you can often get it back accurately enough to avoid the need for alignment.

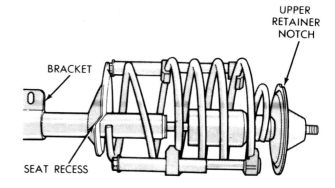

Omni spring compressor details.

If you note these front end symptoms on cars with struts, you may need new shock absorbers: Front end instability; when you push up and down on the front bumper it continues to move when you release it quickly; poor steering control at high speed; and leaking oil from shock absorbers. It's also a question of mileage. If your car has over 30,000 miles without attention to shock absorbers, and exhibits one or more of the above symptoms, it is probable that you have or will have shortly a need to replace one or more shock absorbers.

MacPherson struts are all anchored at the top with some form of bracket assembly—an anchoring nut and two or more bolts that attach the strut to the wheel well area. At the bottom the shock absorber either fits into a mounting bracket or is bolted on to a frame. You cannot change shock absorbers on the car, since the strut is built around the shock absorber.

Removal procedure for struts varies from make to make, but not by much. At the top you unbolt the upper mounting nut and the bolts that hold the top mounting plate. At the bottom you unbolt the bracket that attaches the strut to the wheel. In VW cars this bottom bracket contains two bolts that hold the strut to the wheel housing, and the top one is the camber adjusting bolt. Before removing this bolt, scratch a line across it and the mounting bracket so as to get the camber back where it was. These bolts are heavily torqued; the camber adjustment bolt is 58 ft lb and the bottom bolt is 43 ft lb (80 Nm and 60 Nm). It is extremely important that these torques be observed—or something very close to them.

Before removing the strut from the car, it might be helpful to start the top nut off, as you would discover if you tried to start it with the strut mounted in a vise. It should be easier to start while in the car.

You will also have to remove the brake oil line, in some models, but not in all. If you do, put some kind of stopper in the open ends, so oil doesn't leak out and air in.

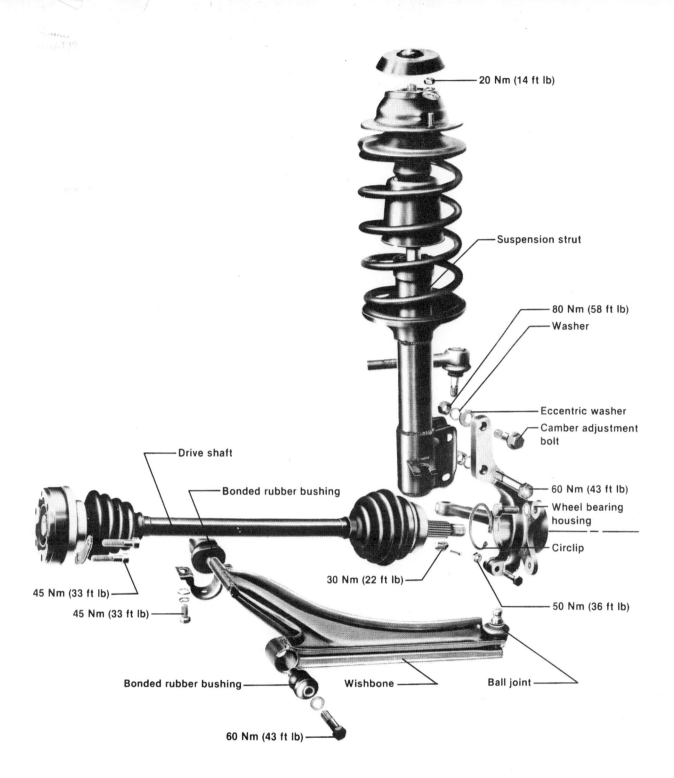

20 Nm (14 ft lb)

Suspension strut

80 Nm (58 ft lb)

Washer

Eccentric washer

Camber adjustment bolt

Drive shaft

Bonded rubber bushing

60 Nm (43 ft lb)

Wheel bearing housing

Circlip

30 Nm (22 ft lb)

45 Nm (33 ft lb)

45 Nm (33 ft lb)

50 Nm (36 ft lb)

Bonded rubber bushing

Wishbone

Ball joint

60 Nm (43 ft lb)

Details of the strut mounting assembly.

All MacPherson struts, no matter what details of fastening, and how they may differ, are alike in one requirement; the coil spring must be compressed to release pressure on the upper mounting bracket so you can get the shock absorber out and the new one in. This operation must be done with the strut in a vise.

Attach the spring compressors so as to grip four or five coils of the spring, and turn the long compressor bolts two or three turns each in sequence, first one then the other. Turn them down just enough to free the upper spring seat and whatever else is on top—a dust shield, a "jounce bumper," washers or whatever—these details vary. Then remove the re-

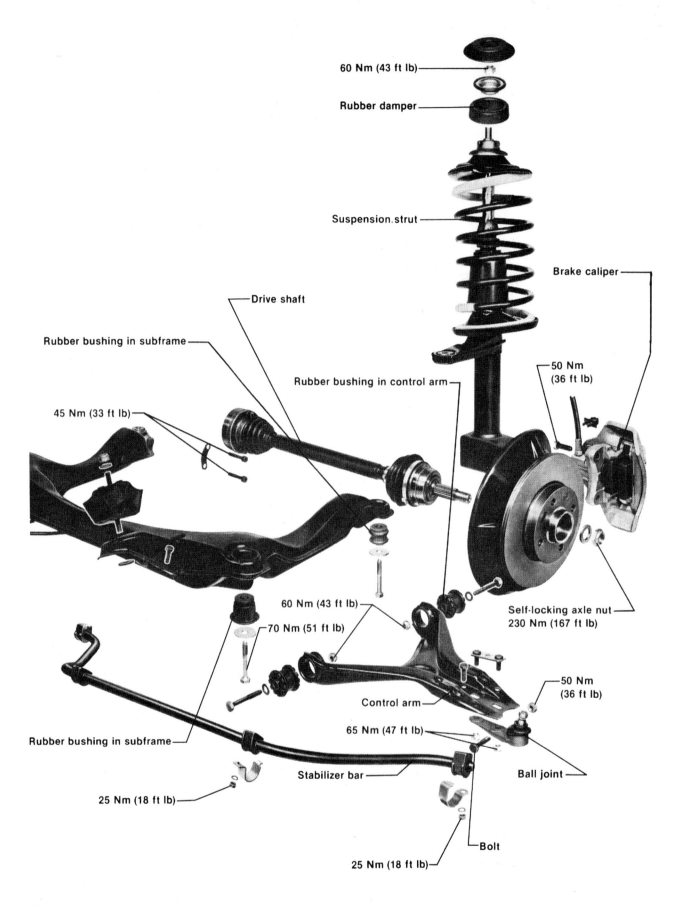

60 Nm (43 ft lb)

Rubber damper

Suspension strut

Brake caliper

Drive shaft

Rubber bushing in subframe

Rubber bushing in control arm

45 Nm (33 ft lb)

50 Nm (36 ft lb)

Self-locking axle nut 230 Nm (167 ft lb)

60 Nm (43 ft lb)

70 Nm (51 ft lb)

50 Nm (36 ft lb)

Control arm

65 Nm (47 ft lb)

Rubber bushing in subframe

Stabilizer bar

Ball joint

25 Nm (18 ft lb)

Bolt

25 Nm (18 ft lb)

VW front suspension details. Similar to Audi, it has its own nuances and details of fastening, including the warning that any undercoating must be removed from nuts and bolts before tightening.

170

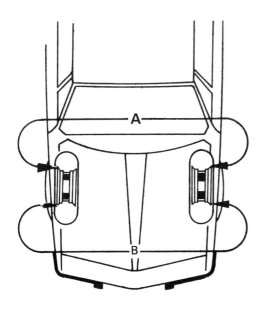

In Fiats—X 1/9, for example—front wheel toe-in requires wheels straight ahead. Measure distance between rear side of rims. Mark the wheels. Turn wheel 180 degrees until mark is in front (push car). Measure distance in front of wheels. Dimension A must be .0787 to .1575 inch greater than Dimension B. To adjust, loosen nut (1), turn ball joint (2) in or out until toe-in is right.

taining nut at the top—carefully to make sure that the spring is compressed sufficiently.

A typical VW installation combines the camber adjusting bolt and the retaining bolt on the lower attaching bracket, and so do U.S. types—Omni/Horizon.

Some cars such as the Fiat 131 use strut suspension with conventional front engine/rear drive, with lower control arm and sway bar. Shock absorber replacement is similar, though the details differ.

Here's the way Chrysler details their strut suspension system in Omni/Horizon. First, wheel alignment.

In order to undertake your own alignment you need a caster and camber gauge, which you can buy inexpensively, since it's little more than a leveler, such as carpenters use, and a good steel tape to measure toe-in and toe-out.

The upper cam bolt, when rotated, moves the top of the wheel in and out (that's camber). Inward tilt is negative; outward tilt is positive camber. Negative camber causes wear on the inside of the tire; positive camber causes outside tire wear. Toe measurement is the distance the front edges of the tires are closer or farther apart than the rear edges.

Chrysler specifications for these adjustments are: $-\frac{1}{4}$ degree to $+\frac{3}{4}$ degree or in other words you don't

want any camber, necessarily. However, there is a "preferred setting," which is $+0.3$ ($+\frac{5}{16}$ degree). A camber gauge is marked in degrees.

For toe setting, $\frac{5}{32}$-inches toe-out to $\frac{1}{8}$-inch toe-in are acceptable. In other words, a generous range, including none at all, and a preferred setting of $\frac{1}{16}$-inch out, which is slicing that pie pretty thinly.

Also, with strut suspension you have to worry about rear wheel alignment. For Chrysler (and these specifications are fairly typical of small front-drive cars) the rear specifications are camber -1.5 degrees to $-.5$ degree ($-1\frac{1}{2}$ degrees to $-\frac{1}{2}$ degree) with preferred setting -1 degree. Toe adjustments in inches are $\frac{5}{32}$ to $\frac{11}{32}$. Both toe and camber adjustments at the rear wheels are accomplished by putting shims behind the rear wheel axle hub at bottom or top (camber) or front or rear (toe).

Front suspension on Omni/Horizon centers around the strut. (So does steering; struts are also part of the steering movements.) To remove the strut, remove the wheel and tire assembly, with one jack under the side holding the car up and the coil spring free of tension. Remove the nuts that hold the strut at the top wheel well. Mark the cam adjusting bolt, then remove it and the through bolt which hold the bracket to the wheel hub. Remove the brake hose bracket retaining screw. The strut will come out.

171

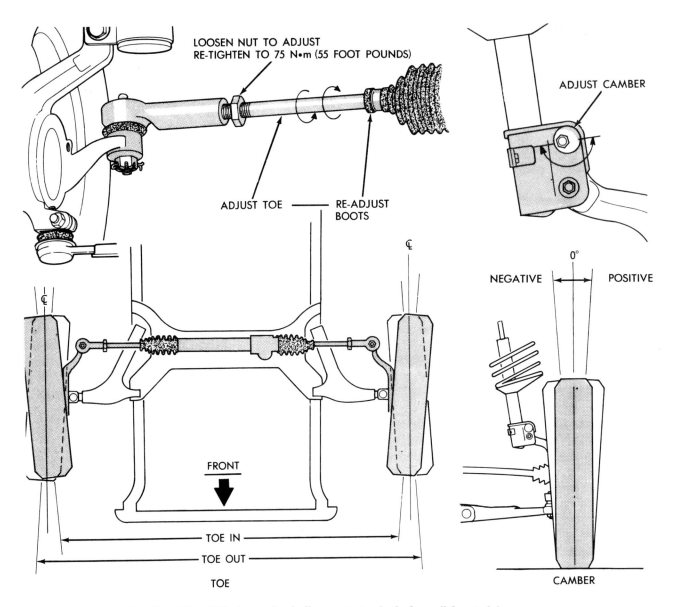

LOOSEN NUT TO ADJUST
RE-TIGHTEN TO 75 N•m (55 FOOT POUNDS)

ADJUST CAMBER

ADJUST TOE — RE-ADJUST BOOTS

0°

NEGATIVE ←→ POSITIVE

FRONT

TOE IN

TOE OUT

TOE

CAMBER

Details of Omni/Horizon wheel alignment, typical of small front-drive cars.

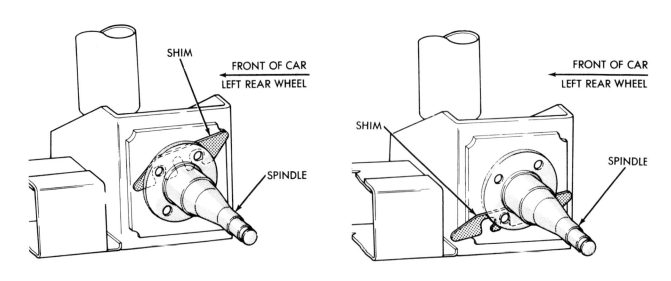

SHIM

FRONT OF CAR
LEFT REAR WHEEL

SPINDLE

SHIM

FRONT OF CAR
LEFT REAR WHEEL

SPINDLE

Omni/Horizon camber adjustment on rear wheels is done with shims at top and bottom.

172

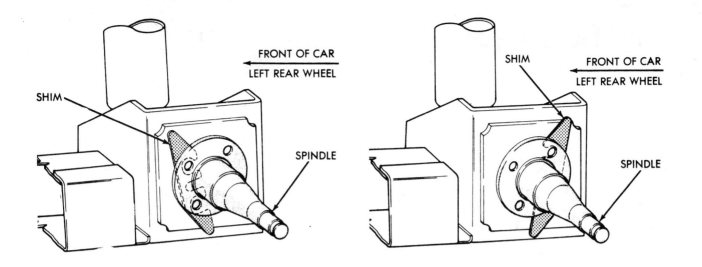

Rear wheel alignment on Omni suspension. Shim installation for toe-out (left), toe-in (right).

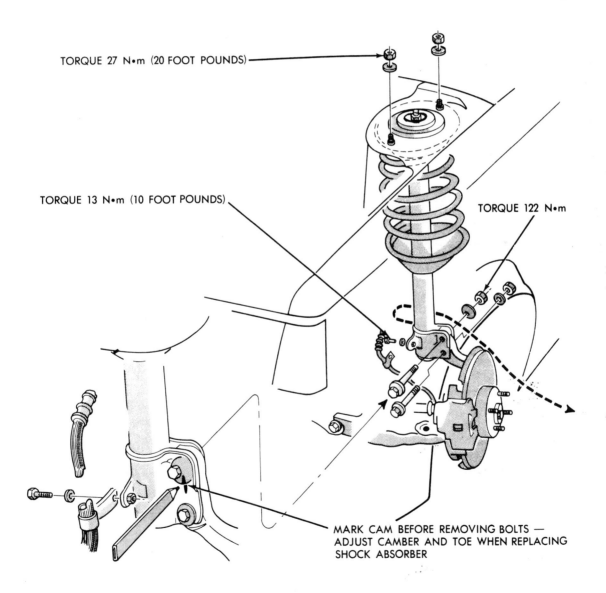

TORQUE 27 N•m (20 FOOT POUNDS)

TORQUE 13 N•m (10 FOOT POUNDS)

TORQUE 122 N•m

MARK CAM BEFORE REMOVING BOLTS —
ADJUST CAMBER AND TOE WHEN REPLACING
SHOCK ABSORBER

Strut removal and installation, Omni/Horizon.

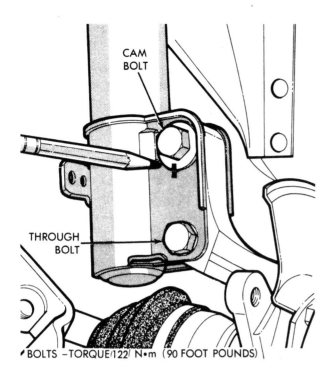

Marking the cam bolt on strut suspension, Omni.

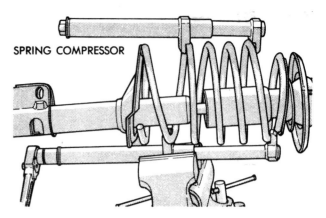

Coil spring compressed.

To take the strut apart, put the coil spring compressors on it, attaching them over four turns of the coil and depressing the coil by alternate turns on the long bolts of the two compressors. Don't overdo it; start with the jaws at 9¼-inches, and you may have to push down on the coil by hand to get it into that measurement.

Then loosen the strut rod nut at the top, with the strut compressor in a vise, preferably (don't take chances with the coil spring). Remove the nut using something to turn it and something to hold it—that means an open end or closed end (box) wrench to turn. With the nut off, remove the strut damper mount assembly, then the coil spring and mark it so you know which end is up. Examine all the parts for wear, cracks and distortions. Examine the bearings for absence of lubricant and binding; remember, the bearing is what the strut turns on when you turn the wheels, so it must be free and smooth.

Replace the shock absorber. Reverse the order of disassembly, in effect. Put the bumper dust shield assembly on the strut rod (top of the shock absorber rod). Put the spring in the seat, with the bottom end in the seat recess. Add the upper spring retainer, bearing and spacer, the mount assembly, rebound bumper, retainer and rod nut. The upper spring retainer has an alignment notch on it which must parallel the lower attaching bracket of the strut. The rod nut on top must be 60 ft lb (81 Nm) which Chrysler says should be torqued before you release the spring compressors.

Fiat X 1/9 suspension uses struts with coils and shock absorbers inside them. The shock absorbers are of a type that can be refilled with oil and rendered like new again. Since that is one type of shock absorber you find with strut suspensions it is well to look closely at disassembly procedures. Bear in mind that not all strut shock absorbers can be refilled and thus repaired. Nor are their details similar to what follows.

Fiat color-codes its coil springs—yellow and red strips. Don't mix them up.

The front shock absorber has a threaded plug at the top which comes out if you tap it with a piece of wood and a small hammer. This is best done with the stem of the cylinder in a vise. The plug at the top, when removed, allows removal of the inner cylinder. It must then be removed. Inner cylinders may be serviced by replacing missing oil, or replacing them entirely. In either case you have to fill the cylinder, since new ones for Fiat X 1/9 are empty when unpacked.

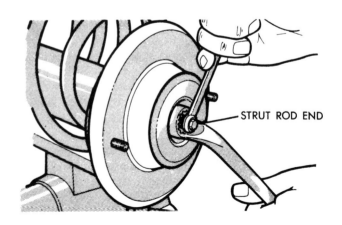

Loosening the strut rod nut.

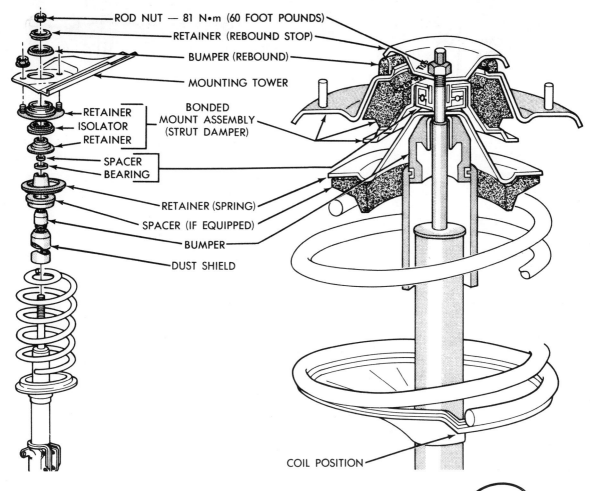

ROD NUT — 81 N•m (60 FOOT POUNDS)
RETAINER (REBOUND STOP)
BUMPER (REBOUND)
MOUNTING TOWER
BONDED
MOUNT ASSEMBLY
(STRUT DAMPER)
RETAINER
ISOLATOR
RETAINER
SPACER
BEARING
RETAINER (SPRING)
SPACER (IF EQUIPPED)
BUMPER
DUST SHIELD

COIL POSITION

1. Stem.　2. Inner cylinder.　3. Valve.　4. Outer cylinder.　5. Threaded plug.　6. Cap.　7. Ring seal.

Disassembly of the strut damper.

You must remove the valve from the cylinder by tapping carefully to loosen it so you can unthread it. Fluid, supplied with a new inner cylinder, or obtainable at the parts counter for an old one, must fill the inner cylinder. What is left over is added to the outer cylinder.

Then put back the valve on the inner cylinder and place the unit into the outer cylinder as before, using a new ring seal and cap. Replace the threaded plug.

The attaching components of the shock absorber consist of bushings, retainers, washers, bolts, and other devices. Their removal requires the spring compressor as in all struts.

Toyota Celica's front shock absorbers resemble the X 1/9's in that they can be refilled. However, the job is rather more complicated. Removal involves dismembering a lot of the front suspension system before you can get at the shock absorber—steering knuckle arm, brake caliper and hoses, backing plate and hub, coil spring (compressed) and other details. The shock absorber itself can be taken apart and

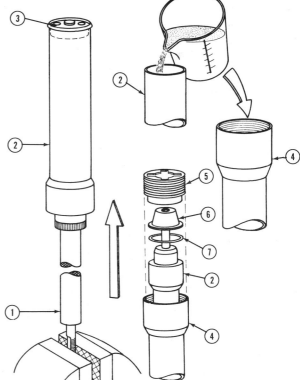

Fiat X 1/9 front suspension assembly/disassembly procedures and details.

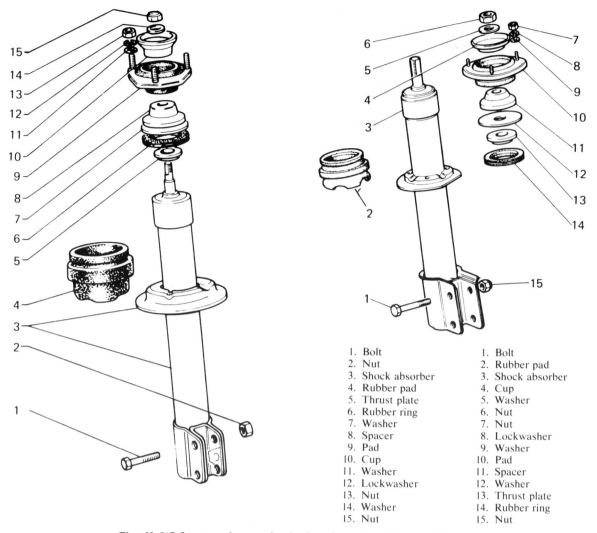

1. Bolt	1. Bolt
2. Nut	2. Rubber pad
3. Shock absorber	3. Shock absorber
4. Rubber pad	4. Cup
5. Thrust plate	5. Washer
6. Rubber ring	6. Nut
7. Washer	7. Nut
8. Spacer	8. Lockwasher
9. Pad	9. Washer
10. Cup	10. Pad
11. Washer	11. Spacer
12. Lockwasher	12. Washer
13. Nut	13. Thrust plate
14. Washer	14. Rubber ring
15. Nut	15. Nut

Fiat X 1/9 front and rear shock absorber attaching details.

rebuilt, or replaced. Replacement cylinders are available. There is little point in replacing the oil unless you check out the seals and other components —the valve, piston and cylinder surface for wear. So it is best to buy a replacement cylinder.

Dealing with other aspects of strut suspension involves the single ball joint which is bolted or riveted on to the wishbone control arm. When the ball joint is bolted on, its replacement is easy. Unbolt the steering knuckle clamp bolt that holds the top shaft of the ball joint, and unbolt the ball joint from the control arm. If riveted, drill or file off the rivets and replace them with bolts. If you can. Chrysler suggests buying a whole new control arm and ball joint.

Bushings in the control arm may need replacement. They must be pressed in and out.

The only other aspects of the front system that you may have to repair are the constant velocity joints. A lot of disassembly is required to get at them. Remove the wheel and the hub nut that retains the front drive shaft. (It is best to loosen the hub nut while the car is on the ground.) Unbolt the top of the ball joint and

separate it from the steering knuckle, by prying it loose. But don't damage the rubber boot. Move the wheel assembly away (the car is now jacked securely in two places) and pull out the outer constant velocity joint shaft. Support the shaft. Remove the allen head screws that attach the inner constant velocity joint to the transaxle drive flange. Remove the driveshaft assembly, avoiding loss of grease by holding both inner and outer housing parallel and turning the outer assembly down while pivoting the inner housing up at the drive flange. It's a neat trick if you can do it. You can't avoid all lubricant loss. You replace it. If you removed the shaft for replacing the boots, due to tears, you also have to replace an adequate amount of special lubricant. But in Chrysler cars, lubricant requirements and quantities are different for inner and outer joints. To replace boots, you cut off the clamps—rubber and metal clamps, and the boot itself. You can buy boot joint kits, which contain clamps and packets of grease. Check out and remove the tripod by removing the snap ring.

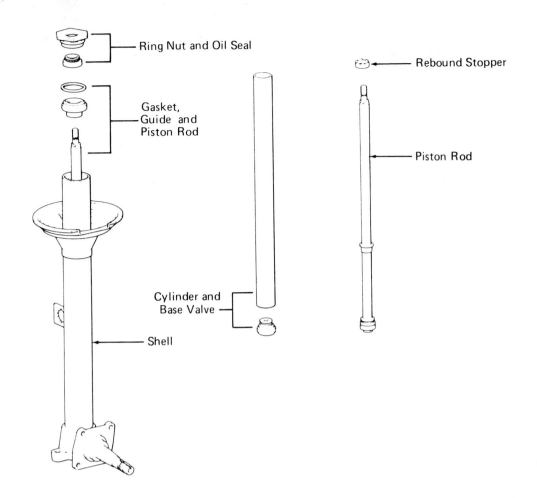

Celica shock absorber can be refilled, if you replace seals and gaskets, and oil.

To install a new boot, slide the small rubber clamp on the shaft, then slide the small end of the boot over the shaft. Position the boot lip face in line with the mark on the shaft where you removed the old one—there are differing shafts; the tubular requires that the boot lip be in line with a mark on the shaft, while the solid shaft has a machined groove in which you position the small boot end. Clamp the small boot end by putting the rubber clamp over the boot groove. Put the tripod back and lock it in place with

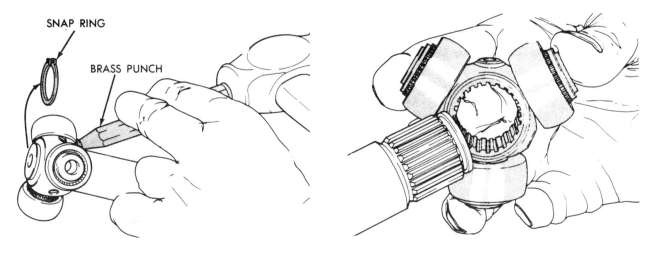

Disassembly of constant velocity joints begins with removal of metal clamps and boots. Next remove tripod, and shaft from housing. To disassemble the tripod, if necessary, remove snap ring and tap lightly.

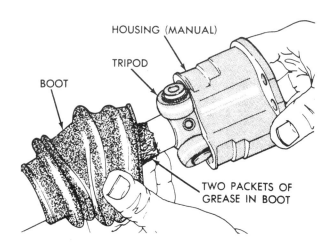

Use two packets of grease in boot before placing tripod into housing. Kits contain necessary supplies.

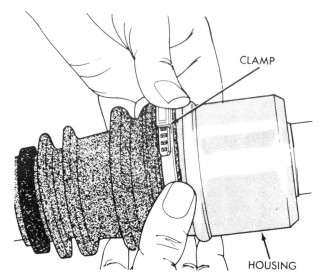

Clamp must be tightened by hand, then by a tool. Great care must be taken to avoid damaging the rubber boot.

the retaining ring in the groove on the shaft. Put two packets of grease in the boot. Install the housing over the tripod and position the large end of the boot in the groove on the housing. Add two additional packets of grease after securing boot to housing (total of four packets). Fit the large metal clamp on the boot and tighten the clamp by hand. Then you have to squeeze the clamp tightly with a tool of some sort—an electrician's pliers. There are special tools—as there are for everything—but any thin-nosed pliers will do. Be very careful not to cut the clamp bridge or damage the boot. Push the grease gently forward in the housing.

The instructions above are for Omni/Horizon manual transmission. Automatic differs slightly; you use a total of three packets of grease and add one instead of two at the first "add instruction."

We've been dealing with the inner constant velocity joint and grease boot repair. The joint nearest the wheel may require similar attention. Details are somewhat different, but you get the picture. To get the joint off you pull the entire shaft out of the wheel hub, as you did for the inner joint. Take it to a bench and with a soft hammer (rubber) tap the joint from the internal circlip installed in the groove at the outer end of the shaft. Don't remove the slinger or the lock ring from the shaft. Boot installation is the same.

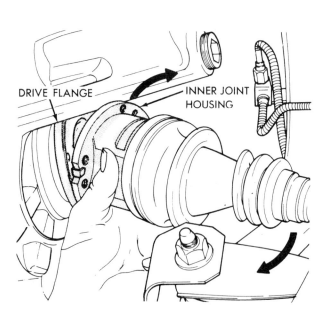

When you remove the housing, watch out for lubrication. Avoid spilling by tilting the housing up.

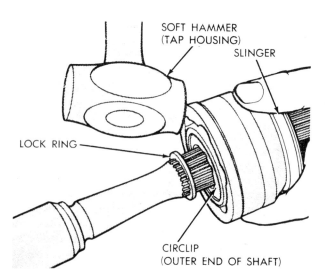

Tap off the housing.

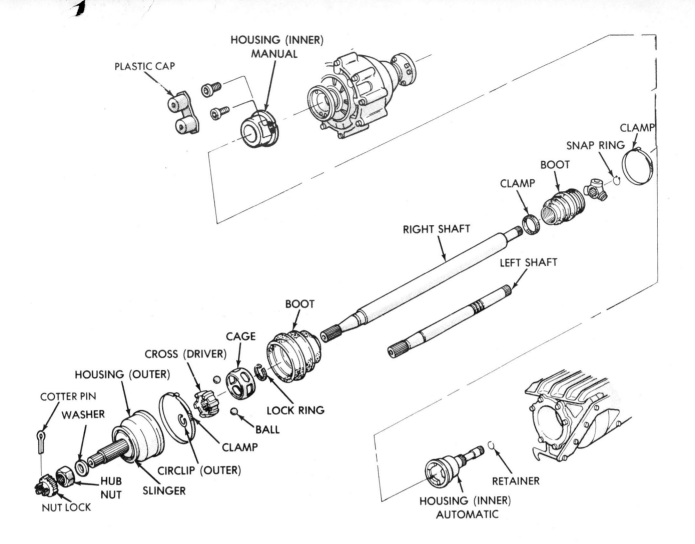

PLASTIC CAP

HOUSING (INNER)
MANUAL

CLAMP

SNAP RING

BOOT

CLAMP

RIGHT SHAFT

LEFT SHAFT

BOOT

CAGE

CROSS (DRIVER)

HOUSING (OUTER)

COTTER PIN

WASHER

LOCK RING

BALL

CLAMP

CIRCLIP (OUTER)

HUB
NUT

SLINGER

NUT LOCK

RETAINER

HOUSING (INNER)
AUTOMATIC

Drive shaft components on Omni/Horizon are not untypical of other front drive cars.

Rear suspension details with rear struts are similar to those above for the front strut, only a bit less complex. You do have to compress the coil spring to replace shock absorbers. But wheel alignment isn't disturbed in the process.

Front wheel drive, combining steering and power thrust through the same wheels, rather than separating these activities as in front engine/rear drive, is a much more complex thing. Therefore you can expect unusual wear to occur if the parts get out of adjustment or simply break down from metal fatigue. Yet the strut suspension system is amazingly foolproof and durable as well as ingenious.

Stabilizers

One aspect of front suspension instability in front engine/rear drive cars is the stabilizer bar and the type of anchor it has at each end. Often, as in the case of Toyota, the stabilizer bar is anchored by two small strut bars. These attach through brackets to the lower control arm. Wear can appear first at the two small strut bars, throwing the stabilizer bar out of adjustment, affecting caster and camber, and general front end stability. If the strut bar assemblies wear out—as they often do—the steering and wheel movement are also affected.

The easiest test is to use a socket wrench long bar and push the strut bars. Since the bars are designed to absorb movement, they will move when you push them. But if their rubber bushings wear out, they cause movement and don't absorb it and when you push on them you can see this. Tight strut bars and stabilizer bar move together; worn strut bars move by themselves.

The strut bars are easily replaced. Squirt penetrant on their bolts—they will almost certainly be rusted badly—and get them off, top and bottom. You will notice that the bolts are fairly but not excessively tight. On Toyota the torque is 11-15 ft lb, which is

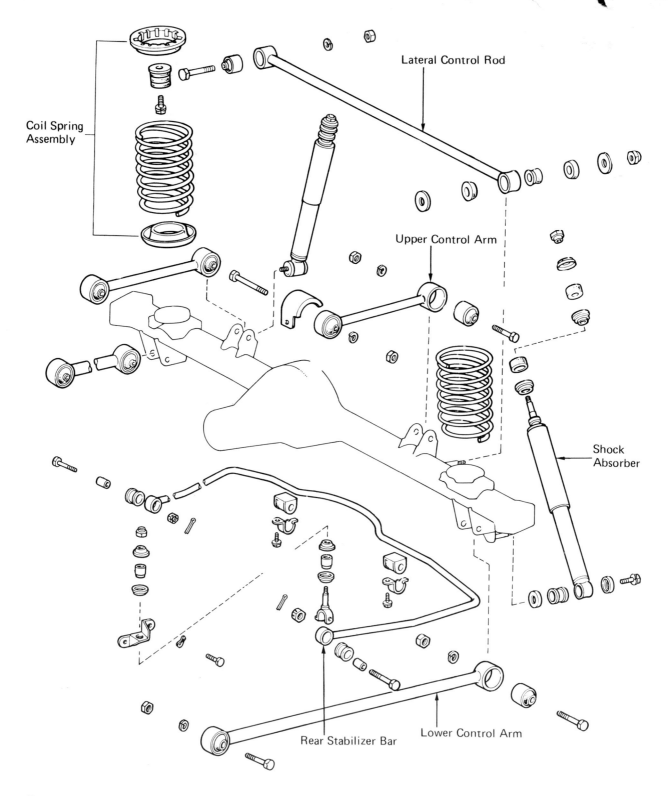

Coil Spring Assembly

Lateral Control Rod

Upper Control Arm

Shock Absorber

Rear Stabilizer Bar

Lower Control Arm

Toyota's rear suspension control system has stabilizer bar, lateral control rod, and upper control arm systems, with bushings and fasteners that wear out exactly as in the front.

about spark plug torque. Strut bar bracket bolts, however, are 29-39 ft lb, which is tight. Incidentally, on Toyota, as on many other cars, there is an engine undercover which has to be removed before you can do any of this.

If the stabilizer bar is also anchored in the center or at other points on the front end, as is the case in some cars (not Celica), you must make the same examination of these housings as with the strut bars. Replacement usually is not difficult.

Chapter Eight

Body Repair

To undertake body repairs on a modern car would seem to be a form of extreme recklessness, if one considers the botched jobs that peer out at you on any parking lot. But if you consider the costs of body work, and what is involved, the problems may be worth solving. They can be.

Body work is more expensive than anything else on a car. Collision work, involving body and mechanical parts and frame damage, is the most costly of all and is the cause of the total wreck. But major rust damage can rival it in destructiveness and cost. Rust, allowed to go on for several years, can also result in a "total wreck"—a condition where the cost of repair exceeds the replacement price of the car.

The price of body work is largely labor and time, since the materials involved in sheet metal work (or plastic, as the case may be) aren't very expensive. Paint, though going up in price rather steeply, still isn't expensive. So it follows that if you are willing to learn and put in the time, you can save the most expensive part of body work.

The statement above that materials are inexpensive is true only if you repair old parts. If you buy new fenders you soon discover why body work is expensive. New body parts, unlike typical mechanical parts, are extremely expensive.

What skills and tools are required?

Skills are not particularly mechanical. In fact, they are closer to sculpture—shaping of forms, using body putty. Ingenuity is also at issue. If you examine a typical bashed front end objectively instead of traumatically you notice that some of the parts might be repairable, some are obviously destroyed, and some are marginal. So, you have to sort out the issues. Smashed bumpers are rarely salvageable. A slashed radiator is junk; so are mechanical parts such as water pumps, fans, alternators and anything else that suffers obvious damage. But, if the front is merely pushed in, with a fender that is riding on a tire, a radiator pushed against the water pump but not destroyed, and other components that appear to be merely out of joint rather than ruined, you can do certain salvage operations.

You start with a jack that will fit between bashed parts and push them out. This could be a fender jack, a scissors jack (that's the usual winner) or even a hydraulic jack—they won't work unless in vertical position in many cases. With a jack you can often push a lot of things back where they belong. You can do a major salvage job on things like rear ends, using only a jack or two.

But you can also do wonders with a piece of two-by-four. It can give you enough leverage to do a lot of pushing on bent body components. It won't straighten anything out, but it can put some things in a position to be straightened.

That development is what interests us.

Pushing damaged areas out is the first aspect of restoring contour. To do that requires a combination of force, imagination, and—correct estimation and the right tools.

The right tools in body work can be anything from a two-by-four to a powerful compressor.

Getting the contours back where they belong is the first major task in any body work. Tools involved can be anything from the informal, improvised tools such as a piece of lumber or a bumper jack, to a pull hammer and regular body tools.

Before you can restore a contour you have to know what it is. Fortunately, most contours are not unique. A right front fender is exactly like the one on the left. To be sure, a rear deck lid, when bashed in, has no counterpart, at least on your car, nor does a front hood. However, parts have to fit together and hoods and deck lids must be able to do what their function requires, so the unique parts don't present unimagineable problems of contour. But problems of fit are something else. A deck lid or hood can cause fits before you get it to fit. You may conclude that it isn't worth trying to salvage, and you could be right. Used car salvage lots exist precisely for your problem. It is possible to pick up a perfectly good deck lid at a fraction of the cost of a new one, as long as you are willing to paint it.

Painting raises the biggest question of tools—a compressor. To paint a car requires a compressor or an equivalent tool. However, the newer types of painting equipment don't produce air, and compressed air is useful in many contexts, so the old style compressor has more uses. You may object that a compressor is terribly expensive and not often very useful. That is only partly true. Compressors can do many things in a garage and around a house, and if you consider that a good one costs several hundred dollars, which almost every body repair job will exceed, the cost isn't very great. It certainly isn't excessive. In fact, a compressor is a marvelous tool that will pay back what it costs in fairly short order.

But if you doubt all this, you can always rent a compressor for a day, and try it out. (Rent a good one.)

PAINTING

The compressor/sprayer requires some expertise in the use of it. You can master the intricacies of it with a little practice on the under side of the hood or deck lid, a fender underside—all places usually preempted by rust. The sprayer must be the internal/external mix type, which means two air jets and the paint meet outside to mix in the act of emission toward the target. You mix the paint itself with thinner before putting it in the sprayer. The ratio is two parts of thinner to one of paint, though it can vary somewhat depending on your results. If you add too much thinner, the paint will run; too little, it won't go on properly. Also, you need to paint in warm weather, preferably around 80 degrees. That means outside, because the spray is toxic inside. But it means an absence of wind, too. Wind will blow dirt on the paint and ruin it.

If you ruin it, wipe it off at once—don't try to salvage a ruined patch. Auto paints dry quickly and if you don't wipe off the running portion instantly, you will have a mess. Then you'll have to sand off the ruined part and start over. Wiping is easier than sanding.

These general remarks about painting obscure other aspects of preparation, but you ought to know about them right away because your willingness to take on body work is related directly to your interest in learning to use a compressor and acquiring one. But even if you don't want to consider a compressor, you can buy spray cans of paint to match your car that will do a passable job and require virtually no skills.

So, painting is a kind of dividing line that separates the men from the boys, the women from the girls. Men and women will paint, boys and girls will use spray cans (and those adults who are closet boys and girls may steal an occasional spray can to use). Be warned, however, that spray can paints do not match as exactly as the stuff you buy at the auto paint store. Nor do results in other ways equal the compressor spray job when it is done excellently. When it is not, you are better off with the spray can. So, the order of procedure is to try out the spray can to test your interest in it and your tolerance for its results. If you are satisfied, don't buy a compressor.

The spray can is preceded by the touch-up brush, which comes in a vial of paint more suited to Roman imperial poison than to car body repair. The vial is a primitive rejoinder to rust—the first step into car painting. It covers the first peeping rust spot on your new car, at a time when the car is too new to be the subject of something as vulgar as body shop work. It is a reminder that a new car loses its novelty within months, and the facts of life must be faced. It is also a reminder that rust is an invisible hand that will not be stayed by cosmetic touching-up.

To spray paint on a car requires a firm hand and the right mixture of thinner to paint, as well as the right spray pattern. But it also requires the right amount of spraying force. That comes from the compressor, which should be no less than 5½ to 6 cfm ("cubic feet per minute"). The horsepower to generate that amount won't be less than one and maybe two. You will need a 20 ampere outlet to run such a motor. An outlet that handles any major appliance will work. A 220-240 volt compressor will require a line with that voltage. An electric dryer or electric stove will have such a line.

The sprayer, as noted, must be an internal-external mix type to go with the compressor. Sprayers are rated for their capacity, and when you buy the compressor it is well to buy a matching sprayer simultaneously.

Spray pattern is something to experiment with, but generally you want a pattern that looks like this () but closed at top and bottom. Spraying should be done in smooth, controlled movements across the panel—left right, right left. Always test the spray pattern and the amount of "run" in the mix. There should be none; if paint starts to run and sag, you need more paint in the mix—but not much more. If the paint is too dry as it goes on, you need more thinner, or more

power behind the gun, or warmer weather.

You deal with acryllic lacquer, mostly (or acryllic enamel). These are rapidly setting paints, but drying time takes from a few hours to a couple of days. That means, you can drive the car when the paint has set. However, you will usually have to put on about three coats and it is well to rub each coat down with very fine emery cloth—No. 600.

Montgomery Ward, Sears, Penneys and many smaller stores sell equipment you will need. Compressors will be rated in the number of cubic feet per minute, horsepower, and pounds per square inch (psi), as well as the voltage. Needless to say, the more of these numbers you buy, the more dollars they cost. So, don't buy more than you need.

A good compressor, which costs several hundred dollars, is a sturdy tool. Its design is usually a piston with rings, much like an automobile engine, with flap valves that control air flow, with a belt-driven electric motor. On occasion, you will have to clean out the flap valves, (when air starts hissing out from them) and if they lose tension you can replace them inexpensively. The motor has a re-start button, in case of overloading. It is important to keep oil levels up, with occasional change of oil. The rubber hose cracks and may need replacement, and the air valves in the tank may sometimes require new gaskets or even replacement. Basically, maintenance is simple and rare. The gauges rarely require attention, nor does the pressure switch that cuts the motor off when the tank is full of air. Obviously it is important that the pressure gauge work—or the pressure switch. Preferably both.

BODY WORK BASICS

Okay, so you know how to paint. But getting the surfaces ready for it is the basic name of this game. Once you have pounded, pushed and pried the contours into rough, acceptable position, you must obtain the smooth, glassy finish that alone guarantees professional-like results in painting. For the painting will not conceal blemishes in your body work; on the contrary, painting will reveal them. The sprayer will highlight the smallest flaw in your body work technique.

Professionals go about preparing surfaces one way; we take another path. Professionals use power equipment most of the way, or they replace parts, and use welding techniques. We replace parts only as a last resort. If you bang in a door so lumpishly that you can't get it to close no matter what you do, it may be necessary to go around to the used car parts lot to find a replacement. But you will be surprised at what you can do to an apparently demolished part. For one thing, the metal isn't very sturdy, which is one of the reasons it's in apparently terminal condition. For another, a heavy hammer and wood block can work wonders in straightening some things out. The thin sheet metal may stretch, making it impossible to obtain the best possible contour with the original surface. What you do then, is pull it into the best shape you can, using the hammer and wood block, or a slide hammer if you can't use any other kind.

A slide hammer is rather essential for amateur body work. It pulls out dents. Some slide hammers have suction cups that grab areas and pull whole panels out. That's rarely possible. Others screw in or hook into a drilled hole of a bashed area and pull it out in cases where you can't enter from the rear with your hammer and two-by-four or other wood block and bang it out. One of these amateur techniques will work in every situation—I speak from the experience of banging up every conceivable location on a car. Lest you interpret this as a sign of such wantonness and recklessness that everything in this discussion is to be disbelieved, let it be noted that three other family members contributed stoutly to the demolition, over many years.

Each panel has its own peculiarities. Doors contain many parts which are easily disrupted. Window and locking mechanisms are easily ruined, glass is too quickly broken. But if the only damage is to the sheet metal, the tactic is either to remove the inside door pad cover and bang the door out from that side with hammer and wood block, or use a slide hammer from the outside. Usually you will have to do both.

Once you get the door sheet metal pounded out, you must make sure that the window and all other mechanisms continue to operate, and the door opens and closes as before. Nobody will congratulate you for repairing a door that they cannot use. The first aim always is to make body work usable as well as artistic. You are not creating an original work of art.

Rust damage is insidious because it can make a pile of junk out of a perfectly usable car. Cars more than two or three years of age are candidates for major rust damage. It begins innocuously enough. One day you notice rust on a seam somewhere; inside the trunk, or under the hood, or you see it below the door, or under a decorative strip somewhere. You look closely at it and see that the problem is bigger than it seems. Rust damage always is; when you can see it, much erosion has already occurred. That is why used car salesmen call rust damage cancer. It is insidious.

However, you can cure it in cars, if not in people.

If you are willing to cut away all the rust damage, and replace it with body putty, you can save the day, and the car. Fiberglass is also a good substitute for rust-rot. You can use either body putty or fiberglass. I prefer body putty, because it is somewhat easier to handle. But others will disagree.

Rust damaged areas have to be removed, if rust is severe. You judge severity of rust easily enough—is it surface rust which sanding can remove, or does it go all the way through? Keep sanding until you reach solid metal, using a hand drill and heavy sanding discs. If you can't reach it with the drill, use a metal cutter of some sort or whatever it takes to pull off the rust area. Rusted body metal won't resist; it peels away fairly easily. But surface rust can be treated with naval jelly or some other chemical that neutralizes it. Then you can paint over it with primer and surface paint.

If gaping holes are left when you remove rusted areas, you can patch them with fiberglass, which will provide a surface as strong as the original, and one that can be painted with a good finish. But you can also use any metal backing and body putty. The body putty becomes part of the surface.

Fiberglass, which is used in boats most prominently, can be used to patch or rebuild rust-damaged areas—to replace a hole—more readily than body putty. The fiberglass resin mixture goes over a cloth or woven mat. If you are working with a hole of any size, the mat is best because it holds its shape better than the cloth. You prepare the surface exactly as with body putty, sanding away all rust and paint. Metal makes the best bonding for either fiberglass or body putty, so sand off the paint at the edges of the surface you're repairing.

The key to successful use of fiberglass is to work it while it's still soft. Once it hardens you will contend with an almost impossible surface. So keep working it—when it's soft, use wood or cardboard or a metal scoop to smooth it out, then use a block wrapped in sandpaper to continue the process. Use rubber gloves and work it with your fingers and palms, when it's still at a malleable stage.

Once fiberglass hardens sufficiently to sand, begin with coarse pads and work up to 320 or finer, until you get a perfectly smooth finish. You will have to apply several coats on a large hole patch.

Small holes are easily filled with body putty. Buy a gallon of it, if you have a lot of body work to do, or any smaller quantity you need.

The way to use body putty is to use just the right amount of hardener cream in it—follow instructions exactly—and then keep working it, first by the type of applicator you use, then as it starts to harden, smooth it over continuously with your fingers until it hardens. Then start immediately with sandpaper and water and keep working over it until you get it smooth. Final smoothing is done when it hardens completely.

In all this there is a progression of the right sanding materials. Final sanding is done with No. 320 emery cloth or finer, which gets you a good surface. Then fill in any small holes that appear; a process that will take several applications. Use emery cloth such as 3M Wetordry Tri-M-Ite paper. It's a waterproof silicon carbide and No. 320 is a good finishing weight, though you may wish to go to an even finer grade. Use coarser grain for earlier steps. For big jobs, when you have to apply several layers of body putty, and have to do a lot of initial sanding to get contours shaped correctly, use the heaviest, coarsest discs you can find—those that will also cut metal—and preferably on a hand drill, though you don't need the drill. Wet sanding is generally better than dry.

Body putty is the hardest part of any major body work. It takes quite a few applications to get a final finish that is the right, glassy surface ready for painting. It will test your patience as well as your skill.

How do you get perfectly flat surfaces? Use a block of wood wrapped in the sanding paper to sand the area, or use a piece of metal. I have found that a large old spark plug socket wrapped in the sanding paper, from the days when spark plugs were much bigger, makes an excellent tool. Some people advocate sanding tools designed especially for the job. But these tools tend to dull quickly and soon become useless.

Using body putty is difficult—more difficult than anything else involved in body repair. But a gallon of body putty costs only a few dollars, whereas every part it saves can cost hundreds of dollars. The difference is labor; the labor is yours. It is wise to know what you get into when you start to use it. Because it is difficult, there are many ways to use it. I have found that the easiest method is to keep after it during its drying phase, which takes only a few minutes. Once it starts to set, brush it with your fingers, rub over it with your palms, using a damp rag wrapped in a block of wood, if necessary. Smoothing the damp putty can save enormous dry sanding work.

PRIMING

After you get the flattest, smoothest surface possible, you have to prime it. That means you start the painting process and you have to mask what you don't want to paint. That includes all glass, ornamentation, tires, wheels, the driveway and the house.

Put the car where it is close enough to the electrical outlet but not so close to the garage or house so that they are affected. You don't want to use an extension on the compressor, if that's what you're using, unless you have an extension of sufficiently heavy gauge wire to avoid overheating. The extension must be as heavy as or perferably heavier than the compressor cord.

Masking means covering precisely. You use masking tape and newspaper. Anything that shows through or isn't covered tightly will be painted, if it's near the paint stream. If you use spray cans there is less paint stream since there is less power. If you use the compressor you must cover extra territory. If you are painting a door panel with a spray can, you can get by without covering the nearest wheel and tire. With a compressor you cannot. If you do only the door, you cover the glass and door frame at the top and part of the roof, as well as everything below and alongside the door. Probably you will also paint the rocker panel below. It is best to remove ornamentation strips and decals, because they usually conceal rust which it is well to remove while you're doing the job. To replace strips and decals that are merely pasted on, use epoxy glue and masking tape to hold the strips and ornaments securely in place— use tape generously, putting small tape strips across the ornamentation. Some ornamentation pieces may have rubber gaskets inside that often come loose. Glue them before putting the ornament back. Many ornamental strips are held by small clips and expansion fasteners that plug in. They're vastly preferable to glue.

With everything masked and the weather and all other elements cooperating, spray the primer coat first. Primer paint is slightly different from the final glossy coat. Primer also requires the right mix of thinner to paint—the same as acryllic, about two parts thinner to one part primer—and the same spray pattern from the compressor-sprayer. It's good finger exercise for the final painting. If you make a mistake you can correct it easily enough; rub it off quickly, let it dry and paint over sufficiently to cover any vestige of the error. Errors in painting, like errors in anything, can be corrected with enough gloss. That is the final product in body work and other deceptive activities.